The Value of Poetry

Eric Falci's *The Value of Poetry* ...rary, cultural, and political value of po... that some of the most vital, significant, and enduring human actions ... oiced and held in poems. Poems marble civilizations: they catch courses of thought, tracks of feeling, and acts of speech and embed these shapes in language that is, in some fashion, poised toward the future. Falci argues that poetry is a vital medium in addressing and understanding some of the most pressing issues of our time. Ranging widely across canonical and contemporary poetry, *The Value of Poetry* shows how poems matter, and what poetry offers to readers in the contemporary world.

Eric Falci is Professor of English at the University of California, Berkeley. He is the author of *Continuity and Change in Irish Poetry, 1966–2010* (2012) and the *Cambridge Introduction to British Poetry, 1945–2010* (2015), as well as a number of essays on twentieth- and twenty-first-century Irish and British poetry. Along with Paige Reynolds, he is the co-editor of *Irish Literature in Transition, 1980–2020* (2020). His first book of poetry, *Late Along the Edgelands*, appeared in 2019.

The Value of Poetry

Eric Falci
University of California, Berkeley

CAMBRIDGE
UNIVERSITY PRESS

University Printing House, Cambridge CB2 8BS, United Kingdom

One Liberty Plaza, 20th Floor, New York, NY 10006, USA

477 Williamstown Road, Port Melbourne, VIC 3207, Australia

314–321, 3rd Floor, Plot 3, Splendor Forum, Jasola District Centre, New Delhi – 110025, India

79 Anson Road, #06-04/06, Singapore 079906

Cambridge University Press is part of the University of Cambridge.

It furthers the University's mission by disseminating knowledge in the pursuit of education, learning, and research at the highest international levels of excellence.

www.cambridge.org
Information on this title: www.cambridge.org/9781108429559
DOI: 10.1017/9781108676915

© Eric Falci 2020

This publication is in copyright. Subject to statutory exception and to the provisions of relevant collective licensing agreements, no reproduction of any part may take place without the written permission of Cambridge University Press.

First published 2020

A catalogue record for this publication is available from the British Library.

Library of Congress Cataloging-in-Publication Data
NAMES: Falci, Eric, author.
TITLE: The value of poetry / Eric Falci.
DESCRIPTION: Cambridge, UK New York : Cambridge University Press, 2020. | Includes bibiographical references and index.
IDENTIFIERS: LCCN 2020024239 (print) | LCCN 2020024240 (ebook) | ISBN 9781108429559 (hardback) | ISBN 9781108676915 (ebook)
SUBJECTS: LCSH: Poetry – 21st century – History and criticism. | Poetry – Social aspects.
CLASSIFICATION: LCC PN1281 .F35 2020 (print) | LCC PN1281 (ebook) | DDC 808.1–dc23
LC record available at https://lccn.loc.gov/2020024239
LC ebook record available at https://lccn.loc.gov/2020024240

ISBN 978-1-108-42955-9 Hardback
ISBN 978-1-108-45447-6 Paperback

Cambridge University Press has no responsibility for the persistence or accuracy of URLs for external or third-party internet websites referred to in this publication and does not guarantee that any content on such websites is, or will remain, accurate or appropriate.

Contents

Acknowledgments	*page* vi
Introduction	1
1 **Attention and Play**	19
2 **Worlds and Selves**	49
3 **Feeling Thought**	89
4 **Recollection**	120
Conclusion	156
Index	180

Acknowledgments

Thank you to my colleagues in the Berkeley English department, in particular Charles Altieri, C. D. Blanton, Josh Gang, and Lyn Hejinian; to Ray Ryan for his longstanding support; to Edgar Mendez, Mary Bongiovi, and Gayathri Tamilselvan for seeing this book through the production process; to Beverley Winkler for her copyediting; to Jim Diggins for constructing the index; and to anonymous press readers for their tremendously helpful suggestions on the project. Thank you to Amanda Post Whitehead, for everything.

Thank you to the following for permission to reproduce copyrighted material from the poems listed:

- Bloodaxe Books for excerpts from "Gish" by Jen Hadfield (from *Nigh-No-Place*, 2008); and *A Furnace* by Roy Fisher (from *The Long and the Short of It: Poems 1955–2005*, 2005);
- Reality Street for excerpts from "Starlings" by Maggie O'Sullivan (from *In the House of the Shaman*, 1993);
- Wesleyan University Press for excerpts from "Anchor" by Rae Armantrout (from *Partly: New and Selected Poems, 2001–2015*, 2016); "To See the Earth Before the End of the World" by Ed Roberson (from *To See the Earth Before the End of the World*, 2017); and *Zong!* by M. NourbeSe Philip (2011);
- Claudia Rankine for the use of 171 (one hundred and seventy-one) words and 7 (seven) lines from *Citizen: An American Lyric* by Claudia Rankine published by Penguin Press, 2015. First published in the United States of America by Graywolf Press, 2014. Text copyright © Claudia Rankine, 2014. Reproduced by permission of Penguin Books Ltd;
- Claudia Rankine for excerpts from *Citizen: An American Lyric*. Copyright © 2014 by Claudia Rankine. Reprinted with the

permission of The Permissions Company, LLC on behalf of Graywolf Press, www.graywolfpress.org;
- Layli Long Soldier for excerpts from *Whereas*. Copyright © 2017 by Layli Long Soldier; Reprinted with the permission of The Permissions Company, LLC on behalf of Graywolf Press, Minneapolis, Minnesota, www.graywolfpress.org;
- Tongo Eisen-Martin for excerpts from "Faceless" from *Heaven Is All Goodbyes*. Copyright © 2017 by Tongo Eisen-Martin. Reprinted with the permission of The Permissions Company, LLC on behalf of City Lights Books, www.citylights.com;
- Coach House Books for excerpts from "The Middle" by Lisa Robertson (from *3 Summers*, 2016); and
- Commune Editions for excerpts from "Dynamic Positioning" by Juliana Spahr (from *That Winter the Wolf Came*, 2015).

Introduction

Two questions sit intertwined at the heart of a volume entitled *The Value of Poetry*. Does poetry have value? What are the particular kinds of value that poetry has, has had, or might have? This book presumes an answer to the first and concentrates on sorting through the second. Poetry of course has value. That value is not universal, but it is transhistorical: poets and poetry have been important parts of every human culture that we know about, although what those terms designated and what roles poets and poetry played vary from culture to culture and from historical period to historical period. For thousands of years, certain kinds of speech, song, chant, and text have been described by the cultures from which they emerged as "poetry," and many of them have had immense importance within those cultures and well afterwards. Some of the most vital, the most moving, and the most lasting notions that have occurred to humans have been articulated and held in poems. Whether in oral performances, circulated manuscripts, or published books, poems have mattered quite a lot to quite a few, and poetry has functioned in manifold ways within its specific landscape – as a mode of historical memory, as a repository for a culture's myths and stories, as a means of political intervention and social mediation, as an aspect of ritual and religious practice, as a form of ceremonial discourse, and as a medium of individual expression and subjective construction. Not all of these functions have been active at all moments or in all cultures, and, as a broad generalization, poets in premodern societies tended to have a much more robust and rangy place than do modern poets.[1] However, even as we understand that the

---

[1] For several influential and wide-reaching accounts of poets and poetry in early periods, see Emily Thornbury, *Becoming a Poet in Anglo-Saxon England* (Cambridge: Cambridge University Press, 2014); M. L. West, *Indo-European Poetry and Myth* (Oxford: Oxford University Press, 2007); Gregory Nagy, *Poetry as Performance: Homer and Beyond* (Cambridge: Cambridge University Press, 1996); Morton W. Bloomfield and Charles W. Dunn, *The Role of the Poet in Early*

place and force of poetry shifts significantly depending on where and when we look, and even if we understand that poetry designates a relatively small literary and artistic sphere within the totality of contemporary cultural practices, it is incontrovertible that poetry's importance has been ubiquitous. Poems marble civilizations.

For a number of reasons, my own account in this book has a much more limited purview than the previous sentences might suggest, one of whose limitations I am all too well aware. *The Value of Poetry* can't pretend or dare to be a comprehensive account of poetry across the globe and throughout time, nor can it help being a book written, primarily, about English-language poetry for an English-language audience. Thus, it is largely a book about poetry's value in the contemporary Anglophone world: I aim to show how poetry matters and what poems in particular offer in the present and might offer in the future. In large part, this is a concession to my own abilities and areas of knowledge. But there are additional reasons for this aspect of the volume. *The Value of Poetry* aims to speak of and to the present and so draws its materials from its own surround. While there are occasional forays into poetry from earlier periods and while I place my account within a much longer history of poetic practices and traditions, my argument rests on and revolves around a particular body and understanding of poetry: English-language poetry since the early nineteenth century. While I often use the simple term "poetry" to designate my topic rather than more unwieldy literary-historical terms ("modern Anglophone poetry" or "nineteenth- and twentieth-century poetry in English"), it should be understood that such a seemingly universal term is much more specific in practice. My use of the term "poetry" throughout is primarily a stylistic convenience, and certainly not an assumption that my account is comprehensive and holds good for all poetry, in all languages, from all times. I wish that I could write that book.

At the same time, this book is not intended as a survey of or all-inclusive argument about contemporary poetry in English. Because

---

Societies (Woodbridge, Suffolk: D. S. Brewer, 1989); and Albert B. Lord, *The Singer of Tales*, ed. Stephen Mitchell and Gregory Nagy (Cambridge, MA: Harvard University Press, 2000 [1960]).

my intention is to demonstrate both what poems afford to readers and how readers might approach contemporary poems, I tend to concentrate on a small handful of texts in each chapter, and while I hope that the total array of poems on which I focus is seen to be interestingly diverse, I did not aim for that array to be representative of contemporary Anglophone poetry in all of its shapes and styles. Some of the poems that I land on are by poets who are canonical or on their way to becoming so, but others are written by poets who are earlier in their careers or who have only gained notice in a quite particular corner of the poetry world. In addition, it is probably worth mentioning that just as my argument about poetry's value recognizes that poetry has been held to be important everywhere and at all times and also that it hasn't always or everywhere been valued for the same reasons or fulfilled the same roles, so does my focus on contemporary poetry proceed from the notion that poems are neither entirely hooked to nor free from their historical conditions. Instead, they often appear as formal switch points between diachronic and synchronic perspectives, attentive to and enmeshed in the terms of their world, but also poised to reassess or reimagine those terms. At a practical level, this means that while my argument about the significance of poetry draws from contemporary examples, it does not account for contemporary poetry in a strictly literary-historicist way, and it does envision that at least some of the interpretive strategies and claims that I make throughout are seen to be portable – or at least generative – for poetry from other periods and traditions. Finally, this book is primarily concerned with poems, rather than poets. There is a long tradition of defending or explaining poets as particular sorts of individuals – in the Romantic and post-Romantic context especially – or by rebutting that notion (in modernist arguments about impersonality, for example). *The Value of Poetry* is much less interested in the value of poets than it is in the value of poems, and so it does not argue for poetry as a particular sort of vocation, but for the significance of a poem as a nexus of writerly practice, textual occurrence, and readerly activity.[2]

---

[2] Although my own volume has a tremendously different approach and intended audience than does Stephanie Burt's *Don't Read Poetry: A Book about How to Read Poems* (New York: Basic Books, 2019), we both privilege the particular

We might give this nexus a name: form. Although it is an overstatement, it isn't very much of one to suggest that nearly every interesting question about poetry has to do with form, and I will spend a bit of time here previewing the approach to form that shapes this book.[3] I am not overly invested in advancing anything like an airtight definition of poetry: if the history of poetry has suggested anything, it is that no single definition of or homogeneous standard for poetry can possibly account for the varieties of significant poetry, even within a single literary-historical period or linguistic tradition. However, it is probably safe to suggest that – at minimum – poetry names a practice and art of shaping language, and my sense of the term "form" gathers the different aspects of this shaping: the compositional activities, assumptions, and implications that are involved in the shaping; the nature and structure of the shape that results; and the ways that a poem is realized within the processes of reception. Any notion of form that doesn't include these nodes will likely become thin in practice, unable to account for the complex and processual dynamics involved in what we must think of capaciously as a poem's making. As Lyn Hejinian points out in "The Rejection of Closure" (1983), "form is not a fixture but an activity."[4]

At the heart of a poem's activity is its bearing toward its materials – words, phrases, sentences. Poetry makes language chimerical. A poet uses our basic system of communication and signification as, simultaneously, artistic material. In a poem, words function both as words – those transparent and shared ciphers that lead on to referents and concepts – and as artistic stuff – more opaque, denser, less

---

textures of poems over poetry or poets. Indeed, it is clear that the unstated positive imperative that goes along with Burt's negative mantra – "Don't Read Poetry" – is "Read Poems."

[3] Nearly all of the texts referenced in this book spend time on form, but for several influential reconsiderations, see Caroline Levine, *Forms: Whole, Rhythm, Hierarchy, Network* (Princeton, NJ: Princeton University Press, 2015); Denise Gigante, *Life: Organic Form and Romanticism* (New Haven, CT: Yale University Press, 2009); Angela Leighton, *On Form: Poetry, Aestheticism, and the Legacy of a Word* (Oxford: Oxford University Press, 2007); and Susan Wolfson, *Formal Charges: The Shaping of Poetry in British Romanticism* (Stanford, CA: Stanford University Press, 1997).

[4] Lyn Hejinian, "The Rejection of Closure," in *The Language of Inquiry* (Berkeley, CA: University of California Press, 2000), 40–58, at 47.

amenable to quick transfer. If language is our common means for conceptualizing the world and our experience in and of it, and for communicating aspects of that experience to others (informing, expressing, describing, explaining, stating, questioning – all the things that language does), then poetry is certainly involved in many of those activities, but it isn't principally interested in conveying information or communicating in a straightforward sense. By way of rhythm, sound, rhyme, figuration, rhetoric, genre, and diction, poems aim to activate the entire bodies of words and their combinations. The good poem asks its reader to look closely at the configuration of words that constitute it rather than to see straight through them to their denotations. This density is the source both of poetry's pleasure and its difficulty, and I devote Chapter 1 to expanding on the implications and significance of this claim. We think of poets as "creative writers," but poets do not "create" the materials with which they work, nor do they fundamentally transform their materials as a sculptor does stone. Poems don't result from acts of creation, but from those of combination, arrangement, and assembly – poetry is often a practice of foraging, tinkering, meddling, melding, and suturing. And poets work with open source material. The words that poets use keep their usual, agreed-upon semantic and denotative freight when they are brought into a poem, even as they gain a certain density or viscosity that is generally not granted to them – or, not actively noticed – when they occur in the run of everyday use. The features of words that typically would be passed over as we tune in to their literal meaning – that is, their phonological and morphological structures, their etymologies, their figural and idiomatic propensities, their consonantal and vocalic patterns – are all turned to use. In poems, words become both enlivened and estranged.

Poems thus take on a peculiar sort of materiality. The specific verbal arrangement of a poem is inextricable from its content in a way that isn't the case for many kinds of prose, which lend themselves more easily to rephrase or paraphrase. And so, like a sculpture or painting, a poem is often granted a certain kind of objecthood: a "well wrought urn" or a "machine made out of words," to cite just two of the more well-known instances, by, respectively, Cleanth

Brooks and William Carlos Williams.[5] A poem's form is, most straightforwardly, the particular words that comprise it in the particular order and pattern in which they appear. At the same time, however, the materiality that we often attribute to poems is peculiar because it is largely immaterial. A poem is strangely free from any single material occurrence of it. When reading a poem – whether online, in a thin volume, or in an anthology – few readers are troubled by the fact that the text is a replica of a replica of a replica of a replica, and so on. A poem keeps its verbal body even as it mutates from format to format, from font to font, and from edition to edition; it is "particular" in that it is only and precisely the words that constitute it (leaving room for variants and alternate versions), but it doesn't exclusively inhere in any specific instance of itself. The "original" of a poem, unlike a painting or sculpture, isn't necessarily a more privileged aesthetic object than any other accurate textual manifestation of it. To be sure, an original manuscript by the poet often has immense scholarly and economic value, and different editions and versions of poems often exist and are differently meaningful, but a reader of Keats' "To Autumn" in its original manuscript has no better *interpretive* "claim" on the poem than does one who reads it on a photocopy's photocopy. Broadly speaking, both have read the same poem. In most cases, the differences that might obtain between a poem's manuscript or typescript and the text of that poem as it appears in the poet's published volume or a later edition are less significant that their fundamental convergence. This is perhaps to belabor the obvious, but it does seem an important aspect of poetry's aesthetic value: a poem isn't attached to any specific manifestation of itself. Any aura that it might have is, paradoxically but crucially, already abstracted: its materiality is imagined.

At the same time that poems might partake, though strangely, of some of the aesthetic features that we more readily associate with the visual arts, they also share with music and dance (as well as with

---

[5] Cleanth Brooks, *The Well Wrought Urn: Studies in the Structure of Poetry* (New York: Harvest Books, 1947); and Williams Carlos Williams, "Author's Introduction to *The Wedge*" [1944], in *Selected Essays of William Carlos Williams* (New York: New Directions Books, 1969 [1954]), 255–257, at 256.

other literary forms) a temporal structure. A poem unfolds in time, both as a compositional arrangement and also as something like a score for a performance by a voice (even if that voice is the subvocal one of a silent reader). However, the "time" of a poem is indeterminate as compared to that of a musical performance, and compared to a musical score a poetic text, while typically affording and encouraging a vocalization, is much less dependent on the formalized conditions of performance in order to be fully realized. In "The Defence of Poesy" (1595), Sir Philip Sidney catches something of poetry's complex commitments: "Poesy therefore is an art of imitation, for so Aristotle termeth it in the word *mimesis* – that is to say, a representing, counterfeiting, or figuring forth." Sidney goes on to describe a poem as "a speaking picture," and this sense of simultaneous verbal mimesis and verbal performance remains central to the work of poetry.[6] A poem is both artifact and happening, and central to our understanding of poems is some kind of account of how they move or proceed. A sonnet, for instance, is both a shape and a path: it provides a notional template that embeds its own formal history and includes both a series of already-established alternative maneuvers and the possibility of crafting new variations. It offers a particular procedure, a set of conventions that have traditionally been linked to that procedure, and the space for both compositional freedom and moments of happenstance and accident – spaces in which the text might be revealed immanently, rather than generated as a function of its chosen design.

A sonnet, then, might be thought of as a conventional form, a procedural form, and a revealed form all at once. And many poems develop according to such hybrid or mixed models, tacking between the procedure or set of conventions to which they have committed themselves and the impulse for invention, play, and deviation. Some poems that I'll highlight in this volume proceed according to no recognizable or easily describable form, generating their structure as they go – freely, haphazardly, or according to a pattern of intention

---

[6] Sir Philip Sidney, "The Defence of Poesy," in Katherine Duncan-Jones, ed., *Sir Philip Sidney: The Major Works* (Oxford: Oxford University Press, 2008 [1989]), 212–251, at 217.

known only to the writer. Others rely wholly or nearly so on a particular compositional rule or procedure, whether a conventional form or genre or a *sui generis* process or concept. Certain compositional choices might be front-loaded – the source of a poem's language (as in found poetry), the principle of its ordering (say, via the alphabet), its metrical patterning, the number of lines or stanzas it contains – while others might be left to disclose themselves as the poem develops. At times a poem might proceed along familiar lines – narrative, catalog, description, meditative reflection – maintaining normative modes of discursive coherence. While at others it might proceed paratactically or according to an inscrutable logic that doesn't seem to cohere into continuous units of sense or significance, such that we are able to hold the poem together only by positing a centripetal force to balance its centrifugal textual energies. We have terms to describe such seemingly unruly poems – such as collage or montage – but we often motivate our interest in them by framing them as the contemplation or thinking-in-language of a person: what knits such a poem together is our attribution of a subject intending it. Thus, in addition to describing the perceptible shapes that a poem takes, the only sometimes evident compositional logic behind those shapes, and the principles and patterns by which those shapes develop, form also gives us a way to think about these shapes and movements within a structure of intention, or at least a way to impel a poem's particulars, especially when those particulars are disjunct or inscrutable.

This brings us to the complicated matter of poetry's relation to expression and subjectivity, a topic that I'll focus on more fully in Chapters 2 and 3, but which I'll introduce here. One line of thought, and one that has tended to dominate since the early nineteenth century, is that a poem is the emanation of a subject. A poem, as John Stuart Mill has put it, is overheard thought, "feeling confessing itself to itself in moments of solitude."[7] A poem, then, isn't primarily a mimetic representation, as Sidney's Aristotelian view has it, but an expressive representation of a person's (and, implicitly for Mill, the

---

[7] John Stuart Mill, "Thoughts on Poetry and its Varieties" [1833/1859], in *Dissertations and Discussions: Political, Philosophical, and Historical* (Boston, MA: W. V. Spencer, 1864), vol. 1, 89–120, at 97.

author's) thoughts, feelings, emotions, or beliefs. Modernist poetics rewired, rather than wholly abandoned, this tenet of Romanticism. As T. S. Eliot notes in "Tradition and the Individual Talent" (1919), "the emotion of art is impersonal."[8] It isn't that poems don't offer emotions, but rather that the emotions they offer are not those of the poet. A poem constructs, in its phrasings, rhythms, images, and figures, an "objective correlative" – a textual object that correlates emotions and patterns them via poetry's shaping forces.[9] In both the Romanticism of Mill and the modernism of Eliot the poem is framed as the delineation of an affective and intellectual experience – a thinking-and-feeling-in-words – however much the two accounts differ in so many other respects. Part of the force of such a poem is that it successfully feigns immediacy; it is not only the recounting of an experience, but the in-process enactment of one.

Central to these enactments is the idea of lyric poetry as what Paul de Man described (and deconstructed) as "the instance of represented voice."[10] If we often imagine poetry as being about a self of some sort, then it is a self that speaks. Poems can catch the shapes of experience and acts of speech – the structure of a feeling, the branching course of a thought, the many-minded play of a mind, an emotion's uncertain curve – and embed these shapes in a bundle of language that is, in some fashion, poised toward the future and addressed to another.

The notion that a poem has a "voice" is a fiction – there's no body or self threaded into the page, just inky (or digitized) marks – but it is a remarkably enduring one. Even in a postmodern, poststructural, post-enlightenment, post-humanist context, we still abide the thought that poems construct voices. Speaking to other people, speaking to animals, speaking to gods, speaking to themselves, speaking to

---

[8] T. S. Eliot, "Tradition and the Individual Talent" [1919], in Anthony Cuda and Ronald Schuchard, *The Complete Prose of T. S. Eliot: The Critical Edition: The Perfect Critic, 1919–1926* (Baltimore, MD and London: Johns Hopkins University Press and Faber and Faber, 2014), 105–114, at 112.

[9] T. S. Eliot, "Hamlet" [1919], in Anthony Cuda and Ronald Schuchard, *The Complete Prose of T. S. Eliot: The Critical Edition: The Perfect Critic, 1919–1926* (Baltimore, MD and London: Johns Hopkins University Press and Faber and Faber, 2014), 122–128, at 125.

[10] Paul de Man, *The Rhetoric of Romanticism* (New York: Columbia University Press, 1984), 261.

no one and nothing. And so one of the core ideas underlying our notion of poetry, and of lyric poetry especially, is that of address.[11] Poems are often construed as confected acts of speech, as potentially vocalizable, but poems as we have them tend to be written: their vocalization is always disjointed, at odds with whatever we might understand to be their original voicing (itself another kind of fiction). In a too prototypically Derridean fashion, poems are estranged from their origin. The chimerical quality of poetry, then, also inheres in its incessant ventriloquizing of a voice that has no source.

Vital to such textual performances is the play of pronouns. A love poem like Prufrock's doesn't simply describe or recount his vexed thought or his wavering feeling – it acts them out in the "real time" form of an address. Of course, such immediacy is radically mediated. Unlike a real-life scenario, deictics have nowhere, or too many places, to attach; unlike a play (or a movie or television show), terms like "us," "you," and "I" aren't connected to characters with actual bodies (or filmed or digitized ones); and unlike a novel, those shifters don't function within the established logic of a diegetic space. Like all of its pronouns, a poem's "I" is also chimerical – a fissile amalgam of writer, speaker, and reader that is built to be unmade. The idea of vocal performance that underlies lyric's constitutive fiction, along with the concomitant construction of a virtual diegesis within which that voice speaks, must be understood as a recessive shadow play that produces both readerly uncertainty and readerly involvement. One is caught between the familiarity of one's own voice speaking (silently or otherwise) and one's own mind reading a poem and, so, being called into it (as "I" or as "you," "here" and "now"), and the knowledge that such a call is provisional, fictional, and something of a ruse. Even the simplest present tense verbs become compound and multivalent. "I walk through the long schoolroom questioning" is neither statement nor update nor reminiscence nor

---

[11] On speech acts, voice, and address in lyric, see Jonathan Culler, *Theory of the Lyric* (Cambridge, MA: Harvard University Press, 2015), esp. 109–131 and 186–243; David Nowell Smith, *On Voice in Poetry: The Work of Animation* (Basingstoke: Palgrave Macmillan, 2015); and William Waters, *Poetry's Touch: On Lyric Address* (Ithaca, NY: Cornell University Press, 2003).

declaration.¹² It is, in its context at the start of "Among School Children," a script for an absent drama. And this is precisely where a reader intervenes and recollects its ghosted scenario, neither taking ownership of the "I" nor fully alienating it. A poem's capacity for deictic metamorphosis also allows for instances of impossible speech. Chidiock Tichborne's famous poem written just before his execution in 1586 for his part in a conspiracy to kill Queen Elizabeth, referred to as Tichborne's Lamentation or Tichborne's Elegy, provides a stark example: "And now I live, and now my life is done."¹³ Only within the tensed, vibratory space of poetry can the "I" here absorb so many contradictions, such that the poem can speak to itself from either side of the gallows. A poem, then, is a verbal performance, but one that isn't assimilable to the form of a monologue or an oration. By being both context-dependent and context-less, poems offer a unique kind of aesthetic experience. As readers, we fill in the pronouns (with ourselves, with our situations, with an imagined authorial situation, with a persona, with a fictional scenario suggested by the poem), but we also understand those shifters to be radically empty. This crowded hollow – "the nothing that is" there at the end of Wallace Stevens' "A Snow Man" – is the catalytic space from which a poem builds its energy.¹⁴

A poem's capacities for rendering complex subjective states and multiform scenarios of address are not merely in the service of personal expression or the delineation of psychological interiors. Because poems are made from shared materials – words – they necessarily take part in social and political spheres, even when they seem exclusively focused on a self and its concerns. Although poems are not necessarily the best vehicles for the clear presentation of a political position, an exposition of a feature of social life, or a straightforward account of a historical topic, poems can provide particularly useful vantage points from which to consider underlying

---

¹² Richard J. Finneran, ed., *The Collected Poems of W. B. Yeats*, rev. 2nd ed. (New York: Simon & Schuster, 1996), 215.
¹³ Margaret Ferguson, Tim Kendall, and Mary Jo Salter, eds., *The Norton Anthology of Poetry*, 6th ed. (New York: W. W. Norton & Co., 2018), 156.
¹⁴ Wallace Stevens, *The Collected Poems* (New York: Vintage Books, 1990 [1954]), 10.

aspects of those matters: how individual life is structured via the social world; how our understanding of that which lies beyond us – the past, the dead, other lives – relies on the construction of imaginative relations of all sorts; how our own experiences are shaped, and even constituted, by what is exterior to us. In this way, poems sketch the limen between subjects and the world, and even when a poet writes of something that seemingly has to do exclusively with her own experience – love, desire, fear – we understand it as part of a social and ideological network and therefore to have, however submerged, political force. This is not to reverse Auden's too-famous claim that "poetry makes nothing happen" – which is true – but to place more emphasis on his slightly later claim in the same poem: poetry is "a way of happening, a mouth."[15] Poems don't necessarily have an overt (or covert) political content – although some certainly do – but they are striated by ideological contexts that are significant aspects of their forms. Part of this volume's concern – one that is apparent throughout but is perhaps most clearly visible in Chapter 4 and the Conclusion – is to apprehend the full import of poetry's "way of happening" and to test the vitality of contemporary poetry's ability to think about social, political, and historical relations.

Earlier, I discussed poetic genres and conventions within the rubric of composition, but it is just as important to understand them within the space of reception – that is, both as part of a literary tradition and as socially mediated. Poems inflect the world by way of their occurrence. The kinds of inflections, as well as their specific intents, have varied throughout history and from culture to culture, but we can name a few: charm, chant, prayer, confession, elegy, spell, lament, satire, meditation, curse, riddle, ode, love poem. Within those generic markers are not only formal models but also social scenarios. As speech acts and as textual performances, poems historically had social functions and so presumed audiences of some kind. These markers and scenarios shape a poem's mode of

---

[15] W. H. Auden, *Collected Poems*, ed. Edward Mendelson (New York: The Modern Library, 2007 [1976]), 246.

vocalization or inscription. Of course, most poems in the past several centuries have not had a definite or prescribed social function, or have mustered or feigned one. To return to Auden, they make nothing happen, but they remain ways of happening, albeit untethered to some specific social context and so often ambiguous. This is part of a much larger sense in which poetry's own place in culture is ambiguous, and I'll conclude by introducing a few points about that uncertain place.

"Poetry" remains a deeply ambivalent cultural signifier. It often signals elitism or hermeticism and has done so for quite a while. More than other literary genres, poetry still radiates a sense of "high culture" even after the divide between high and low has been so thoroughly dismantled. Poetry often produces a blanket dismissal – "I don't do poetry" or "I don't get poetry" – in ways that other genres or art forms tend not to. And even among poets and readers of poetry, commitment often comes with a definite measure of skepticism, disdain, and self-loathing, as has been captured most famously by Marianne Moore's "Poetry," both the sentiments offered throughout much of the poem and in the way that Moore hacked away at the text until it was just a stub of itself.[16] It would be difficult to make a case for the wider value of poetry based on its reach or direct impact within the churn of contemporary mass culture – which may be no bad thing – but it is remarkable just how much staying power is had by an idea of a now-lost time in which poetry had widespread, mainstream cultural relevance. Most attacks on the obscurity of poetry or the insularity of the subcultures of poetry are premised on the assumption of a bygone golden age – one that is never quite named or placed – and many laments about poetry's obsolescence similarly rely on a stated or unstated narrative of retreat, one that has been, ironically, quite stable in its broader outline for quite a long time.

---

[16] For an account of this widespread structure of feeling and one spurred by Moore's poem, see Ben Lerner, *The Hatred of Poetry* (New York: Farrar, Straus and Giroux, 2016). Lerner's "hatred" is more like a constitutive disappointment that actual poems never live up to the idealizations around poetry that lead to their existence.

Alongside this view of poetry's exclusivity, difficulty, and obsolescence is the fact of its utter accessibility. Many, many people have tried their hand at a poem at some point in their lives, in part because the materials and competencies that one requires to compose a poem are remarkably cheap and widely available. What one needs is what one already has: language. And some sort of writing or recording device. Compared with other forms of artistic and cultural activity, poetry is very near to hand. If a person of whatever socioeconomic background happened to come across a poem and found herself intrigued, then the task of finding more poems and writing some herself would present few significant material obstacles. This is especially pronounced in the contemporary period. The internet is strewn with poems, and the explosion of small press, desktop, and digital publishing has allowed many more people to publish their work than in earlier eras. Although there are of course still a small handful of publishers within the Anglophone literary world that play an outsize role in shaping the cultures of contemporary poetry, it is less the case now than it was the 1950s or 1960s that an exceedingly narrow pipeline of editors and publishers in New York and London – likely to be white, upper-class men – control the entire production and field of poetry. While this shift has spurred a significant increase in access and publishing opportunities – a democratization of poetry in a number of respects, although inequities of many sorts remain – it must also be coupled with the fact that unlike most other forms of contemporary literature, there are likely as many practicing poets at any one time as there are regular readers of poetry.

While we tend not to equate poetry's significance with its sales figures – in fact it is most often the case that poets who move more product are downgraded within certain sectors of the poetry world, as though popularity always signals too-easy accessibility or mediocrity – it is important to recognize the basic asymmetry that structures the poetry market. There are significantly more volumes of poetry published each year than there are expected readers of most individual volumes of poetry, apart from those of a few figures who sell exponentially more copies than anyone else. There are around 4,000–5,000 volumes of poetry published in English each year and the average print run for a volume is perhaps 1,000 copies (and much lower in many cases).[17] These figures do not account for chapbooks or other printed volumes that don't have ISBN numbers, and they don't account for work published exclusively in digital formats. There is a contradiction at the heart of poetry's place in contemporary culture: it is evident that writing poems is an important practice for many people, with many thousands publishing volumes of poetry and individual poems in print and digital periodicals, and many more desiring to publish poems and books of poetry for which they cannot find a platform or outlet. But it is just as evident that this desire to produce poetry isn't matched by the desire to read the poetry of others. This is an intriguing sign of the poetry world's unusual formation, in which the line between practitioner and adherent or fan (or between

---

[17] As Craig Dworkin points out, "the typical print run for a book of small press poetry" is "somewhere between 200 and 1,000 copies" ("Seja Marginal," in Craig Dworkin, ed., *The Consequence of Innovation: 21st Century Poetics* [New York: Roof Books, 2008], 7–24, at 15–16). Prints runs for poetry volumes published by university presses are typically between one and two thousand copies, with somewhat higher runs for the larger trade publishers. There have been periods over the past half century when a very small number of living poets accounted for a large proportion of total poetry sales. For instance, Seamus Heaney's volumes accounted for two-thirds of the total sales of poetry in the United Kingdom in 2007 (see Jamie Smith, "Nobel Prizewinning Poet Seamus Heaney Dies," *Financial Times*, August 30, 2013, www.ft.com/content/ab96 a37c-116b-11e3-a14c-00144feabdc0, accessed August 31, 2018). And for long periods in the late twentieth century, the combined sales of volumes by Philip Larkin, Ted Hughes, and Heaney constituted the bulk of Faber and Faber's poetry sales as well as the bulk of UK poetry sales in general. In the United States, a small handful of poets, such as Mary Oliver and Billy Collins, sell exponentially more copies than do major figures. As Jahan Ramazani makes clear, low sales figures for poetry volumes are by no means a contemporary phenomenon. Many key books from canonical modern poets, whose volumes are now coveted properties for their publishers, were printed in quite low numbers: "the press run of T. S. Eliot's *Prufrock and Other Observations* was 500, of William Carlos Williams's *Spring and All* 324 (largely unsold), of Marianne Moore's *Observations* 250, and of Ezra Pound's *Hugh Selwyn Mauberley* 200" (*Poetry and Its Others: News, Prayer, Song, and the Dialogue of Genres* [Chicago and London: University of Chicago Press, 2014], 17). There have been a number of indications that poetry, both in terms of sales and overall readership, has increased in popularity over the past several years. According to Nielsen BookScan, 2018 was the best year ever for poetry sales (see Natasha Onwuemezi, "Poetry Sales are Booming, LBF Hears," *The Bookseller*, April 13, 2018, www.thebookseller.com/news/poetry-summit-766826, accessed August 31, 2018). Also see data from the NEA: Sunil Iyengar, "Taking Note: Poetry Reading Is Up – Federal Survey Results," *NEA Art Works Blog*, June 7, 2018, www.arts.gov/art-works/2018/taking-note-poetry-reading---federal-survey-results, accessed August 31, 2018.

professional and amateur) is blurry or nonexistent. It is also, in sheer terms of audience size and cultural scope, a drawback. The contradictory nature of poetry's market is just one among many. The idea of poetry in contemporary culture exists at the nexus of a handful of contradictions: elitist and utterly accessible; an enduring (though perhaps vestigial) acme of literary achievement and entirely ignored by many readers of literature; an anachronistic art form and important because of its outmodedness. This is fitting, for it may be that the significance of poetry more broadly has everything to with its ability to reckon with contradiction and ambiguity. The chimeric doubleness that I have described as a basic circumstance of poetic activity means that poetic texts comprise particularly promising spaces in which to both model and scrutinize the systemic complexities and contradictory conditions of contemporary life. In such cases, a poem will be active on every level, as J. H. Prynne suggests: "Formal and structural features within the language system, the selective-discourse system, the prosodic and formal verse system, all within the contrastive perspectives of historical development, compete to provoke the formation of shifting hybrids across boundaries of sometimes radical counter-tension. The active poetic text is thus characteristically in dispute with its own ways and means, contrary implication running inward to its roots and outward to its surface proliferations: not as acrobatic display but as working the work that, when fit for purpose, poetry needs to do."[18] The poems that appear in the chapters that follow operate in such ways, working with and against the grain of their words and galvanizing all of language's features and aspects within the crucible of their forms. This results in poems that are often "difficult," but such difficulty isn't simply a sign of navel-gazing or willful obscurity. It is part of a broader project of resistance to the instrumentalization of language. Clearly, linguistic instrumentality isn't necessarily a bad thing – one very often wants the language that one employs and

[18] J. H. Prynne, "Mental Ears and Poetic Work," *Chicago Review*, 55.1 (Winter 2010), 126–157, at 141.

encounters to convey some quickly apprehensible meaning. However, there is a more dangerous aspect to the necessary instrumentality of language, one that characterizes much too much of our political and cultural discourse: language can too quickly stiffen into an ideological tag, can be used to coerce and dictate, can serve to cover over the intricacies of feelings and ideas, and can become a mere vehicle by which to provoke unthought, consumption, or reaction. Poetry's value is that it both resists such oversimplifications and resides elsewhere.

In the chapters that follow, I frame poetry's significance in a number of ways: as providing a space for attentiveness and linguistic play, as a site where the vicissitudes of individual experience might be made considerable and shareable, as a locus wherein the complexities of mental and affective life might be mapped, and as a means of constructing an imaginative and textual relation with the dead and the past. In the conclusion, I gather and braid these strands in order consider briefly the place of poetry in a time of large-scale crisis. Each chapter isolates a different aspect of poetry's significance, but each one takes on board issues raised in previous chapters and projects them into those that follow. The chapters collate the basic features and shapes of poems in different, though interlocking, ways, which is to say that each attends to the cache of concepts that typically drives considerations of poetry: form, genre, voice, inscription, subject, rhythm, sound. If, as this volume will show, poetry's unique charge is based in its handling of ambiguity or multiplicity, and if, simultaneously, poetry is often invested in the rendering of deep feeling and intellection that both goes to a self's quick and exceeds and eludes the self, then the value of poetry is an uncertain one. This isn't to say that poetry's primary good is to produce incessant uncertainty. It is rather to claim that a poem's consequence is uncertain – unfixed, in flux, negatively capable – and that such uncertainty makes it possible for a poem to both resist the seeming certainties of current conditions and to potentially remake our common store – language. In this way, poetry is something of a counterforce. It appears both as emerging and residual, it can gesture toward that which cannot yet be seen or is seen no more, and it can bring to the surface some aspect of what has been overlooked. It is, then, usually on the move, what Stevens calls "a pheasant disappearing in the brush."[19] *The Value of Poetry* aims to show the patterns and tracks made by contemporary poems in order to suggest that what might be found there is vital for our present, that ever more precarious moment.

[19] Wallace Stevens, *Opus Posthumous: Poems, Plays, Prose*, ed. Milton J. Bates (New York: Vintage Books, 1990 [1957]), 198.

1 Attention and Play

Poems spurn skimming. They entreat our full attention. A distracted age such as ours, then, seems an unpropitious time for poetry. Dense, oblique, relatively lengthy, or difficult poems – and at least one of this quartet of terms fits many of the poems in the modern and contemporary canon – ask to be read closely, carefully, and often without an instrumental or definite end in mind, one point that differentiates poems – and literature more broadly – from other categories of "difficult" texts, such as legal contracts, philosophical treatises, or scientific papers. Some poems require so many readings and so much study before anything like sense breaks through that even the most dedicated reader may find herself asking, "is this worth the effort?"[1] Even short poems that would seem to be ideally suited for a civilization that unspools in Twitter-sized bursts necessitate, for howsoever brief a span, readerly attention, as do poems that provoke a quick reading pace, as in a number of Frank O'Hara's "I do this, I do that" poems or much of the work of Tom Raworth. If poetry is viewed as antiquated, then that is because attention seems antiquated as well. At the same time, however, if poetry now is, like Hugh Selwyn Mauberley, "out of key" with its time, then this may be the source of its most profound value within contemporary culture (and one might say, along with Walter Benjamin, that poetry has been out of key with its time since Baudelaire).[2] In such unpropitious conditions, a poem can serve as a counterforce to governing cultural logics, a space in which dismal

---

[1] On difficulty and contemporary poetry, see Charles Altieri and Nicholas Nace, eds., *The Fate of Difficulty in the Poetry of Our Time* (Evanston, IL: Northwestern University Press, 2018).

[2] Ezra Pound, *Personae: The Shorter Poems*, ed. Lea Baechler and A. Walton Litz (NY: New Directions, 1990), 185. In "On Some Motifs in Baudelaire," Benjamin begins with the premise that "Baudelaire envisaged readers to whom the reading of lyric poetry would present difficulties," because the larger cultural situation in which he wrote was one in which the "conditions for a positive reception of lyric poetry have become less favorable." Such conditions, Benjamin goes on to point

instrumentalization, constant distraction, and ceaseless consumption can be – even momentarily – checked and turned back. This is not to position poetry as a form of pseudo-religious practice or simply a pretext for mindfulness. Nor is it to imbue the writing or reading of poems with some innate moral or ethical consequence. Rather, it is to suggest that in order to begin to comprehend the significance of poetry more broadly, we must first understand the particular space that a poem constructs as one that affords distinct forms of readerly engagement and responsiveness.[3] In this chapter, I'll focus on several dimensions of this double space.

Typically, a poem asks to be read closely, to be read more than once, to be lived with rather than rushed through. At the same time, the kind of attention that a poem requests is not ends-oriented, nor does it offer something apart from its own unfolding: no paraphrase-able gist, or take-away message, or nub of detachable knowledge. For all of the rhetorical, figurative, and sonic energy that poems muster, they harness such energy in quite different ways than, say, a politician giving a speech or a protester at a rally. They certainly have the power to enthrall, but perhaps less so to coerce. To be sure, there have been numerous arguments about the manifold powers of poetry to ensorcell and persuade, whether such power was framed as dangerous to the polis, as by Plato, or as necessary and central, as by Percy Bysshe Shelley. However, describing poetry as "indeed something divine … the centre and circumference of knowledge" and poets as "the hierophants of an unapprehended inspiration … the unacknowledged legislators of the world," as Shelley does in his "A Defense of Poetry" (1821/1840), seems somewhat extraneous to any argument to be made about

---

out, continue from Baudelaire's time to Benjamin's own (and, of course, further). Walter Benjamin, "On Some Motifs in Baudelaire" [1939], trans. by Harry Zohn, in *The Writer of Modern Life: Essays on Charles Baudelaire*, ed. Michael W. Jennings (Cambridge, MA: Harvard University Press, 2006), 170–210, at 170 and 171.

[3] Recent accounts of attention in poetry include Andrew Epstein, *Attention Equals Life: The Pursuit of the Everyday in Contemporary Poetry and Culture* (New York: Oxford University Press, 2016); Lily Gurton-Wachter, *Watchwords: Romanticism and the Poetics of Attention* (Stanford, CA: Stanford University Press, 2016); and David Marno, *Death Be Not Proud: The Art of Holy Attention* (Chicago and London: University of Chicago Press, 2016).

poetry's value in the twenty-first century.[4] First, the kind of power with which Shelley (and, differently, Plato) endows poets is both utterly improbable and deeply suspect; as Auden writes a century and a half after Shelley's "Defense," "'the unacknowledged legislators of the world' describes the secret police, not the poets."[5] And second, it can't be said that poetry is "the centre and circumference of knowledge"; poetry is, however one shades the term, a marginal practice within the totality of contemporary global culture, which isn't the same as saying that it's insignificant. Arguing that the importance of poetry in our world is bound up in the consequence of "Poets" or in the value of some aggrandized notion of "Poetry" is misguided. Rather, the value of poetry inheres in the value of poems and what they offer to readers: an experience of open intellection, aesthetic pleasure, and affective intensity that is vital to but often absent from the general run of contemporary culture, a point made by William Carlos Williams in one of his magnificent late poems, "Asphodel, That Greeny Flower":

> It is difficult
> to get the news from poems
>   yet men die miserably every day
>   for lack
> of what is found there.[6]

Poems generally do not offer "the news," and so they are too easily disregarded in a time when all are "distracted from distraction by distraction," as Eliot puts it in *Four Quartets* (1943), his own crucial late work. And how much more so now than in the mid-twentieth century in which Williams' and Eliot's poems are situated.[7] And so, how much more vital now is poetry's capacity to provoke and shape forms of attention.

---

[4] Percy Bysshe Shelley, "A Defense of Poetry," in *The Critical Tradition: Classic Texts and Contemporary Trends*, ed. David Richter (Boston: Bedford Books, 1998), 339–356, at 353 and 356.
[5] W. H. Auden, *The Dyer's Hand and Other Essays* (New York: Random House, 1962), 27.
[6] Christopher MacGowan, ed., *The Collected Poems of William Carlos Williams: Volume II, 1939–1962* (New York: New Directions, 1988), 318.
[7] T. S. Eliot, *Collected Poems, 1909–1962* (New York: Harcourt Brace & Co., 1991 [1963]), 178.

A poem's ability to enthrall but not coerce has everything to do with its linguistic texture and complexity. The poetry that I most value does not lead the reader down a single path or to an inevitable end but rather leaves multiple routes open, eliciting a flexibility and many-mindedness on the part of the reader. This is often described (or denigrated) as poetry's ubiquitous ambiguity or unwarranted difficulty. Why, so many have asked, can't poets simply say what they mean? The trouble with this formulation is that it assumes that the text of the poem (what is "said") is somehow a cover for a buried meaning, one that the poet either won't articulate clearly or can't – "It is impossible to say just what I mean," bemoans J. A. Prufrock.[8] To be sure, Prufrock's dilemma is by no means limited to poets: we all reckon constantly with the difficulty of saying what we mean.[9] Poems neither replicate nor solve this difficulty: that is, they neither ambiguously or imperfectly render some other meaning that goes unsaid, nor proceed as though language is transparent. Poetry's complexity and ambiguity isn't a failing or a glitch but central to its major tasks: to emphasize the productive but vexing density of language, and to display language's thickness by activating the entirety of words – their denotations, their connotations, their etymologies, their phonetic and phonemic properties, and their histories of use. Contemporary culture is deeply inattentive: distraction, multitasking, and disengagement are among its central features. Many contemporary poems push against these conditions, whether implicitly or explicitly, by offering a space for noncoercive attention. From this perspective, the compaction or density of poetry isn't a sign of its willful difficulty or unapproachability but an index of compositional scope and readerly possibility.

The kinds of attentiveness that poems afford, then, are inextricable from linguistic play. By "play" I do not only mean surface-level verbal invention – puns, rhymes, arresting images or metaphors – but also the extensive series of shaping forces by which poets condense,

---

[8] Eliot, *Collected Poems, 1909–1962*, 6.
[9] For a remarkable exploration of the various aspects of this matter, see Denise Riley, *The Words of Selves: Identification, Solidarity, Irony* (Palo Alto, CA: Stanford University Press, 2000).

arrange, splay, and renovate language, setting additional patterns atop or athwart a poem's system of syntax and grammar. Such varieties of play – those riddling, rhythmic, sonic, hymnic, or mantric aspects of poetic texts – are sources of readerly pleasure and excitement, but they also inflect the social and generic commitments of a poem and help to shape the kind of thought and feeling produced within it. Poetic play, then, is also quite serious, to redirect Johan Huizinga's famous claim in *Homo Ludens* (1938). For both writer and reader, the space of a poem can be one of intellectual and affective seriousness but also one of experimentation – a kind of free and meaningful play. The dual demand that a poem makes of its reader – to attend and to play – evokes the many other double structures from which poems are made, some of which I began to outline in the introduction. A poem, as I suggested earlier, is a chimera. Northrop Frye's famous distinction between "babble" and "doodle" – that is, between poetry's sonic and graphic dimensions – maps onto an entire series of double forms: *melos* and *opsis*, charm and riddle, *carmen* and text, music and speech.[10] This particular dialectic is poetry's crux, as long as we understand that each term is subject to constant and thoroughgoing deconstructions and reformulations at every turn. Poems are founded in both speech and song but fully assimilate themselves to neither. And this chimeric quality is based in a feature that is so plainly evident that it can go under-noticed: a poem is made simultaneously of lines and sentences.[11]

To say that a poem's single string of words is doubly encoded is not to make a new observation. In "A General Introduction for My Work" (1937), W. B. Yeats, borrowing from Robert Bridges a notion he

---

[10] See Northrop Frye, *Anatomy of Criticism: Four Essays* [1957] in Robert D. Denham, ed., *Collected Works of Northrop Frye*, vol. 22 (Toronto: University of Toronto Press, 2007), 257–263.
[11] This definition implicitly sidelines prose poetry and mixed mode poetry, which of course have their own traditions and complexities. In making such a sweeping claim, I do not mean to exclude such work, and I'll consider a number of prose poems and mixed mode forms throughout this volume. However, one could argue that even in the case of prose poetry and mixed verse-prose texts the dialectic between lines and sentences, or the possibility of such, catalyzes – even via negation – their formal dynamics. That is, prose poems still do remake typical patterns of sentence use, even if they do not employ lineation to do so.

himself borrowed from Gerard Manley Hopkins, emphasizes the "contrapuntal" structure of verse, its basis in both the regular pattern of the "'folk song" and the variable rhythms of "passionate prose."[12] In "The End of the Poem," Giorgio Agamben suggests that poetry exists in the schism between language as a semiotic event and a semantic event, what he describes as "the tension and difference (and hence also in the virtual interference) between sound and sense," and "the opposition between metrical segmentation and semantic segmentation." He goes on to call poetry "an organism grounded in the perception of the limits and endings that define – without ever fully coinciding with, and almost in intermittent dispute with – sonorous (or graphic) units and semantic units." For Agamben, poetry is defined at the point when the sentence (the "semantic unit" or segment) and the line (the "sonorous [or graphic]" unit) collide and disjoin: that is, at the end of a line. Poetry lives in "the possibility of enjambment," which, in Agamben's thinking, makes the final line of any poem a profoundly volatile place, a catastrophe "distinguished by the unexpected irruption of prose."[13] Because it cannot enjamb, cannot turn back around to the next line, the final line of any poem is, strangely enough, not a line of poetry because poetry is marked indelibly by the disjunction between lines and sentences rather than their coincidence. It is as though poems embed within their concluding moments a gesture toward their own endlessness, "as if the poem as a formal structure would not and could not end, as if the possibility of the end were radically withdrawn from it."[14]

Even if we do not follow Agamben all the way to his thrilling conclusion – that poems, in a sense, cannot end, or that they can only end by suspending their poetic structure – we can take on board the broader stakes of his argument: poems braid together two different modes of segmentation and significance within their single course of words. To be sure, not all poems actively or constantly exploit this

---

[12] W. B. Yeats, *Essays and Introductions* (New York: Macmillan, 1961), 524.
[13] Giorgio Agamben, "The End of the Poem," in *The End of the Poem: Studies in Poetics* (Palo Alto, CA: Stanford University Press, 1999), 109–115, at 109, 110, and 112.
[14] Agamben, "The End of the Poem," 113.

tension, such as Whitman's "Song of Myself" or Ginsberg's "Howl," long-lined poems whose line endings often coincide with the end of a syntactical unit, but this tension subtends such poems nonetheless. And there are numerous poems that do away with syntax or grammatical structure, or that aim to do away with sentences entirely. Both Yeats and Agamben think in terms of metrical verse, and the presence of a regular meter certainly makes visible the way that lines and sentences interact in a mobius-like fashion as they spiral down the page. However, metrical regularity is not necessary for such structures and effects to be on display, as in Gwendolyn Brooks' iconic poem, "We Real Cool," in which the title's three-word sentence structure provides the poem with its first compositional rule, while the poem's severe and angular principle of enjambment – "We real cool. We" – provides the second.[15] The poem's lines carve an alternate path through the poem's sentences, an effect that bolsters both the text's playful insouciance and its much grimmer import. One of the characteristic qualities of Paul Muldoon's poetry is the use of rhyme to regulate line length and sentence development: many of his poems contain strict rhyme patterns filled with often baroque rhymes, but the rhyme scheme is often decoupled from a consistent meter. Here, for instance, are the opening stanzas of "When the Pie Was Opened," a poem in seven sections, each of which contain three quintains rhymed *aabba*:

> Every morning the water again runs clear
> as it has for twenty years
> of jabs
> and stabs
> where we've joined in single combat, my dear,
>
> on a strand or at a ford.
> Every evening I've fleshed my sword
> in a scabbard.
> The hedgehog bristling on your tabard.
> Behind each of us is arrayed a horde[.][16]

---

[15] Gwendolyn Brooks, *Selected Poems* (New York: HarperCollins, 1999 [1963]), 73.
[16] Paul Muldoon, *Maggot* (New York: Farrar, Straus and Giroux, 2010), 28.

The poem's thematic dialogue between love and combat intertwines with Muldoon's usual mode of free association. It isn't only the case that the line endings frequently perform their content, as in the case of "jabs/and stabs," whose linear brevity replicates the violent rapidity to which they refer. It is also that the unfurling of lines and sentences are subjugated to the rhyme scheme: line endings are determined by the single necessity of maintaining a rhyme scheme rather than by the dual necessity of keeping a meter to which the rhyme scheme is crucial but subordinated. In such poems as Brooks' and Muldoon's, the eschewal of a regular or traditional meter allows another dimension of poetry's line-sentence dialectic to emerge.

Even in those poems in which sentences seem to be entirely eschewed in favor of isolated words and phrases, we continue to attend to the prospect of grammar as we reckon with sequestered words. In the case of a poet such as Maggie O'Sullivan, unmooring words from sentences is part of a much larger project to unmake conventional linguistic practices so as to revivify language. In her performance essay, "Riverrunning (Realisations," she explains that "the works I make Celebrate ORigins/ENtrances – the/Materiality of Language: its actual contractions &/expansions, potentialities, prolongments, assemblages – /the acoustic, visual, oral & sculptural qualities/within the physical."[17] Her poems aim to channel shamanic and bardic energies within a thoroughly disrupted linguistic texture in which words and phrases are under constant transformative pressure, often in texts that concern the natural world, as in "Starlings":

> Lived Daily
>   or both
>
>   Daily
> the Living
>   structuring
>   Bone-Seed,

[17] Maggie O'Sullivan, *Palace of Reptiles* (Willowsdale, Ontario: The Gig, 2003), 64.

>   Pelage,
>   Aqueous,
>
>   *YONDERLY* –
>   lazybed of need –
>   *CLOUD-SANG*
>   Tipsy-bobble, Dowdy
>   wander[18]

Even as we find most of our attempts to make sense of this poem in any conventional way rebuffed, and even as we are constantly foiled in our attempts to link word to word into larger units of normative meaning, O'Sullivan exploits the poem's line-by-line occurrence in order to produce something like a verbal analogue – all babble and doodle – of the titular birds' life in the sky. To be sure, O'Sullivan's poem doesn't contain sentences, but it harnesses the potential of sentence-making by continuing to rely on articles, conjunctions, and prepositions alongside of her newfangled nouns, verbs, and adjectives. This is to say, while O'Sullivan's poetry wouldn't be conceivable in Yeats' or Agamben's understanding of the contrapuntal structure of verse, it is still propelled by the doubleness at the core of poetry.

As is clear from the introduction of O'Sullivan's work, which mobilizes many of poetry's earliest archetypal forms (riddles, charms, chants, incantations), another dimension of this tension between a poem's sentences and its lines has to do with matters of genre and the context of a poem's verbal and textual performance (whether actual or imagined): how a poem is shaped and arrayed has to do with compositional choices, to be sure, but also with generic conventions and expectations. The kinds of attention that a poem aims to produce and the sorts of linguistic and aesthetic play that it elicits are guided by the demands of the generic matrix in which it takes part. As acts of speech and inscription, poems have often been called upon to do particular kinds of cultural work: naming, celebrating, marking, commemorating, praising, cursing, praying, memorializing. By means of

---

[18] Maggie O'Sullivan, *In the House of the Shaman* (London: Reality Street, 1993), 41.

its verbal music, for instance, a charm or spell or prayer or ode is meant to ensure the completion of a task, the fulfillment of a rite, the performance of a practice, or the representation of a set of values. By means of its placement, an inscription or epitaph is meant to mark an event or person. Genres carry with them certain formal tendencies or entailments, and some formal constraints are guided by the social context of the genre (the necessity of brevity and pithiness on an epitaph; the importance of rhythmic repetition in a chant or spell). However, this isn't to say that generic categories (which tend to be quite baggy) dictate particular forms. As Jahan Ramazani has pointed out, genres are capacious, open categories that can accommodate a great deal of revision, reinvention, and hybridization. He argues for "a dialogic understanding of poetry" in which "poetry is infiltrated by and infiltrates its generic others."[19] This is especially the case for twentieth- and twenty-first-century poems, many of which cultivate an ironic, subversive, or transgressive stance toward traditional genres, whether poetic genres or what Ramazani calls poetry's "generic others," a massive range of texts and styles that includes everything from literary prose and journalism to instruction manuals and menus, as well as the huge range of discourses and styles that bloom in digital space. Just as we understand the relationship between lines and sentences in poetry to be mutually generative and mobile rather than fixed or determined, so can we see genres as constructive matrices rather than as closed and fixed classes.[20] Poems habitually partake of multiple generic and modal drives, and such discursive fluidity impels the kind of noninstrumental attention that poetry affords.

Questions about genre are inextricable from questions about the kind of linguistic event or speech act – both written and oral – that a poem is or approximates. Traditionally, part of poetry's task – very broadly defined – has been to delineate events or occurrences, to indicate a shift from one set of conditions to another, or to separate "everyday" time

---

[19] Jahan Ramazani, *Poetry and Its Others: News, Prayer, Song, and the Dialogue of Genres* (Chicago and London: University of Chicago Press, 2014), 5.
[20] In addition to Ramazani on genre, see Ralph Cohen, "History and Genre," *New Literary History*, 17.2 (1986), 203–218; and Erik Martiny, ed., *A Companion to Poetic Genre* (Chichester, UK and Hoboken, NJ: Wiley-Blackwell, 2012).

from ritual or special time.[21] Often the saying of the poem itself stages such a shift. At the same time that poetry is understood to be a "heightened" sort of language that formalizes events or conditions, as an intensification of everyday speech, it is also the case that poetry is thought to be precisely everyday speech, arranged or distilled in such a way that it is both how "one" talks and, to reroute Eliot once again, "how [one] should talk if [one] could talk poetry."[22] This argument has been active since Wordsworth's "Preface" to *Lyrical Ballads* (1800): instead of marking a break with the everyday or existing in some rarified zone away from the grain of daily life, a poem articulates such life. The impulse to create poetry that remains close to speech certainly preceded Wordsworth, but poetry in the last two centuries has been catalyzed by repeated attempts to write poetry in the dialect, register, and idiom that is near to that of the poet's own community (however such community is conceived). To list the significant poets of the twentieth and twenty-first centuries who at some point in their careers wrote with their ear close to their local sociolinguistic ground would be to list many of the significant poets of the twentieth and twenty-first centuries. And just as poets can splice and meld genres, so can they solder linguistic codes and dialects and rotate among registers. In any case, the simple act of framing or presenting a stretch of language as a poem, even if that poem is a "found text" of the most banal sort, takes that text out of the realm of everyday speech. It is an imitation or embedding of everyday speech into an aesthetic context: the piece of slang that a writer absorbs into a poem is no longer simply that but is also reconceived, ironized, or made reflexive. The banality is no longer simply uttered, it is brought to attention. For the most part, then, poems are neither simple instances of everyday speech nor heightened, formalized linguistic constructions entirely removed from the spoken and written language environment out of which they surface. To return sidewise to an earlier point, poetry's propensity to absorb,

---

[21] On modern poetry's adaptation of ancient poetic modes and genres, see Andrew Welch, *Roots of Lyric: Primitive Poetry and Modern Poetics* (Princeton, NJ: Princeton University Press, 1978). Also see Eleanor Cook, *Enigmas and Riddles in Literature* (Cambridge: Cambridge University Press, 2006); and Daniel Tiffany, *Infidel Poetics: Riddles, Nightlife, Substance* (Chicago and London: University of Chicago Press, 2009).

[22] T. S. Eliot, *The Music of Poetry* (Glasgow: Jackson, Son & Co., 1942), 16.

refract, and redirect the multiple vernaculars and registers that surround it makes it an especially important mode of immanent critique, especially in a time of inattention and unthinking. Sifting a language's multifarious registers and sorting the finds, a poem can display the ways that language is used in everyday life, can ask a reader to attend both to the surfaces of language and the forces at work beneath it, and can critique those forces by reflecting upon them and so pointing toward alternatives. The task of poetry is not "to purify the dialect of the tribe," as is suggested by the "familiar compound ghost" during the Dantean encounter in Eliot's "Little Gidding."[23] Rather, it is to restage the messiness of converging idioms at every turn and to shape that mess into a compelling form.

The utopian strains of the above sentences must be tempered, at least a bit. The force or consequence that I've attributed to poetry in the contemporary world must be countered by acknowledging that the kind of social and cultural privilege or place upon which such consequence must rely is, at least a bit, defunct. It isn't only that poetry is "out of key" with its time or a peripheral form within the broader landscape of cultural production. It is also that the social and cultural scenarios that have long underpinned poetry's generic and performative patterns have long been relics. The energy that poems continue to draw from much earlier generic and contextual conditions is inevitably a pseudo- or gestural energy. A poet like O'Sullivan who aims to channel the mantric or shamanic within her metamorphic forms is not simply making a bid for shamanic powers. This notion is central to post-Kantian and modern aesthetics: key to art's consequence is its uselessness; its noninstrumentality allows it to potentially find a space outside the logic of capital and cold rationality. I'll take up this topic more fully in the following chapters.

This chapter on poetry's tactics of producing attention and provoking readerly play has slowly backed into the most important matter, that of sound. The general topics I've broached so far are inextricably connected to the role of sonic play in poems. Matters of line, sentence, genre, and register are all central to a poem's import but they are also at least a bit submerged. A reader's consideration of those

[23] Eliot, *Collected Poems, 1909–1962*, 204, 203.

aspects is likely to be preceded by (and spurred by) a surface-level allure – a phrase's unexpected turn, an image's stark weirdness, a strand of word-sounds that compel notice. Poems often elicit attention via their sonic patterns – not only overt displays of rhyme, assonance, or consonance, but also the subterranean tessellations generated by any poem's chimeric venture: that is, to constitute both sensible, cognizable speech and thought, and to approach-though-never-reach the condition of a wordless song made of words. For the remainder of this chapter, I'll delve into poetry's basis in and manipulation of linguistic sound.

Reuven Tsur's central claim about how sound works in poetry (and in literature more broadly) concerns the existence of what he calls a "poetic mode" within human auditory capacity.[24] The basic modes of human audition in Tsur's account are the "speech mode" and the "nonspeech" mode. When we hear a set of sounds, we almost immediately (and subconsciously) categorize the sound as either speech or nonspeech. If the sound is cognized as speech, then the vast array of auditory information that constitutes that sound – pitch, tone, volume, timbre – is deprioritized as the sound is converted into language. If the sound isn't immediately transformed into speech, then certain acoustic information remains in the ear as sonic material, rather than being encoded phonetically, a capacity that Tsur describes as the "poetic mode of speech perception." The "poetic mode" is something of a delaying effect. Instead of instantaneously attending away from acoustics and toward phonetics, some of the sonic richness of words lingers and registers subliminally. He suggests that poetry's multifarious nonsignifying structures (rhyme, assonance, phrasal rhythm, and so on) have a particular effect on auditory processes. Even though we hear words and so should immediate strip the sounds of their acoustic granularities and recode them as language, what happens instead is that some of what Tsur calls "the rich, precategorical auditory information" lingers in the ear and brain.[25] The activation of the "poetic mode"

---

[24] Among Reuven Tsur's many works, see in particular *What Makes Sound Patterns Expressive? The Poetic Mode of Speech Perception* (Durham, NC: Duke University Press, 1992).

[25] Tsur, *What Makes Sound Patterns Expressive?*, 37.

provides a brief span of auditory "negative capability": a string of words can seem at once like speech and wordless sound.

Tsur's argument rests on his hypothesis about a capacity within human audition. Whereas we typically sort sounds either as language or noise (with the caveat that "noise" here designates any kind of non-linguistic sound, from birdsong to Bartók to jackhammers), Tsur's "poetic mode" provides a framework for explaining what sound can do in certain linguistic contexts. In so doing, it builds upon Roman Jakobson's influential notion of the "poetic function," one of six basic functions that comprise the language system. Each of Jakobson's six functions is geared toward a different aspect of language's primal scenario: addresser-message-addressee. In addition to these three explicit components (the sender of the message, the receiver of the message, and the message itself), there are three others: the "code" (the language that must be shared so that the receiver can receive the sender's message); the "contact" (the medium or channel via which the message is transmitted); and the "context" (by which Jakobson indicates the meaning or referent of the message). Jakobson's six linguistic functions map onto these basic components: the emotive (or expressive), the conative, the referential, the phatic, the metalingual, and the poetic. In most actual instances of communication, whether oral or textual, each of the six functions will be active, but one or several might predominate. For instance, in a message focused on the receiver of the message – a command, a request, a plea – the conative function is the dominant one, but of course the others are active as well.

Jakobson describes the poetic function as that which focuses "on the message for its own sake." A message in which the poetic function predominates promotes "the palpability of signs," that is, their graphic and sonic shapes, even as the other linguistic functions are present, as they must be.[26] The "poetic function" isn't exclusively the province of poetry, and Jakobson's most famous example of the poetic function – "I like Ike," the iconic slogan of Dwight D.

---

[26] Roman Jakobson, "Linguistics and Poetics," in *Style in Language*, ed. Thomas A. Sebeok and John W. Ashton (New York and Cambridge, MA: John Wiley & Sons and the Technology Press of the Massachusetts Institute of Technology, 1960), 350–377, at 356.

Eisenhower's 1952 presidential campaign – demonstrates quite clearly that the poetic function is at work in a range of discursive and rhetorical scenarios beyond literary poetry, from political slogans, protest chants, and mnemonics to lullabies and nursery rhymes. We tend to differentiate between forms of speech and writing that function poetically – to tweak Jakobson's phrasing – and "poetry" proper in one of two ways. The first rests on a determination about a difference in intent and the second about a difference in value. On the first: the difference between a political or advertising slogan that is sonically compelling and a poem is that the aim of the slogan's "catchiness" is typically persuasion, coercion, or ideological mystification. (To be sure, a different, gentler form of persuasion can be at work in a lullaby or nursery rhyme.) A poem usually doesn't have such overt designs upon its reader or receiver (or, if it does, then its complexity or obliquity will likely muffle or topple any such designs). On the second: we tend to differentiate between the huge corpus of sonically, rhythmically charged language forms and poems by elevating the latter into the realm of art and placing the former into a massive, amorphous category that includes everything from jingles and versified taunts to mantras, the banalities of greeting cards, and the constitutive clichés of much popular music. Such work is "poetic" in Jakobson's sense, but – to state the case in the bluntest terms – it is uncompelling as literature. It isn't only, as Jakobson points out, that the "poetic function" can't be confined to poetry, it is also that poetry can't be considered simply as a display of the "poetic function." In fact, verbal messages (again, whether oral or textual) that are flagrantly reliant on the poetic function are likely to be actively sidelined or passively overlooked by many critics and scholars of poetry, either shunted into the marginal category of "light verse" or nonsense verse, as in Lewis Carroll's "Jabberwocky," or cordoned off into the zone of "sound poetry," including important modernist experiments such as Kurt Schwitters' "Ursonate" or Hugo Ball's Dadaist *lautgedichte*, as well as more recent works by Bob Cobbing, Tracie Morris, and O'Sullivan.

Such experimental, transgressive works cause difficulties for readers and critics because their radical linguistic playfulness unbalances the relationship among the linguistic functions that Jakobson maps. Verbal texts that seem to give up on sense and reference ask readers to reverse engineer Tsur's "poetic mode." If our auditory system tends to be tuned to the possibility of language, switching into "speech mode" whenever it seems like language is being heard, and thereby stripping the richness of word-sounds so that they can be encoded as words, then sound poems – texts built from the bits of language, phonemes, syllables, word-parts – start up the speech mode only to stall the ear, leaving it in a sonic lurch. We have such trouble experiencing and understanding such works because we are being asked to hear words or word-like sounds simply *as* sound, which cuts harshly against the grain of our linguistic capacity and auditory tendencies. We tend to be on the lookout for language, and a poem like "Jabberwocky" or Wallace Stevens' "Bantams in Pine Woods," both gives us what we seek and refuses to attune itself to our desires to simultaneously hear and comprehend.

One of the best-known comments on the importance of sound in poetry is from a letter that Robert Frost wrote in 1913: "The best place to get the abstract sound of sense is from voices behind a door that cuts off the words."[27] The scenario that Frost presents is a proleptic dramatization of Tsur's poetic mode: the sounds of language can be heard but the words themselves cannot be deciphered, so the overhearer is in the position of constantly listening for language that never arrives. Such a listener can tune into patterns of sound and articulation, the rhythms of conversation or speech, and the quasi-melodic run of grammar. At the same time, however, that listener is assuming that language is happening and so is listening differently than if, say, it was apparent that the voices on the other side of the door were simply vocalizing nonspeech sounds (such as singers or actors warming their voices). If Frost's overhearer opened the door and encountered not people speaking but a set of machines programmed to produce speech-like nonsense, then the evocative beauty of the unseen, muffled voices would be shattered. This is the point that T. S. Eliot

---

[27] Robert Frost, *Collected Poems, Prose, and Plays*, ed. Richard Poirier and Mark Richardson (New York: Library of America, 1995), 664.

makes in his 1942 lecture, "The Music of Poetry." For Eliot, the "music of poetry" is not separate from its status as sensible language: "we can be deeply stirred by hearing the recitation of a poem in a language of which we understand no word; but if we are then told that the poem is gibberish and has no meaning, we shall consider that we have been deluded – this was no poem, it was merely an imitation of instrumental music."[28] If for Frost the "sound sense" of language can be ascertained before the actual sense of the words can be apprehended, then Eliot introduces a further condition: a listener might register the beauty of a string of words framed as a poem (even if the listener is unfamiliar with the language of the poem), just as Frost's overhearing listener senses something of the muffled language's "abstract sound of sense," but it is crucial that any "music" that a poem evinces is grounded in its status as potentially meaningful language.

Well beyond Eliot's expectedly commanding pronouncement, the importance of sound in poetry, and in literature more broadly, typically has been understood to exist in an inextricable ratio with sense. The signifier is a visual and sonic mark bound to a concept or idea that it signifies. The specific visual and aural densities of the signifier largely dissolve when it is cognized and so transformed into its signified. Both Jakobson's "poetic function" and Tsur's "poetic mode" operate within the bounds of this broader account of signification: Jakobson's "poetic function" indicates a particular force within the linguistic system and Tsur's "poetic mode" theorizes how this force transpires within audition. Both accounts rely on the fundamental bind between the sound of a sign and its sense. True sound poems are so hazardous to readers because they untie this bind: they invite a reader to read or hear the poem as though it were made of words, and then – extravagantly or subtly – cancel this invitation.

In many ways, our understanding and expectation of sound's significance for poetry is still governed by Alexander Pope's famous declaration in "An Essay on Criticism" (1711) that "the sound must seem an echo to the sense." In the passage from which this line is

[28] Eliot, *The Music of Poetry*, 15.

drawn, Pope demonstrates that "art, not chance" is all, that a writer must ensure that the form of a poem fits its content: a line about a "smooth stream" must flow in "smoother numbers," while a text that features "loud surges lash[ing] the sounding shore," likewise so "the hoarse, rough verse should like the torrent roar."[29] For Pope, and many after him, the sound of a poem and its sense are commensurable. But Pope's line signals not only a relationship but also a teleology: sense comes first and is then echoed or bolstered by sound.

We can read against the grain of Pope's line to understand something not only about the ways in which sound and sense interact, but also about the ways that they don't. Contra Plato's "Cratylus," the sound of a word or phrase can reinforce, amplify, augment, or counteract the sense of the line, but it can't inaugurate sense. Apart from certain special cases in which the sound and sense of a word have a natural or iconic relation – most familiarly in the case of onomatopoeia – the bind between signifier and signified is arbitrary and differential. The meaning of a word is not inherent to that word but rather relies on its place within an entire system and storehouse of words from which it can be differentiated. At the same time, while the relationship between the sound of a word and its sense is arbitrary, it isn't insignificant or nonmeaningful. Benjamin Harshav argues for a "two-directional process" in which a sound pattern is established and then the meanings of certain words within the pattern bolster or refract the sound pattern, which then turns back around and reinforces the composite meaning of the passage.[30] For Harshav, this is a dialectical process in which autonomous patterns intersect and reshape one another at various crucial points in a poem and in variable ways (Harshav goes on to provide a general typology of sound-meaning relations), and much relies on a reader or listener activating "potentials of meaning impressions" as they occur within a poem.[31] The necessary point is that while particular language sounds don't have

---

[29] Margaret Ferguson, Tim Kendall, and Mary Jo Salter, eds., *The Norton Anthology of Poetry*, 6th ed. (New York: W.W. Norton & Co., 2018), 639.
[30] Benjamin Harshav, *Explorations in Poetics* (Stanford, CA: Stanford University Press, 2007), 144.
[31] Harshav, *Explorations in Poetics*, 146.

automatic, innate meanings, they do have a range of tendencies, having to do with a number of factors such as acoustic properties, articulatory properties, and associations with other words. Relations between sound and meaning, therefore, are rife but not codifiable or reducible to a general model.[32] Certain sounds don't necessarily link up with certain meanings; rather, poetry's habit of patterning sound has the effect of, as Harshav puts it, "deautonomizing the sound itself and making it conspicuous."[33]

In this way, a poet's manipulation of linguistic sound – playing with it, attending to it – is basic to what Viktor Shklovsky has described as art's central function, which is to "defamiliarize" the world and our experience of it. In "Art as Technique" (1917), he provides the canonical description of defamiliarization:

> art exists that one may recover the sensation of life; it exists to make one feel things, to make the stone *stony*. The purpose of art is to impart the sensation of things as they are perceived and not as they are known. The technique of art is to make objects "unfamiliar," to make forms difficult, to increase the difficulty and length of perception because the process of perception is an aesthetic end in itself and must be prolonged.[34]

If we gather up Tsur's notion of the "poetic mode," Jakobson's of the "poetic function," and Harshav's sense of the interactivity of sound and sense, and route them all through Shklovsky's formulation of defamiliarization or estrangement, then we can understand that key to the value of poems is their revivification of language and linguistic conventions, the reactivation of what I. A. Richards called "the full bodies" of words.[35]

---

[32] For an account of the importance and function of such secondary features of language that quite independently approaches a somewhat similar conclusion, albeit from a very different theoretical and methodological path, see J. H. Prynne, "Stars, Tigers, and the Shapes of Words," The William Matthews Lecture, Birkbeck College, London (1992).

[33] Harshav, *Explorations in Poetics*, 152.

[34] Viktor Shklovsky, "Art as Technique," trans. Lee T. Lemon and Marion Reis, *The Critical Tradition: Classic Texts and Contemporary Trends*, ed. David Richter (Boston: Bedford Books, 1998), 717–726, at 720 (emphasis original).

[35] I. A. Richards, *Science and Poetry* (Cambridge: R. I. Severs, 1935 [1926]), 17.

Any given word or phrase might have a range of potential sound effects, and we have a variety of terms – alliteration, assonance, consonance, rhyme, paronomasia – to indicate what sort of effect is at work. It remains the task of reading to consider the import of such effects: a rhyme pair is bound sonically because of the rhyme, but a reader must weigh the implications of such binding. Adjacent rhymes (as in Pope's heroic couplets in "An Essay on Criticism") work differently than rhyme pairs separated by one or more lines. Rhyme pairs whose meanings bolster or reflect one another will function quite differently than pairings whose semantic freight tends in opposite directions, as in the conventional rhyme on *breath* and *death*: the words occupy each other's negative space, and depending on which comes first, the poem at hand might offer either a confirmation of death – *breath* stopped by *death* – or a resurrection – *death* overturned by new found *breath*.

Often, particular rhymes can encapsulate an entire poem, as though fractally. The final word in Seamus Heaney's famous early sonnet, "Requiem for the Croppies" – an elegy for the Irish rebels (the "croppies") battling the British at Vinegar Hill during the 1798 Irish Rebellion that is spoken in the collective voice of the dead fighters – is, appropriately enough, "grave." "Grave" completes the second triple rhyme that constitutes the sestet, which tells of the croppies' defeat and death in battle: "the final conclave," "our broken wave," "grave." Here the rhyme triplet enacts the battle in miniature. Even more stunning is the triple rhyme that is braided around the *conclave/wave/grave* triplet. This second trio is built out from a description of the Irish fighters taking cover from British cavalry behind hedges, "where cavalry must be thrown." The next member of this rhyme chain again focuses on the asymmetry of the battle, as the croppies shake their "scythes at cannon." The final instance of this rhyme chain occurs in the sonnet's penultimate line, which then gives way to elegiac recompense in the final line:

> They buried us without shroud or coffin
> And in August the barley grew up out of the grave.[36]

---

[36] Seamus Heaney, *Poems: 1965–1975* (New York: Farrar, Straus and Giroux, 1980), 54.

There is a remarkable range of sound effects in these final lines, most of which are catalyzed by "coffin." Although the poem does not aspire to the form of a Shakespearian sonnet with its final, clinching couplet, it manages to include a figural rhyme in a concluding quasi-couplet: *coffin* and *grave* "rhyme" metonymically. There is also a partial internal rhyme on *buried* and *barley*, with the opening consonance (/b/) and the double assonance (/ur/ and /ar/; /ie/ and /ey/) holding the two words together, while the consonantal differences end up doing significant work: the /d/ in *buried* indicates a finality that is subtly (subterraneanly) undone by the medial "l" in *barley* that literally rises out of the middle of the two words' shared midsection just as the actual barley – which, as the poem's first line tells us, filled the pockets of the croppies' "great coats" – sprouts the following season, so as to fulfill the poem's elegiac economy. All of the soundwork on "buried" and "barley" occurs within the mass, coffin-less grave of the croppies. The place of "coffin" within the rhyme scheme is perhaps even more complex. The first word in the chain – "thrown" – initially refers to what would happen to the British cavalry riders should the horses attempt to rush the hedges. However, when it is pulled into the orbit of its rhymefellows, "cannon" and "coffin," it can be redirected to describe the croppies, who are "thrown" by the British "cannon" and then "thrown" sans "coffin" into the unmarked pit – save for the following spring's barley – that is their grave. We can even take the pararhyme on *cannon* and *coffin* to encode the croppies' burial. The two words share opening and closing consonants, but the middle of *cannon* is emptied out so as to produce *coffin*: the grave pit is enciphered within the rhyme.

Of course, not every sound effect will ramify so intensely within a poem's formal and semantic logic, but two points should be clear. What is in many ways a quite traditional form – Heaney chooses a sonnet template that combines a Shakespearian or English octave (quatrains rhyming *abab cdcd*) with a variation on a Petrarchan or Italian sestet (*efefef*) – becomes the site of extensive sonic play that goes to the quick of the poem's generic and discursive core. It is much less straightforward than Pope suggested, but the sound of the poem and its sense are inextricable. The relation between them isn't linear or unidirectional, and readers are simultaneously activating and constructing various paths of meaning, depending on the multivalent set of formal patterns suggested by the text. To stay with Heaney's poem for a moment longer, these patterns are not only sonic, rhythmic, or metrical, but also structural and generic. At a larger level, the two most notable features of "Requiem for the Croppies" are its formal status as a sonnet and its generic status as an elegy. It is a weird elegy, to be sure, as it is spoken by the dead who are elegized, but it certainly partakes of the basic elegiac conventions, just as it clearly partakes of the many of the conventions of the sonnet. At the same time, its form and its genre sit askance: traditionally, sonnets tended to be poems of love and desire, and so Heaney's adaptation of the sonnet form to write an elegiac poem cuts against convention. Readerly attention to matters of sound can't but be shaped by a poem's generic investments and, more generally, by the kind of poem it is – what it seems to be about, what are its principles of construction, how it positions the reader in relation to what it represents and how it progresses. As we read a poem such as "Requiem for the Croppies," we do not simply notice or admire the varieties of its sonic patterning; instead we are implicitly asked to restage the poem's elegiac scenario as we locate significant patterns and revivify the workings of sound that lay waiting on the page.

Considerations of poetic sound, then, are underwritten by matters of poetic genre and mode, as I have suggested earlier, and the significance of any given set of sound effects is shaped inexorably by the kind of poem it is. Craig Dworkin describes the predominant notion of poetry in the twentieth century and beyond as "a kind of text that deviates from conventionally utile language by self-reflexively foregrounding elements other than the referentially communicative." Nestled within Dworkin's usefully broad gesture are many of the most prominent modern accounts of poetry, from those of the Russian Formalists and Jakobson to Wittgenstein and Adorno. Dworkin goes on to gloss how the sound/sense ratio appears within this account: "sound is to sense as poetic language is to conventional language, but the relation of sound and sense, understood in this way, is nested within the category of the poetic. Taken as the opposite of sense, sound, in the formalist economy, encapsulates the logic of the poetic. One among the material, palpable, quantifiable facets of language, sound contrasts with the ideas conveyed by the referential sign."[37] As sound is to sense in a poem so is the "logic of the poetic" to "conventional language." Missing here, however, are exactly the kind of interactive energies that Harshav maps. The value of sound within any given poem does not stand opposed to the value of the poem's sense: they may operate by way of different logics, but they work in tandem.[38]

At the same time, such interactivity is not limited to the logic of echo that Pope proposed and that has guided most critics since, even though this sort of interaction may still predominate. Heaney's "Requiem for the Croppies" is one of many, many such examples of this kind of sound-sense play. In that poem, aspects of the text's topic, diegesis, theme, or meaning are spurred by a formal feature, which then rebounds upon and ramifies upon the meaning. I paid the most attention to matters of sound, but one might also think about such enactment in terms of figure, stanza, meter, or overall shape. A pattern poem such as George Herbert's "Easter Wings" is the prototype of such a technique: the poem, both visually and metrically, embodies its content. Marianne Moore's complexly patterned syllabic stanzas often display some aspect of their topic, especially in her animal poems, as in "The Pangolin," which opens with a description of the animal that doubles as a primer to the poem:

> Another armored animal – scale
> > lapping scale with spruce-cone regularity until they
> form the uninterrupted central
> > tail-row![39]

---

[37] Craig Dworkin, "The Poetry of Sound," in Marjorie Perloff and Craig Dworkin, eds., *The Sound of Poetry/The Poetry of Sound* (Chicago and London: The University of Chicago Press, 2009), 9–17, at 10.

[38] On sound in poetry, also see the essays in Perloff and Dworkin, eds., *The Sound of Poetry/The Poetry of Sound*; Susan Stewart, *Poetry and the Fate of the Senses* (Chicago and London: University of Chicago Press, 2002), esp. 59–105; Angela Leighton, *Hearing Things: The Work of Sound in Literature* (Cambridge, MA: Harvard University Press, 2018); Adalaide Morris, ed., *Sound States: Innovative Poetics and Acoustical Technologies* (Chapel Hill, NC: University of North Carolina Press, 1998); and John Hollander, *Vision and Resonance: Two Senses of Poetic Form* (New York: Oxford University Press, 1975).

[39] Marianne Moore, *Complete Poems* (New York: Macmillan Publishing Company/Penguin Books, 1994), 117.

The poem proceeds "with spruce-cone regularity" for nine eleven-line stanzas whose jagged lines realize the opening line's performative enjambment – "scale/lapping scale" – so as to align the poem's form with that of its titular animal. Elizabeth Bishop provides an analogous effect in "At the Fishhouses," in which the speaker describes the scene at the docks:

> Down at the water's edge, at the place
> where they haul up the boats, up the long ramp
> descending into the water, thin silver
> tree trunks are laid horizontally
> across the gray stones, down and down
> at intervals of four or five feet.[40]

The long lines quietly take on a kind of specular objecthood, metamorphosed into the "thin silver/tree trunks" "laid horizontally" down to the water. The pun on "feet" allows one to transfer the "four or five feet" interval between tree trunks into a moment of formal self-reflection: for the most part, "At the Fishhouses" is composed of lines that are "four or five feet" long. A different sort of rhythmical play can be seen in Yeats' early lyric, "The Song of Wandering Aengus," a poem in long ballad meter (tetrameter lines rhyming *abxb*). The first stanza ends with the speaker fishing:

> I dropped the berry in a stream
> And caught a little silver trout.[41]

Thus far, the poem had been largely iambic, but the last half of the second line "speeds up" metrically: the front-heavy stresses on "little" and "silver" mimic the fishing line as it is abruptly pulled from the water with a fish on its hooked thread. Such species of metrical or quasi-metrical self-reflexivity are ubiquitous, even in a twentieth-century canon partly defined by the rise of nonmetrical poetry and free verse,

---

[40] Elizabeth Bishop, *The Complete Poems, 1927–1979* (New York: Farrar, Straus and Giroux, 1983), 65.
[41] Richard J. Finneran, ed., *The Collected Poems of W. B. Yeats*, rev. 2nd ed. (New York: Simon & Schuster, 1996), 59.

by what Ezra Pound describes in *Canto* LXXXI: "to break the pentameter, that was the first heave."[42]

The enactive play that is apparent in the examples from Heaney, Moore, Bishop, and Yeats – in which some aspect of a poem's form sparks and is sparked by its sense – is perhaps the most typical species of poetic sound effect. But there are myriad other ways for poets to galvanize sound, especially since the heaves of modernism. Many poems rely explicitly on sound's relation to sense, some aim to abandon sense altogether and function exclusively as wordish sound, and some aim to alter the ratio, letting the play of linguistic sound generate new styles of sense. Jen Hadfield's poetry is characterized by its immersion in the dialect and lexicon of the Shetlands, where she has long lived. In the notes to her T. S. Eliot Prize-winning volume, *Nigh-No-Place* (2008), she states that she is "not a Shetland dialect speaker," but the Shetlandic words that "flitted through [her] vocabulary" become the building blocks of many of the volume's pseudo-dictionary poems, such as "Gish":

> **Gish**, *noun*: a channel of water strained through the wet red grass of a Fair Isle field, where a conger eel, like a swathe of gleaming liquorice, might thresh till nightfall; or, the water that wells in hoof shaped holes in the pasture; the two rails of faint light in a flooded *gaet* (*footpath, path leading to a beach*); or, a leak from a washing machine; the black liquor that cooks out of mushrooms; or **gish** – if drinking means a person sleeps, the sound of breath like drowning; or **gish** – a pish in the dark, in a severe to moderate wind.[43]

Unlike many of the unfamiliar words in Hadfield's books, "gish" appears neither in the volume's "notes" (which are largely devoted to glossing Shetlandic dialect terms) nor in John J. Graham's *Shetland Dictionary*, an important source for Hadfield. Neither does it appear in the *Oxford English Dictionary*. Reminiscent in certain ways of

---

[42] Ezra Pound, *The Cantos of Ezra Pound* (New York: New Directions Books, 1996 [1970]), 538.
[43] Jen Hadfield, *Nigh-No-Place* (Northumberland: Bloodaxe Books, 2008), 64 and 36 (emphases original).

Heaney's place-name poems in *Wintering Out* (1972) (such as "Toome" or "Broagh") and in others of Ambrose Bierce's *The Devil's Dictionary* (1906) or Jorge Luis Borges' *The Book of Imaginary Beings* (1957), Hadfield's "Gish" begins by recording what seems to be the word's ultra-local origin – a "channel of water" that flows through the red grass of Fair Isle (one of the Shetlands) – and then unspools a series of lexical concoctions based on the initial definition ("a channel of water") but ever further removed from the local context. The word's onomatopoetic character carries its meaning across a range of contexts, with the /-sh/ sound acting as a binding agent ("liquorice," "thresh," "-shaped," "washing," "machine," "mushrooms," "pish") even as the definitions become more outlandish. In this short prose poem, Hadfield moves from definition to invention, using the "full body" of "gish" to generate new meanings and leveraging the capacity of sound to invent sense. A word that is presumably specific to a particular linguistic community is launched into wider circulation via sonic and figural play, transforming from a noun – "a channel of water" – into a verb: the act of producing a very different stream of liquid in precise meteorological circumstances. Of course, as a dictionary entry, this is utterly fanciful; Hadfield's point isn't to provide a straight-faced definition. Rather, "Gish" helps us to see that part of poetry's value lies in its continual sifting of what Heaney called the "word-hoard," as an act of both reclamation and invention.[44]

We might say that Hadfield's "Gish" belongs in what Harryette Mullen calls the "recyclopedia." In the preface to *Recyclopedia* (2006), which gathers three volumes of Mullen's poetry, she writes: "If the encyclopedia collects general knowledge, the recyclopedia salvages and finds imaginative uses for knowledge. That's what poetry does when it remakes and renews words, images, and ideas, transforming surplus cultural information into something unexpected."[45] Mullen's own work, particularly in *Sleeping with the Dictionary* (2002), is committed to producing such unexpected renewals. *Sleeping with the Dictionary* is part of a lineage of texts emerging from modernist avant-garde practices, and especially from the kind of procedural work

---

[44] Heaney, *Poems: 1965–1975*, 175.
[45] Harryette Mullen, *Recyclopedia* (Saint Paul, MN: Graywolf Press, 2006), vii.

of mid-century figures like John Cage and Jackson MacLow. Mullen's volume is based on a variety of procedures, some of which derive from Raymond Quenau and the *Oulipo* writers, in particular a form of textual manipulation called "n plus 7" (sometimes "s plus 7"), in which every noun is replaced by the noun that appears seven words away in the dictionary or another pre-set text.[46] Just as more familiar forms of conceptual poetry are generated out of a single principle or notion (for example, Kenneth Goldsmith's massive *Day* [2003] is a verbatim rewriting of the entirety of a single issue of the *New York Times*), so are procedural poems generated out of a formal rule or set of rules.[47] Christian Bök's *Eunoia* (2001), for instance, is a series of page-length prose poems in five chapters, each of which uses words that only contain a single vowel: the book proceeds from *a* through *u*. Such projects draw from the energies of the avant-garde, but conceptual and procedural poetry is also connected to, if radically, the main line of the poetic tradition. What else is a sonnet but a kind of procedure? Even after the governing concept of the sonnet tradition (that is, poems of love and desire) is submerged, the procedure remains. The sonnet form has continually morphed over centuries – swelling to sixteen lines in George Meredith's "Modern Love" (1862) and to eighteen in John Berryman's *Dream Songs* (1969), shedding its rhyme scheme and internal structures in Ted Berrigan's *Sonnets* (1964), Lyn Hejinian's *The Unfollowing* (2016), or Terrance Hayes' *American Sonnets for My*

---

[46] *Oulipo* is short for "Ouvroir de littérature potentielle" – "workshop of potential literature" – and emerged in France in the 1960s. See Warren F. Motte, Jr., ed., *Oulipo: A Primer of Potential Literature* (Normal, IL: Dalkey Archive Press, 1998 [1986]); and Alison James, *Constraining Chance: Georges Perec and the Oulipo* (Evanston, IL: Northwestern University Press, 2009).

[47] On contemporary conceptual and avant-garde poetry, see Marjorie Perloff, *Unoriginal Genius: Poetry by Other Means in the New Century* (Chicago and London: University of Chicago Press, 2010); Timothy Yu, *Race and the Avant-Garde: Experimental and Asian American Poetry Since 1965* (Stanford, CA: Stanford University Press, 2009); Kenneth Goldsmith, *Uncreative Writing: Managing Language in the Digital Age* (New York: Columbia University Press, 2011); Linda Kinnahan, *Lyric Interventions: Feminism, Experimental Poetry, and Contemporary Discourse* (Iowa City, IA: University of Iowa Press, 2004); Lynn Keller, *Thinking Poetry: Readings in Contemporary Women's Exploratory Poetics* (Iowa City, IA: University of Iowa Press, 2010); and Brian Reed, *Nobody's Business: Twenty-First Century Avant-Garde Poetics* (Ithaca, New York: Cornell University Press, 2013).

Past and Future Assassin (2018) – but it persists as a generative scaffolding.

In the most important procedural and conceptual poetry of the past fifty or sixty years, the text has outdistanced its governing concept, procedure, or project. That is to say, the poem retains an interest beyond an acknowledgment of its concept or the fulfillment of its predetermined schema. If procedural and conceptual poetry can't but be playful, appearing as the outcome of a game of some kind, then the most significant such work also requires readerly attention; and Mullen's *Sleeping with the Dictionary* is a signal twenty-first-century text in this regard. Most of the poems are generated via a procedure, either an alphabetic process or an *Oulipian* rule, and so for the most part sound or chance determines sense rather than echoes it, with common idioms, slogans, and phrases often serving as the grist for linguistic transformation. In Mullen's hands, the alphabet becomes – explicitly, flagrantly – exactly what it is: an infinitely rearrangeable sequence, a multiform catalyst, the grounds of metamorphosis.

"Any Lit" is both typical of the book's style and exceptional in its ultimate import. At its surface, it is a straightforward procedural poem constituted by a repeated verbal formula, "you are a u- beyond my my(i)-." For thirty-three lines, Mullin spins variations, beginning with "you are a ukulele beyond my microphone" and ending "you are a uselessness beyond my myopia."[48] The poem abides by its rule, producing lines of sidewise historical comment ("you are a eugenics beyond my Mayan"), encrypted wisdom ("you are a union beyond my meiosis"), or high comedy ("you are a Uranus beyond my Miami"). Certain lines seem like freakish premonitions, such as "you are a Euterpe beyond my Mighty Sparrow," which links the Greek muse of music and lyric poetry and the iconic Trinidadian Calypso singer. Others seem conveniently preordained: "you are a unicorn beyond my Minotaur." Compelled by its structural logic, the poem can go nowhere but where it's bound to go. And yet, beneath the inevitability

---

[48] Harryette Mullen, *Sleeping with the Dictionary* (Berkeley, CA: University of California Press, 2002), 6–7.

of its surface movements, and perhaps despite them, "Any Lit" taps poetry's most deeply laid line.

Readers would be very hard pressed to coalesce around a conventional interpretation of "Any Lit" or to arrange its sound and sense according to the kind of enactive logic that I outlined earlier, and most readers would likely place the poem in the realm of experimental or innovative poetry – that baggy category derived from varieties of modernist and avant-garde practices. However, at its formulaic core, "Any Lit" restages lyric poetry's primal scene: the encounter of a speaker and a spoken-to. It is a little machine of lyric address, one that both distances addressee from addresser – "you are a you beyond my my/me" – and places them in relation. Its lexical pyrotechnics are premised upon poetry's central toggle switch: *you/I*. And so "Any Lit" appears not only as a textual game but as a love poem. It takes an archetypal gesture of lyric desire – as in the opening of Christopher Marlowe's "The Passionate Shepherd to His Love" or Eliot's "The Love Song of J. Alfred Prufrock" – and inverts it. Instead of a speaker who attempts to draw in the beloved – "Come live with me and be my love"; "Let us go then, you and I" – Mullen's speaker insists upon the agency, even autonomy, of the addressee, who is always "beyond" the speaker.[49] Mullen's reformulation has an ethical drive: the lyric "I" aims not to engulf or capture the "you," but rather to emphasize its simultaneous independence from ("you are a you") and relation to the speaker.

Beneath its set of lexical games and sonic manipulations, Mullen's "Any Lit" asks a question that has vitalized and vexed poets, especially in the twentieth and twenty-first centuries: how can and should a poem render a person as well as the social worlds in which persons live? While poetry has not always been linked so intimately with matters of individual feeling, thought, and sensation, these notions have predominated within accounts of poetry, especially since the early nineteenth century. William Wordsworth's definition of poetry – "poetry is the spontaneous overflow of powerful

---

[49] Christopher Marlowe, *The Complete Poems and Translations*, ed. Stephen Orgel (New York: Penguin Books, 2007), 207; Eliot, *Collected Poems, 1909–1962*, 3.

feelings; it takes its origin from emotion recollected in tranquillity" – is, however much that it has been the subject of critique and modification, still with us.[50] As is John Stuart Mill's: "poetry is feeling confessing itself to itself in moments of solitude, and embodying itself in symbols which are the nearest possible representations of the feeling in the exact shape in which it exists in the poet's mind."[51] By now, when the concept of the autonomous, Cartesian subject has been severely problematized if not entirely undone, it is nearly impossible to abide Mill's notion of a poem as the precise representation of an inner feeling or of the utter sovereignty of the writing subject. Contemporary poems that unproblematically assume a coherent, independent self at the center of things exercise a form of discursive power or privilege that is deeply suspect. And yet poetry has not given up on – nor should it – the project of constructing, construing, and modeling forms and instances of subjective being and social life. It is understood that individuals are constituted by the larger codes, structures, and systems in which they are enmeshed; that our feelings and thoughts and words are never entirely (or even partly) *ours*; that what we think of as our inimitable, singular "self" is always partial, multiple, and constituted by that which is exterior to us; and that a poem, or any form of writing that presumes to render the texture of selfhood, is shot through by ideological mediations and external determinations. And yet, the broader questions still remain. How does a poem – a strange sort of textual performance located in some third space that is neither nonfiction nor fiction – represent the experience and inner life of a person? And how can a poem represent the ways in which persons are embedded in the world? The following chapter will burrow into these two questions.

[50] William Wordsworth, "Preface to *Lyrical Ballads*" [1800/1802], in Stephen Gill, ed., *The Oxford Authors: William Wordsworth* (Oxford: Oxford University Press, 1984), 593–615, at 611.
[51] John Stuart Mill, "Thoughts on Poetry and its Varieties" [1833/1859], in *Dissertations and Discussions: Political, Philosophical, and Historical* (Boston, MA: W. V. Spencer, 1864), vol. 1, 89–120, at 97.

2 Worlds and Selves

For the last several centuries, poetry has been understood primarily as an expression or construction of an individual subject. The features traditionally associated with lyric poetry – intensity and granularity of thought and feeling, a commitment to the textures and peculiarities of the inner life, sonic and figural density, and relative brevity – have become defining features of poetry more generally. In part, this is evidence of a conflation of *lyric* and *poetry*, one that a number of critics have worked to disclose and untangle.[1] But this conflation is

---

[1] Virginia Jackson uses the twin terms "lyricization" and "lyric reading" to describe the process by which critics read all poetry according to conventions of lyric reading that were established within twentieth-century literary-critical protocols. A number of critics over the past two decades have worked to elaborate the premises upon which the study of poetry in the twentieth century unfolded, and to approach the poetry of earlier periods in a more historically minded fashion. Traveling under several names – "lyric theory," "new lyric studies," and "historical poetics" – such scholarship has been key to the revival of poetry's status within literary scholarship after a period in the late twentieth century when literary-critical and literary-theoretical methods tended to look toward narrative fiction rather than poetry for examples and models. (Of course, the careers of the three great American poetry critics of the late twentieth century – Charles Altieri, Marjorie Perloff, and Helen Vendler – were centered in these same decades; their achievements, working across the aesthetic spectrum, helped to shape the foundation upon which was built the revival of poetry scholarship in the early twenty-first century.) Jackson elaborates her notion of "lyricization" in *Dickinson's Misery: A Theory of Lyric Reading* (Princeton, NJ: Princeton University Press, 2005). On lyric theory and lyricization, see Yopie Prins, *Victorian Sappho* (Princeton, NJ: Princeton University Press, 1999); Jonathan Culler, *Theory of the Lyric* (Cambridge, MA: Harvard University Press, 2015); Virginia Jackson and Yopie Prins, eds., *The Lyric Theory Reader: A Critical Anthology* (Baltimore, MD: Johns Hopkins University Press, 2014); and the essays gathered under the heading "New Lyric Studies" in *PMLA*, 123.1 (January 2008), 181–234. On "historical poetics," see Yopie Prins, "What Is Historical Poetics," *Modern Language Quarterly*, 77.1 (March 2016), 13–40. Also see Sharon Cameron, *Lyric Time: Dickinson and the Limits of Genre* (Baltimore, MD: Johns Hopkins University Press, 1979); W. R. Johnson, *The Idea of Lyric: Lyric Modes in Ancient and Modern Poetry* (Berkeley, CA: University of California Press, 1982); and Marion Thain, ed. *The Lyric Poem: Formations and Transformations* (Cambridge: Cambridge University Press, 2013). For considerations of lyric in earlier periods, see Ardis Butterfield, 'Why Medieval Lyric?,' *English Literary History*, 82.2 (Summer 2015), 319–343; Seth

not simply a narrowing of ambition on the part of poets nor a retrospective misprision on the part of twentieth- and twenty-first-century critics. It is part of a larger turn in artistic practice and aesthetic thinking in the late nineteenth and early twentieth centuries as many artists and writers became less interested in the representation of an external reality and more committed to the intricacies and potentials of the materials and shaping forces of their own mediums. It is also an effect of the rise of the novel and related prose genres over the course of the eighteenth and nineteenth centuries and of a variety of filmic genres in the twentieth. Many of the narrative and discursive tasks that, in earlier periods, would have been undertaken in verse – such as the telling of a long, episodic story or the presentation of an epic or a play – increasingly fell within the domain of novelists and playwrights, and, later, filmmakers and show runners. This is not to say that narrative, dramatic, and epic poetry ceased to exist. There are a number of extended poems in the last two centuries that are narrative or epic in the traditional sense, such as Alfred Lord Tennyson's *Idylls of the King* (1859–1885), Austin Clarke's retellings of Irish myths, or Derek Walcott's *Omeros* (1990); as well as a small but steady stream of verse dramas, from Percy Bysshe Shelley's *Cenci* (1819) and Algernon Charles Swinburne's *Atalanta in Calydon* (1865) to modernist plays by W. B. Yeats and T.S. Eliot; and, beginning with Alexander Pushkin's *Eugene Onegin* (1833), a relatively small clutch of verse novels, such as Elizabeth Barrett Browning's *Aurora Leigh* (1856), Vladimir Nabokov's *Pale Fire* (1962), Anne Carson's *Autobiography of Red* (1998), Vikram Seth's *Golden Gate* (1986), and Bernadine Evaristo's *The Emperor's Babe* (2001).

Lehrer, "The Genre of the Grave and the Origins of Middle English Lyric," *Modern Language Quarterly*, 58.2 (June 1997), 127–161; Marissa Galvez, *Songbook: How Lyrics Became Poetry in Medieval Europe* (Chicago and London: University of Chicago Press, 2012); Peter Dronke, *The Medieval Lyric* (New York: Cambridge University Press, 1977); Roland Greene, *Post-Petrarchism: Origins and Innovations of the Western Lyric Sequence* (Princeton, NJ: Princeton University Press, 1991); Heather Dubrow, *The Challenges of Orpheus: Lyric Poetry and Early Modern England* (Baltimore, MD: Johns Hopkins University Press, 2008); and G. Gabrielle Starr, *Lyric Generations: Poetry and the Novel in the Long Eighteenth Century* (Baltimore, MD: Johns Hopkins University Press, 2004).

However, in general the kinds of narrative, epic, and dramatic freight that poetry might have carried prior to the nineteenth century migrated to other genres and mediums. Even the major long poems of the last two centuries have tended centralize the individual subject and the experiences, attitudes, and thoughts of that subject rather than the unfolding of a plot, whether an authorial subject, as in Wordsworth's *The Prelude* (1799, 1805, 1850) or Whitman's "Song of Myself" (1855), a characterological subject, as in the linked dramatic monologues that comprise Browning's *The Ring and the Book* (1868–1869) or in John Berryman's *Dream Songs* (1969), or what amounts to a dialectical contortion of the two, Eliot's *The Waste Land* (1922). The most significant long poem of the twentieth century, Ezra Pound's *Cantos*, aspires to epic in various ways and wrestles with its epic precursors, but the primary centripetal force that holds the *Cantos* together (despite his cry in Canto CXVI that "I cannot make it cohere") is Pound himself.[2] Pound's life – his social world, his reading, his beliefs, his aesthetic and cultural commitments, his particular experiences and knowledge, his complex and disastrous political activities – comprises the arena of the *Cantos* in a manner that may be closer to our expectations of lyric poetry than of epic or narrative, at least in their traditional guises.[3]

I am not arguing that all poetry is essentially lyric poetry, nor that poetry cannot partake of various other literary and discursive genres, a point that I elaborated in Chapter 1. Nor am I suggesting that poetry's value is bound to its role as a vehicle for personal expression, and that as such it is unable to reckon with matters outside of the orbit of the self, such as history or politics – I will examine these topics here and in later chapters. Nonetheless, the significance of poetry in contemporary culture remains inextricable from its inwardness, its attention to matters of thought and feeling, and its position at the

---

[2] Ezra Pound, *The Cantos of Ezra Pound* (New York: New Directions Books, 1996 [1970]), 816.
[3] On modernist epic, see in particular C. D. Blanton, *Epic Negation: The Dialectical Poetics of Late Modernism* (New York: Oxford University Press, 2015); the essays in Nigel Alderman and C. D. Blanton, eds., "Pocket Epics: British Poetry After Modernism," *Yale Journal of Criticism*, 13.1 (Spring 2000); and Michael André Bernstein, *The Tale of the Tribe: Ezra Pound and the Modern Verse Epic* (Princeton, NJ: Princeton University Press, 1980).

limen of individual experience and social life. In this way, a poem's construction and representation of a subjectivity, voice, or identity are evidence both of its inward turn and its outward look: the ways that a text renders the textures and vicissitudes of inner life are, at the same time, that text's emergence into the social.

The lyric subject or lyric "I" (two of the typical phrases by which critics and readers designate the metaphorical locus [both speakerly and psychological] around which many poems are organized) is not only a mark of the personal, individual, or subjective (which isn't necessarily to say the autobiographical – poems can certainly render fictions of selves), but is also shaped by material and historical conditions. Just as modern poetry, broadly construed, has been driven by the historical developments of capitalism, the enlightenment subject, and the bourgeois individual, so has it emerged out of persistent critiques of both enlightenment humanism and the status of the subject under capitalism. The ways that contemporary poets have constructed subjects, or resisted such constructions, have been premised, at least in part, on a systemic crisis of that same subject. John Ashbery, the late twentieth century's great poet of the dispersed self, provides a knowingly glib précis of such conditions in "Definition of Blue":

> The rise of capitalism parallels the advance of romanticism
> And the individual is dominant until the close of the nineteenth century.
> In our own time, mass practices have sought to submerge the personality
> By ignoring it, which has caused it instead to branch out in all directions
> Far from the permanent tug that used to be its notion of "home."
>
> There is no remedy for this "packaging" which has supplanted the old sensations.[4]

In this potted lyric history, Ashbery encapsulates the hazards of modernity. That what is taken to be one's inner, inalienable life is

[4] John Ashbery, *The Mooring of Starting Out: The First Five Books of Poetry* (Hopewell, NJ: The Ecco Press, 1997), 266.

produced from the outside; that it has no core, that its idea of individual experience is in fact a delusion, a "packaging" that has replaced genuine feeling and sensation; and that – as a sixteen-year-old Arthur Rimbaud noted in a letter to Georges Izambard – one's self is somebody else.[5] Or no one. In "As One Put Drunk into the Packet-Boat," the opening poem of *Self-Portrait in a Convex Mirror* (1975), Ashbery dramatizes this wobbly, vertiginous stance:

> A look of glass stops you
> And you walk on shaken: was I the perceived?
> Did they notice me, this time, as I am,
> Or is it postponed again?[6]

Such forms of subjective alienation have only intensified in the twenty-first century. This chapter, then, is motivated by the questions offered at the end of the previous one: how does, if it does, a poem stage the experience and inner life of a person, and how can it represent the ways in which persons are embedded in the world? These tasks are both vital and precarious: vital because poetry's value hinges on its insistence on the importance of the life of individuals, and precarious because such insistence is ideologically fraught and because the substance and significance of individual and social life are exceedingly uncertain.

For many Romantic writers, poetry was not only a space for the articulation of feeling and emotion, but also a mechanism for producing the subject as free, reflective, and autonomous. Implicit within the ideology of this key strand of Romantic poetics (one that long outlived the Romantic period) is a dual understanding: both the poet and the speaker of a poem are figures of imaginative and discursive power. Even in poems in which the speaker is figured as lacking agency or control – as in John Keats' "Ode to a Nightingale," Samuel Taylor Coleridge's "Kubla Khan," Dylan Thomas' "Fern Hill," or Sylvia Plath's "Daddy" – the poem itself is premised upon a

---

[5] The phrase "Je est un autre" appears in a letter from May 13, 1871. See Wallace Fowlie, trans., *Rimbaud: Complete Works, Selected Letters* (Chicago and London: University of Chicago Press, 1966), 304.
[6] John Ashbery, *Self-Portrait in a Convex Mirror* (New York: Penguin Books, 1976 [1975]), 1.

centripetal subject that is the center of the action and its driving force. As I began to suggest in Chapter 1, such a stance has attenuated severely, notwithstanding later reflexes of a Romantic ideology among many twentieth-century poets. Even as we might continue to abide the notion that poems construct a new imaginative set of relations – that, as Stevens has it, "a poet's words are of things that do not exist without the words" – we are much less likely to grant the claim that a poet is the locus of hieratic or special powers.[7] This Romantic poetic subject – self-possessed, autonomous, sovereign, implicitly male, and implicitly white – has been deconstructed as a discursive pawn within an impoverished ideology of enlightenment humanism. Over the course of and beyond the second half of the twentieth century, the lyric "I" has been the object of considerable critique from nearly all sides: it takes no cognizance of racial, ethnic, or gender differences, nor of difference itself; it presumes a discursive and imaginative dominance over its materials, scenes, and objects; it is blind to its privilege; and it is a witting and unwitting carrier for bourgeois consumerism. The "bad" lyric poem, under such an account, is a monologic utterance that relies on a fantasy of individualism and furthers the damaging notion that art is separate from politics or an escape from actual social and material relations. A number of writers and poetic movements in the past half-century – primarily the Language poets and varieties of post-Language poetry in North America, and several nodes within postwar English poetry – have worked to dismantle the false figure of the self-possessed poetic subject, the imperious lyric "I" that comfortably pulls all the strings.

While the unreflective, sovereign lyric subject is a rightly ruined figure, poems still have the capacity to construct more viable modes of subjectivity and self-making. Without reaching back once again to an outmoded model of the Romantic subject, much contemporary poetry seeks to represent the mediated precarity of individual experience and to frame those experiences as more than simply "individual," as, rather, modes of subjective being and responsiveness that are

---

[7] Wallace Stevens, *The Necessary Angel: Essays on Reality and the Imagination* (New York: Vintage Books, 1951), 32.

necessarily embedded in various networks of social, economic, and ecological relations. In this way, the value of contemporary poetry inheres precisely in its continuing and critical interest in the status of subjectivity within world systems that are unthinkable at the level of the human. How, though, might poems maintain their capacity to render inner life and individual experience if, at the same time, the typical frame for presenting such experience – the lyric subject, the lyric "I," the speakerly self that cinches a poem's discourse – is so utterly problematized, if not entirely overturned?

To begin to get a sense of how contemporary poets have reckoned with this charge and to better understand poetry's place within broader debates about subjectivity and selfhood, we might rethink those truisms with which I began: that, for the last several centuries, poetry has been concerned primarily with matters of individual feeling, emotion, and thought; and that the lyric "I" or speaker, whether conceived of as a stand-in for or shadow of the writer or as a kind of character (as in the dramatic monologues of Browning, Eliot, or Carol Ann Duffy), is the locus around which such concerns have been organized and represented. Such an understanding is built into the influential accounts of poetry that have long undergirded poetic theory and practice, and that remain relevant, if much scrutinized, today. To return to John Stuart Mill's trio of claims about the impetus and composition of poetry: "poetry is feeling confessing itself to itself in moments of solitude," this affective confession "embod[ies] itself in symbols," and these symbols – which can be read broadly to indicate both the specific images, figures, and phrases that constitute the poem, and the basic mechanisms of linguistic signification – "are the nearest possible representations of the feeling in the exact shape in which it exists in the poet's mind."[8] Mill binds poet and poem tightly together, and knots the experience underlying a poem with the symbolic embodiment that is the actual text. This presumes a stable, self-governing subject who has coherent feelings (as well as emotions, thoughts, impressions, and so on) and who can more or less

---

[8] John Stuart Mill, "Thoughts on Poetry and its Varieties" [1833/1859], in *Dissertations and Discussions: Political, Philosophical, and Historical* (Boston, MA: W. V. Spencer, 1864), vol. 1, 89–120, at 97.

perfectly render these inner experiences into language. Mill here presents a prototypical understanding of lyric immediacy and intimacy.

However, as I've suggested in several contexts thus far, this understanding of poetry, and of the place of the subject, speaker, or "I" of a poem, does not suffice. To be sure, poems are keen on representing feeling, emotion, and the complexities of interiority – what Ashbery famously called "the experience of experience" – but they also arise out of a fundamental alienation.[9] They simply can't offer the intimacy that Mill's account silently promises; any such bid for intimacy is always alienated or estranged. Although Wordsworth's "Preface" to *Lyrical Ballads* has furnished the most famous encapsulation of poetic intimacy or immediacy – "the spontaneous overflow of powerful feelings" – it is crucial to notice that Wordsworth himself understood poetry's affective spontaneity to be deeply mediated.[10] Unlike Mill, who aligns the feelings that underlie the poem with the poem itself, Wordsworth distances them from each other, both temporally and psychologically. The "spontaneous overflow of powerful feelings" is not simply transcribed "in the exact shape" in which those feelings arise in the poet's mind. Rather, they are "recollected in tranquillity," at a later point in time and in a very different mindset. A fissile doubleness is built into Wordsworth's canonical notion: the phrase that stands on its own toward the start of the "Preface" – "all good poetry is the spontaneous overflow of powerful feelings" – is, in its second appearance, yoked to another that both augments and undoes it:

> I have said that Poetry is the spontaneous overflow of powerful feelings: it takes its origin from emotion recollected in tranquillity: the emotion is contemplated till by a species of reaction the tranquillity disappears, and an emotion, kindred to that which was before the subject of contemplation, is gradually produced, and does itself actually exist in the mind. In this mood

---

[9] A. Poulin, Jr., "The Experience of Experience: A Conversation with John Ashbery," *Michigan Quarterly Review*, 20.3 (1981), 242–255, at 245.

[10] William Wordsworth, "Preface to *Lyrical Ballads*" [1800/1802], in Stephen Gill, ed., *The Oxford Authors: William Wordsworth* (Oxford: Oxford University Press, 1984), 593–615, at 598.

successful composition generally begins, and in a mood similar to this it is carried on; but the emotion, of whatever kind and in whatever degree, from various causes is qualified by various pleasures, so that in describing any passions whatsoever, which are voluntarily described, the mind will upon the whole be in a state of enjoyment.[11]

Poetry is offset from itself: it is both the initiating catalyst and the later recollection of that moment of "spontaneous overflow" in a very different affective space, one that begins in "tranquillity." Out of that tranquil disposition, a poet imaginatively produces a semblance of the original "subject of contemplation," those previously overflowing "powerful feelings." Instead of being overwhelmed by those feelings, the poet remakes emotions "kindred to" the originals within the crucible of art. This is, in many ways, an inversion of Mill's poetic process: instead of a psychic and affective experience that is then represented textually and aesthetically in "the exact shape" in which it initially appeared in the mind, Wordsworth's process requires that the shape and tenor of the original experience (the "spontaneous overflow") be reproduced by its affective negation (with meter serving as the shaping and regulating force that mediates the two). It is a proto-deconstructive process, one that sets an aporia between the experience that spurs the poem and the composition of the poem itself.[12]

Varieties of this chasm have appeared throughout twentieth-century poetics and criticism. The gap that opens in Wordsworth's account of poetry is a central premise in T. S. Eliot's thinking about the impersonality of poetry. In "Tradition and the Individual Talent" (1919), a document as central to ideas about modern poetry as is Wordsworth's "Preface," Eliot argues that the making of a poem involves "a continual surrender" of the poet's self.[13] Far from Mill's alignment of poet and poem, and a furthering of Wordsworth's model,

---

[11] Wordsworth, "Preface," 598, 611.
[12] Wordsworth's argument about the necessity to compose poetry in "the real language of men" is structured along similarly discrepant lines as his argument about the nature of poetic composition (ibid., 608).
[13] T. S. Eliot, "Tradition and the Individual Talent" [1919], in Anthony Cuda and Ronald Schuchard, *The Complete Prose of T. S. Eliot: The Critical Edition: The*

Eliot argues that the autonomy of the poem is assured by cutting the bind between author and text. The compositional process is not a "spontaneous overflow" of feelings, the "turning loose of emotion" in Eliot's terms, but rather "an escape from emotion."[14] The poem does not represent the writer's emotional or psychological dimensions. Instead, "the progress of an artist is a continual self-sacrifice, a continual extinction of personality." The role of the artist in the production of the artwork is a "depersonalizing" one, and here he offers his famous comparison of artistic composition with a catalytic reaction: "the action which takes place when a bit of finely filiated platinum is introduced into a chamber containing oxygen and sulphur dioxide."[15] In this somewhat fanciful analogy, "the mind of the poet" is the "shred of platinum" that catalyzes the reaction that eventuates in the poem, but that remains itself unchanged, "digest[ing] and transmut[ing] the passions which are its material."[16] Poems are based in emotion and feeling, but these emotions and feelings have been abstracted from the person responsible for the creation of the poem: "the emotion of art is impersonal."[17] A poet, Eliot continues, is "a receptacle for seizing and storing up numberless feelings, phrases, images, which remain there until all the particles which can unite to form a new compound are present together."[18] However, the force of a work has nothing to do with the personal emotions of the poet, but with the way in which emotions are worked up into poetry in order to express feelings in the form of a "concentration."[19]

Eliot's distinction between "the man who suffers and the mind which creates" became a touchstone throughout the twentieth century, a bulwark against biographical readings of poems that depend too much on psychologizing an authorial subject behind the work.[20] New Criticism relied heavily upon Eliot's arguments, and we might even understand deconstructive readings of poetry as relocating the sort of chasm or aporia that appears differently in Wordsworth and Eliot. Paul de Man's fundamental insight about lyric poetry, that its bid for

Perfect Critic, 1919–1926 (Baltimore, MD and London: Johns Hopkins University Press and Faber and Faber, 2014), 105–114, at 108.
[14] Eliot, "Tradition and the Individual Talent," 111. [15] Ibid., 108.
[16] Ibid., 109. [17] Ibid., 112. [18] Ibid., 109. [19] Ibid., 111. [20] Ibid., 109.

"presence" is staked upon a suppression of that bid's dependence on figuration, on a rhetorical move that slyly becomes naturalized, has been central to studies of poetry in the past half century. The aporia that de Man locates is not between the feeling subject and the writing subject (as in Wordsworth's "Preface") nor between the author and the text (as in Eliot's "Tradition and the Individual Talent"), but rather exists within the poem itself. In "Semiology and Rhetoric," he notes that "the term *voice*" is itself "a metaphor inferring by analogy the intent of the subject from the structure of the predicate."[21] The split that de Man deconstructs occurs between the metaphor of a text's "voice" and its grammatical subject. As what de Man later calls "the instance of represented voice," lyric poetry, in particular, relies on the illusion by which a metaphorical figure is transformed into the semblance of a speaking subject.[22] The anthropomorphism of lyric poetry "seems to be the illusionary resuscitation of the natural breath of language, frozen into stone by the semantic power of the trope. It is a figural affirmation that claims to overcome the deadly negative power invested in the figure."[23]

A poem's "I," then, is not a locus of subjective coherence or of poetic power, but a hollow, an empty grammatical mark that provides a figment of rhetorical fullness – an ontological will-o'-the-wisp. In *The Words of Selves: Identification, Solidarity, Irony* (2000), Denise Riley follows up on de Man's insights but aims to go beyond his deconstructive method. She acknowledges a subject's linguistic alienation, but finds in that alienation generative forms of "linguistic unease" (the title of the chapter from which the following passage is drawn). For Riley, "'I' is a pretender to an impossible throne" because the very "grammar of the language of self-reference seems to demand, indeed to guarantee, an authenticity closely tied to originality. Yet simultaneously it cancels this possibility. Any *I* seems to speak for and from herself; her utterance comes from her own mouth in the first

---

[21] Paul de Man, *Allegories of Reading: Figural Language in Rousseau, Nietzsche, Rilke, and Proust* (New Haven, CT: Yale University Press, 1979), 18.
[22] Paul de Man, *The Rhetoric of Romanticism* (New York: Columbia University Press, 1984), 261.
[23] De Man, *The Rhetoric of Romanticism*, 247.

person pronoun which is hers, if only for just so long as she pronounces it. Yet as a human speaker, she knows that it's also everyone's, and that this grammatical offer of uniqueness is untrue, always snatched away."[24] This "oscillation at the heart of authorship" derives from a systemic "linguistic unease" founded in what Riley calls the "peculiar anteriority" of the writing subject: any text's supposed interiority or inwardness is externally produced.[25] The "I" of a poem, as well as the "I" more generally, is exterior and prior to the "I" that writes or speaks it.[26] The self or subject figured within a poem is, as we've seen, triply estranged from the person behind the act of writing: distanced from the experience underlying the writing (Wordsworth), cleaved from the totality of the author's personal psychology and experience (Eliot), and internally fissured along the lines of grammar and rhetoric (de Man).

The subject's self-alienation is not only a psychological or linguistic matter, it is also a historical one. Turning briefly to important essays on poetry by Walter Benjamin and Theodor Adorno, we can open up a further dimension of this question before considering how several contemporary poets have reckoned with the constitution and crisis of the subject in modernity.[27] In "On Some Motifs in Baudelaire" (1939), Benjamin focuses on the historical dimensions of the poetic subject's position. For Benjamin, it isn't only – as it was for Eliot and Wordsworth – that there is a divergence or troubled mediation between the experience that initiates the poem and the poem itself. It is also the case that experience *as such* has shifted, that the onset of capitalist modernity has reconfigured the ways in which humans encounter and are situated

---

[24] Denise Riley, *The Words of Selves: Identification, Solidarity, Irony* (Stanford, CA: Stanford University Press, 2000), 59, 57.
[25] Riley, *The Words of Selves*, 90, 89.
[26] In addition to Riley, see Judith Butler, *The Psychic Life of Power* (Stanford, CA: Stanford University Press, 1997). For a psychoanalytically inflected account of poetry along occasionally related lines, see Mutlu Konuk Blasing, *Lyric Poetry: The Pain and Pleasure of Words* (Princeton, NJ: Princeton University Press, 2007).
[27] The major scholar of lyric poetry within the context of the Frankfurt School is Robert Kaufman. Among his many essays, see for instance "Aura, Still," *October*, 99 (2002), 45–80; "Lyric's Expression: Musicality, Conceptuality, Critical Agency," in David Cunningham and Nigel Mapp, eds., *Adorno and Literature* (London: Continuum, 2006), 99–116; and "Lyric Commodity Critique, Benjamin Adorno Marx, Baudelaire Baudelaire Baudelaire," *PMLA*, 123.1 (January 2008), 207–215.

in the world. Baudelaire's poetry becomes the foremost site in which to examine the juxtaposition of lyric poetry and capitalism, and Benjamin accounts for Baudelaire's poetry historically, although without reducing it to a mere historical symptom. Built out of a complex synthesis of Proust's distinction between *mémoire volontaire* and *mémoire involontaire*, Freud's work on memory, consciousness, and shock experiences in *Beyond the Pleasure Principle* (1920), and Marx's understanding of the commodity fetish and the forms of alienation that attend urban life and mechanized labor, Benjamin's argument is based upon the notion of a severing of the bind between those nodes that have been differently figured by Mill, Wordsworth, and Eliot: the experience underlying the poem, the individual who has this experience, and the making of a poem "out of" an experience. The disconnection that Benjamin locates has to do with the loss of "aura" in artworks that occurs when all three nodes are thoroughly commodified. One of the reasons why Baudelaire's poetry is successful is because it powerfully presents these changed circumstances, although at the cost of a certain kind of failure. Baudelaire's poetry is fashioned out of the subject's own flailing against the alienating effects of the city and of urban life: "being jostled by the crowd" is the "decisive, unmistakable experience" that shapes Baudelaire's poetry, which battles the crowd "with the impotent rage of someone fighting the rain or the wind."[28] Unlike the Wordsworthian model of the poet as one who can "see into the life of things," Baudelaire makes his poetry out of the impossibility or collapse of such kinds of experience: "blank spaces hovered before him, and into these he inserted his poems."[29] Benjamin's model of the poet in modernity, Baudelaire is crucial because he understands that aesthetic success is bound up in poetic failure. This failure is not Baudelaire's alone, but is rather inherent to the changed conditions and possibilities of lyric poetry under capitalist modernity. One almost has to offer a ruined poetry as the only option. Only a willing

---

[28] Walter Benjamin, "On Some Motifs in Baudelaire" [1939], trans. by Harry Zohn, in *The Writer of Modern Life: Essays on Charles Baudelaire*, ed. Michael W. Jennings (Cambridge, MA: Harvard University Press, 2006), 170–210, at 210.
[29] Wordsworth, *The Oxford Authors: William Wordsworth*, 133; Benjamin, "On Some Motifs in Baudelaire," 177.

renunciation of aesthetic aura – that sense of human presence and relation that radiates from works of art, what Benjamin describes as "the way an earthen vessel bears the trace of the potter's hand" – would allow a poem to fully register its own modernity: "[Baudelaire] named the price for which the sensation of modernity could be had: the disintegration of the aura in immediate shock experience."[30]

Benjamin uncovers in Baudelaire the contradiction that structures modern poetry. If the aura of an artwork "arises from the fact that a response characteristic of human relationships is transposed to the relationship between humans and inanimate or natural objects," then such a transposition invests works of art with "the ability to look back at us."[31] It is this precise possibility of reciprocity that is shattered by the objectifying, instrumentalizing, commodifying forces of modernity. A poem's "ability to look back at us" is upended, and all that remains is what Benjamin calls "the spell of eyes-without-a-gaze."[32] Its capacity to project modes of inner life and subjective response to social conditions is wrenched by those same conditions. The chasm or gap that has been framed so differently by the writers I've examined is not the problem or glitch that haunts the making of poetry; it is poetry's constitutive space, albeit an incongruous and dizzying one. In "On Lyric Poetry and Society," an essay originally delivered on German radio in 1957, Theodor Adorno aims to elaborate the critical value of lyric poetry under such conditions. As a subjective expression made out of objective and shared materials (that is, language), a poem is well-placed to critique the concepts that govern society and is potentially able to glimpse a space outside those governing concepts. But, for that same reason, lyric poems are always in danger of simply parroting the false beliefs and ideological myths of capitalism and of what he and Max Horkheimer call "the culture industry." As Adorno writes, "the traditional lyric, as the most rigorous aesthetic negation of bourgeois convention, has by that very token been tied to bourgeois society."[33]

---

[30] Benjamin, "On Some Motifs in Baudelaire," 174, 210.   [31] Ibid., 204.
[32] Ibid., 206.
[33] Theodor Adorno, "On Lyric Poetry and Society," in *Notes to Literature*, ed. Rolf Tiedemann, trans. Shierry Weber Nicholson (New York: Columbia University Press, 1991), volume 1, 37–54, at 46.

Adorno tunes Benjamin's account of Baudelaire to his own more abstract mode. Most poems mistake themselves, imagining that they present the individuality and freedom of the subject when they merely carry forward the mystifications that drive consumer capitalism. A relatively weak lyric poem, in Adorno's estimation, will overindulge its own solitary adventures and overestimate its ability to stand outside of or entirely resist society. Such a poem doesn't realize that its bid for individuality or solitude is itself a function of, and determined by, the social: "the lyric work of art's withdrawal into itself, its self-absorption, its detachment from the social surface, is socially motivated behind the author's back."[34]

The kind of critical lyric that Adorno values would not be misled by "false universality" and would instead find ways of using its own materials to express that which lies outside of the social's available terms, concepts, and conditions.[35] In so doing, it doesn't escape from conditions nor does it become merely a symptom of those conditions. Rather, it can point toward that which cannot yet be seen by "giving form to the crucial contradictions in real existence" and "voice to what ideology hides."[36] Adorno argues for a "social interpretation of lyric poetry" in which a poem is revealed to be an "internally contradictory unity" that is premised on a reflective understanding of the discontinuity on which it rests.[37] This "internally contradictory unity" stages the alienated and discontinuous nature of subjectivity in order to begin to see past the illusions that necessarily shape its appearance. Moving beyond the ideological premises of the bourgeois subject by apprehending that "the shadow-side of the elevation of the liberated subject is its degradation to something exchangeable, to something that exists merely for something else," the value of the critical lyric lies in its ability to construct a form of subjective expression that "actually bears the whole in mind and is not simply an expression of the privilege" of the hegemonic class.[38]

There is of course much more to say about Adorno's essay, about the numerous twists, turns, and switchbacks that the argument takes;

---

[34] Adorno, "On Lyric Poetry and Society," 43. [35] Ibid., 38. [36] Ibid., 39.
[37] Ibid., 38, 39. [38] Ibid., 42, 45.

about the oddly unsatisfying readings that close the essay; and about the place of this relatively brief essay within Adorno's broader theories of culture and aesthetics. But such an inquiry would be a project on its own, and the central point is, hopefully, clear. Modern lyric poetry is both constituted and jeopardized by the conditions of modernity: its status as "the subjective expression of a social antagonism" is central to its potential as a mode of aesthetic critique but is also the source of its peril.[39] The crisis of the subject is a crisis for poetry, but Adorno's argument is that what is needed is a more reflective form of lyric subjectivity rather than its abandonment. In "On Lyric Poetry and Society," he doesn't argue that poets should turn away from the conditions of subjectivity, but rather that they should approach those conditions in more rigorously imaginative ways. In part, this is a matter of realizing the necessarily objective nature of what we take to be a subjective art. For Adorno:

> the highest lyric works are those in which the subject, with no remaining trace of mere matter, sounds forth in language until language itself acquires a voice. The unself-consciousness of the subject submitting itself to language as to something objective, and the immediacy and spontaneity of that subject's expression are one and the same: thus language mediates lyric poetry and society in their innermost core. This is why the lyric reveals itself to be most deeply grounded in society when it does not chime in with society, when it communicates nothing, when, instead, the subject whose expression is successful reaches an accord with language itself, with the inherent tendency of language.[40]

The lyric subject's realization of its own objective status in language allows for a further form of subjective expression, one that is – paradoxically it seems – both immediate and fundamentally mediated. The blinkered sorts of subjective expression censured by Adorno are those that fail to realize that one "inherent tendency" of language is to lean both inwards and outwards at once. What Adorno

---

[39] Ibid., 45.   [40] Ibid., 43.

describes as a poem's communication of nothing takes us circuitously back to some of the concerns of Chapter 1: poetry composes itself out of language but reconfigures or reroutes language's primary communicative function. What Adorno names "the highest lyric works" can glimpse an alternative to society's governing conditions by recognizing their simultaneous existence within and resistance to those conditions, comprising a tensed, generative formal space made of "the sounds in which sufferings and dreams are welded," and in which language's potential for subjective expression is routed through its objective dimensions and entailments.[41]

A substantial task for contemporary poets has been to find forms that might both critique and reconstrue the modes of subjectivity stitched into lyric's deep textures, by displaying the sorts of alienation and dispersal that attend the constitution of the modern subject, and by making poetry responsible to matters of difference so that, as Adorno suggests, the lyric "I" isn't – whether by default or design – an naïve expression of privilege or merely an effect of hegemony or domination.[42] Over the remainder of this chapter, I will focus on several recent texts in order to elaborate some of the ways in which writers have taken up this task within projects that revitalize poetry's composition of subjective experience.

As I have emphasized throughout, poetry's significance derives from its multitude of chimerical qualities, and the same can be said of the status of poetic "I," as well as the deictic network in which a poem's

---

[41] Ibid., 45.
[42] For a variety of accounts of the status of the lyric subject within contemporary poetry, see Rachel Blau DuPlessis, "Otherhow," in *The Pink Guitar: Writing as Feminist Practice* (Tuscaloosa, AL: University of Alabama Press, 2006 [1990]), 140–156; "Marble Paper: Toward a Feminist 'History of Poetry'," in *Blue Studios: Poetry and Its Cultural Work* (Tuscaloosa, AL: University of Alabama Press, 2006), 96–121; and "Agency, Social Authorship, and the Political Aura of Contemporary Poetry," *Textual Practice*, 23.6 (2009), 987–999; Juliana Spahr, *Everybody's Autonomy: Connective Reading and Collective Identity* (Tuscaloosa, AL: University of Alabama Press, 2001); Oren Izenberg, *Being Numerous: Poetry and the Ground of Social Life* (Princeton, NJ: Princeton University Press, 2011); Gillian White, *Lyric Shame: The "Lyric" Subject of Contemporary American Poetry* (Cambridge, MA: Harvard University Press, 2014); and Dorothy Wang, *Thinking Its Presence: Form, Race, and Subjectivity in Contemporary Asian American Poetry* (Stanford, CA: Stanford University Press, 2014).

"I" is situated. Just as the "I" of a poem is fissured along multiple lines (as suggested in various ways by Wordsworth, Eliot, Riley, de Man, Benjamin, and Adorno), so is a poem's deictic and diegetic space substantially untethered as compared to other social and discursive scenarios. Unlike a novel, the *I* or *you* or *this* or *here* of a poem do not attach to a fully realized story world. And unlike a scene in real life (or on stage or screen), such contextual words in a poem do not refer to actual bodies or vectors of shared space or time. In a novel, the sentence "I see you there" is most likely to be part of dialogue between characters or perhaps folded into a complex third-person narration. (In a first-person novel, it might also function as a drastic shattering of the fourth wall.) In the real world, such a spoken sentence would have a clear set of referents, as it would in a play or film. Appearing in the context of a poem, however, it would be both awkward and thrilling – the pronouns would all spark, but in too many directions and not quite together. Poems muddy the context of all of their shifters. Each deictic fluctuates between a quasi-diegetic space and an ambiguous pseudo-speech act; the "I" of a poem is a sedimented and multiple figure, attaching nearly simultaneously to the author, the reader, and to some abstracted "speaker" that is neither and both.

In the opening stanza of Jorie Graham's "San Sepolcro," for instance, the "I" and the "you" are both indeterminate and replete:

> In this blue light
>   I can take you there,
> snow having made me
>   a world of bone
> seen through to. This
>   is my house[.][43]

The title cues the poem's setting, but the stanza exists in an unfixed space: a *here* ("this blue light") that is "there" and then *here* again ("This/is my house"). The speaker's bid is that the poem can imaginatively build out a world – the world of a house in San Sepolcro – that

---

[43] Jorie Graham, *The Dream of the Unified Field: Selected Poems, 1974–1994* (Hopewell, NJ: The Ecco Press, 1995), 21.

the reader can somehow access. Graham begins by simply making explicit what drives the bulk of what we might variously call imaginative, creative, or fictional writing. Every text – fictional or not – that aims to transport a reader might as well begin with such an epigraph: "I can take you there." In the context of Graham's poem, however, the diegetic "there" to be fashioned is undone by the rhetorical gambits and generic conventions that underlie the poem. We understand the "I" of the poem to be something other than the "I" of the storyteller or narrator, but rather a compounded and contradictory figure: the single pronominal subject – indicated by "I," "me," and "my" – is bilocated, wrenched between a space of textual enunciation (the "I" of a lyric speech act) and one of diegetic desire (the "I" who wants to be in Tuscany but isn't quite). The only way to cross that aporetic space – from the "blue space" of snow to the "blue space" of San Sepolcro – is to generate another aporia: one in which "there" is "here." The "you" that is taken to there/here is nominally the reader but actually the poet, the authorial "I" who needs to be herself transported in order to effect the transportation that the poem wants to achieve. To be sure, the "I" of the poem solidifies as it turns more fully into a phenomenologically tinged and epiphanically driven account of the particular house and its aesthetic analogues, but this subsequent and more typical lyric space is built on deictic sand.

Just as poems exploit the fluctuational nature of personal pronouns, so do they unmoor those of time and space. We often associate poetry with presence and immediacy, but as I've shown thus far these bids for temporal and spatial intimacy are constituted by distance and displacement: a poem's *here* is neither *here* nor *there*. Its *now* can't but signal *then*. In "Yoohoo," Rae Armantrout describes this recursive scenario as

> The present's chronic
> revision
>
> which a poem
> reenacts.[44]

---

[44] Rae Armantrout, *Partly: New and Selected Poems, 2001–2015* (Middletown, CT: Wesleyan University Press, 2016), 92.

Leaning backwards into a "present" that also projects futurity, Armantrout catches the way in which a poem's temporality is uncanny, just as she catches its unplaceable space in this passage from "Anchor":

> If you watch me
> from increasing distance,
>
> I am writing this
> always[45]

Stitched into this passage (which is, to be sure, fully aware of its ironies) are the privileges and hazards of poetry's temporal and spatial instabilities. The perceived permanence of a poem's present-tense quality ("I am writing this/always") is both internally contradictory and undone by what precedes it, the "increasing distance" (both spatial and temporal) from which any "you" watches the incessant production of "this," which, of course, immediately hollows out and becomes yet another "that." This textual lurch is both key to a poem's generativity and an indication of its incessant untimeliness, a point that is given a somewhat different spin in this well-known moment from Ashbery's "Hop o' My Thumb":

> No worse time to have come,
> Yet all was desiring though already desired and past,
> The moment a monument to itself
> No one would ever see or know was there.[46]

The space of the poem – what Ashbery elsewhere calls "the gap of today filling itself" – is exposed as unpropitious, self-vexed, and navel-gazing.[47] Riffing on Rossetti to riff on the New Critical notion of the "well wrought urn," the poem's "moment" is both embedded in and cleaved by its self-reflexive "monument": the "nu" that differentiates "moment" from "monument" is at once a glib homophonic gesture to the poem's modernist credentials (its "nu-ness"), a suggestion of its inbuilt belatedness ("nu" as "knew," a mode of past tense knowledge), and its own near self-negation ("nu" approximates the

---

[45] Armantrout, *Partly*, 136.
[46] Ashbery, *Self-Portrait in a Convex Mirror*, 31–32. [47] Ibid., 7.

"no" that begins the following line as well as the one two lines previous). The poem is figured as a recursive loop of unfulfilled desire that hardly comes into appearance before giving way to another false monument. What is at stake for Ashbery in such moments – and they appear frequently throughout his massive body of work – isn't simply a need to constantly redescribe forms of estrangement, but an attempt to maintain a poem as a space in which to consider and figure subjective experience while also divesting from an aesthetic ideology in which the poem's subject carries with it a sense of artistic or epistemological mastery or discursive centrality.

Such passages and poems articulate instances of relational or situational subjectivity that do not rely on the presumption of power. They offer a way to represent the enmeshed, aspectual qualities of subjective experience. Just as the lyric "I" can display the objective basis of its subjectively minded discourse, so can that same "I" evoke its own decentralized position: a shifting node within a series of networks and landscapes (social, political, and ecological) rather than a reified and self-contained unit. The "I" of the poem is thus not one of scopic mastery and discursive self-possession, but rather an instance of limited and changeable agency that is at the same time subject to systems and conditions well out of its ken. The "I" in the following passage from Roy Fisher's great long poem *A Furnace* (1986) seeks to limn its own position while recognizing that it is in no position to comprehensively map the in-motion world in which it partakes:

> Something's decided
> to narrate
> in more dimensions than I can know
> the gathering in
> and giving out of the world on a slow
> pulse, on a metered contraction
> that the senses enquire towards
> but may not themselves
> intercept. All I can tell it by
> is the passing trace of it
> in a patterned agitation of

> a surface that shows only
> metaphors. Riddles. Resemblances
> that have me in the chute
> as it meshes in closer, many modes
> funnelling fast through one event,
> the flow-through so
> dense with association
> that its colour comes up, dark
> brownish green, soaked and
> decomposing leaves
> in a liquor.[48]

Sliding among literal description, phenomenological sketch, and metapoetic commentary, Fisher writes at the threshold of individual experience and the outer world. *A Furnace*, like much of Fisher's work, is focused on the complexities of Birmingham and the West Midlands, where he spent nearly all of his life. At various points, *A Furnace* attends to the area's landscapes, histories, politics, and culture, but here we are given something closer to the "experience of experience," to reuse Ashbery's phrase. In a profound way, Fisher is a poet of place, but his work does not simply depict environments (natural or built) so as to render a lyric "I" apart from and overlooking those environments. Instead, "I" is always a function of its location, shaped by a surround with which it is in relation but of which it is not in control: the passing of time and the unfurling of space – the "slow pulse" and "metered contraction" of "the world" – are available to the senses to "enquire towards" but are not able to be "intercept[ed]." As it careens between first-order impressions and second-order reflections, the passage remains relatively abstract until the final moment, when a rich image momentarily arrests the churn of language. However, the image of "dark/brownish green" leaves rotting in liquid does not function to concretize the experiential fuzz that precedes it, because the image itself is untethered: it emerges as the phenomenological description intensifies ("the flow-through so/dense with

---

[48] Roy Fisher, *The Long and the Short of It: Poems 1955–2005* (Northumberland: Bloodaxe Books, 2005), 53.

association") but it exists not in itself (that is, not as a simple verbal image of leaves), but as the figurative comparison for "its colour" that "comes up." "Its" here is ambiguous, referring back either to the "flow-through" or "the event." Either way, the evocative image isn't deployed as a means to epiphanically clinch the more abstract discourse leading up to it, since that image itself is a figural abstraction. What Fisher manages to present here is something like the multifarious and multilayered quality of everyday subjective experience as a combination of sensation, cognition, and reflection as constructed in and refracted by language, "many modes/funnelling fast through one event," with the near-constant enjambment underscoring the text's aspectual elaboration. The lyric subject is refused a position outside the perpetual interleaving of inside and outside that characterizes experience: unable to overlook the scene, the "I" is enmeshed and hemmed-in as it locates spaces of agency and dynamism, even if they are always only "passing trace[s]" amidst flux.

If one tendency in contemporary poetry has been to complicate the ways in which subjectivity is construed in texts so as to render the dispersed, processual qualities of selfhood, then another, related tendency has been to bring to bear upon poems the work of feminist politics and theory, postcolonial thinking, anti-racist politics, and critical race theory so as to show the poetic "I" as it has developed throughout European and Anglo-American literary history to be an adjunct to (or even a function of) Western patriarchy and imperialism. That is, to deconstruct the lyric subject not only along the lines outlined above but also because it carries within it such disastrous ideological freight. The project for many women poets and poets of color in the second half of the twentieth century and into the twenty-first has been to claim space within a poetic tradition that had been typified as male and white, not only by entering into that space but also by overturning the myths and reformulating the conventions by which certain aesthetic and canonical regimes were perpetuated. Since at least the 1960s (and much earlier if one thinks of poets like Gertrude Stein and Mina Loy), writers have engaged in a dual project of poetics and politics, of – as in the title of one of Adrienne Rich's most famous poems – "diving into the wreck" of literature and culture to find what might be salvaged and reclaimed. Of course, to speak of a single poetic "project" of decolonialization, anti-racism, and anti-patriarchy is an oversimplification, and the forms that such disparate projects took have been as various as the political and social commitments that underwrite them. What I aim to show in this chapter are a few ways in which poets have routed political and social critiques through the formal workings of lyric's deictic and formal networks, in addition to writing directly about the politics and history of gender, race, and colonialism. A poem can be a powerful forum in which to expose systemic racism and sexism, critique patriarchal ideologies, and address histories of oppression. But in addition to considering these issues as themes and topics, poems can also generate new possibilities of political and cultural agency by way of their forms, by not only expanding the kinds of identities and subjective experiences that are represented in poetry, but also by upending the terms of representation.

One of the most stunning such works, in addition to being one of the most widely read volumes of poetry thus far in the century, is Claudia Rankine's *Citizen* (2014).[49] Like its predecessor, *Don't Let Me Be Lonely* (2004), *Citizen* is subtitled *An American Lyric* and so activates a set of generic expectations and conventions that it proceeds to both subtly fulfill and drastically overturn. Focusing primarily on the politics of race and blackness in twenty-first century America, the mixed-genre and mixed-media *Citizen* moves between text and image and between lyric and essayistic prose. It often concentrates on particular individuals and incidents, as in the volume's essay on Serena Williams, the bigotry she has faced on and off the tennis court, the particular ways in which she has been objectified as a Black female body, and Williams' own, for some, controversial stance in the face of such vitriol and racism; or the reflection on Zinedine Zidane's headbutting of the Italian Marco Materazzi in response to a vicious racial slur during the final match of the 2006 World Cup, which combines video stills of the event with a collage of quotations from Zidane,

---

[49] According to the volume's publisher, more than 300,000 copies of *Citizen* have been published, an astonishing figure for a volume of poetry. See "Graywolf Acquires Just Us By Claudia Rankine," March 26, 2019, www.graywolfpress.org/news/graywolf-acquires-just-us-claudia-rankine, accessed December 15, 2019.

Maurice Blanchot, Ralph Ellison, Frantz Fanon, James Baldwin, William Shakespeare, Homi Bhabha, and Frederick Douglass. A number of the pieces in the volume are memorials for Black men murdered by white men, including James Craig Anderson, Jordan Russell Davis, and Trayvon Martin; Black men wrongfully convicted of crimes, such as the Jena Six; and Black men killed by the police, including Mark Duggan, Eric Garner, John Crawford, and Michael Brown. A section on the aftermath of Hurricane Katrina collages quotations taken from CNN's coverage of the devastation. In a powerful way, then, *Citizen* trains its gaze on the ideological construction of race, criminalization, and the material brutalities of racism in the public sphere by gathering and constellating a number of significant and well-known incidents within contemporary American and global culture.

Much of the book, however, focuses on the lived experience of the racialized body in everyday life, and many of the page-length prose sections anatomize individual instances of "everyday" and institutional racism rather than the more spectacular or deadly forms of racial violence described just above. These local incidents are nonetheless marked by physiological and psychological damage:

> Certain moments send adrenaline to the heart, dry out the tongue, and clog the lungs. Like thunder they drown you in sound, no, like lightning they strike you across the larynx. Cough. After it happened I was at a loss for words.[50]

Citizen aims to articulate the inner anatomy and force of such moments, moving between concrete anecdotes and more abstract meditations on the psychology of racism, the intersection between racial identity and inner experience, the constant perils of living as a Black person in the United States, and the ongoing trauma that collects in the wake of such an incessant stream of racist slights and affronts, a condition described, as Rankine tells us, by the term John Henryism.[51]

---

[50] Claudia Rankine, *Citizen: An American Lyric* (Minneapolis, MN: Graywolf Press, 2014), 7.
[51] See Rankine, *Citizen*, 11.

At the core of *Citizen*'s critique of systemic racism is a particular rhetorical feature and lyric texture. For the most part, the volume is written in the second person. There is, to be sure, a space from which the discourse emanates, an unsurfaced "I." But *Citizen*'s dominant pronoun is "you," although "you" is not a consistent or coherent figure throughout the volume. The opening passage offers a "you" that is an unspecified lyric projection, one that can be occupied smoothly by a reader, who might also understand the "you" to be the poetic "I" talking to herself. Here is the first paragraph of *Citizen*:

> When you are alone and too tired even to turn on any of your devices, you let yourself linger in a past stacked among your pillows. Usually you are nestled under blankets and the house is empty. Sometimes the moon is missing and beyond the windows the low, gray ceiling seems approachable. Its dark light dims in degrees depending on the density of clouds and you fall back into that which gets reconstructed as metaphor.[52]

All mood and atmospherics, this opening is almost too cozy. It establishes an individual in the contemporary world who is both privileged – a "you" having the means to own multiple devices (iPhones, tablets, laptops) and the freedom to ignore them – and safe. Ensconced among pillows and blankets, "you" does what many of us often do: begins to remember while drifting toward sleep. Thus far, Rankine has provided a prototypical lyric scenario, with a reader able to position herself just as comfortably within the text's "you" as "you" does within the diegetic bedroom.

Here, however, is the beginning of the book's second paragraph:

> The route is often associative. You smell good. You are twelve attending Sts. Philip and James School on White Plains Road and the girl sitting in the seat behind asks you to lean to the right during exams so she can copy what you have written.[53]

The generalized lyric "you" of the first paragraph is replaced by the quite specific biographical "you" in the second paragraph, which (it seems)

[52] Ibid., 5. [53] Ibid.

relates a particular incident from Rankine's childhood. The reader who was initially able to occupy the position of the addressee is shoved out of the pronoun. The first paragraph alerts us to what is to come – "you let yourself linger in a past ... that which get reconstructed as metaphor" – but the second paragraph's swerve still surprises us because we had falsely assumed that the "past" in which the text invited us to linger was our own. Checking this kind of presumption, the second paragraph then retools the "you," pulling it away from the orbit of the reader and toward the orbit of the author and her own past. The third paragraph presents more definitely the volume's dominant concern:

> You never really speak except for the time she makes her request and later when she tells you you smell good and have features more like a white person. You assume she thinks she is thanking you for letting her cheat and feels better cheating from an almost white person.[54]

"You" is now marked racially by the girl who cheats off her, who – in her mind – compliments her "almost" whiteness in order to make herself feel better about cheating. This slow process of diegetic hailing and discriminating is subtly replicated outside the diegesis: the reader is in an analogous position to the cheating white girl, looking over "you's" shoulder and initially positioning that experience and knowledge as the reader's own. *Citizen*'s most keen investigation of racial identification and the politics of blackness occur in this tensed space of the second person.

Rankine has suggested that the use of the second person in the volume is meant to disallow "the reader from knowing immediately how to position themselves. I didn't want to race the individuals." In the same interview, she goes on to say that she was interested in thinking "about blackness as the second person ... [n]ot the *first* person, but the *second* person, the *other* person."[55] Throughout the volume, the second person takes on this dual and discrepant function: whether it

---

[54] Ibid.
[55] Meara Sharma, "Claudia Rankine on Blackness as the Second Person," *Guernica: A Magazine of Global Arts & Politics*, November 17, 2014, www.guernicamag.com/blackness-as-the-second-person/, accessed August 23, 2018.

seems to attach to Rankine herself or to another person at the center of an anecdote that details a racist or discriminatory encounter, the "you" in these passages is not typically identified racially, but the context of the anecdote is usually one in which the "you" is positioned, presumably though not explicitly by a white subject, as the "second" or "other" person, both objectified and overlooked, exposed and elided. *Citizen* presents dozens of these moments, and each one turns around the overdetermined yet ambivalent place of the "you." As she suggests, Rankine systemically disallows "the reader from knowing immediately how to position themselves," but the force of the work is much stronger than this. It isn't only that the "you" is ambiguous and needs to be understood anew with every page. It is that Rankine constructs a rhetorical texture that strategically short-circuits the readerly affordances that lyric usually provides – that is, fissile pronouns that are able to be occupied and moved among. Throughout Rankine's "American lyric," white readers are implicitly invited to inhabit the "you" but are then turned back and must reckon with the implications of this double motion. This complexly orchestrated deictic mechanism discloses the whiteness of a white reader, who initially feels hailed by or included in the volume's ubiquitous "you" but is then dismissed by the terms and specifics of the scenario that unfolds, "the pronoun barely holding the person together."[56] Rankine uses the presumed universality of personal pronouns in order to critique the phony universalism that undergirds liberal politics and white privilege. White readers are by no means excluded from *Citizen*, but white readers certainly experience the book differently, in a way that doesn't allow their own whiteness to go unspoken or to be silently universalized.

It isn't simply that certain readers are meant to recognize themselves or fail to do so within the volume's many scenes, anecdotes, and meditations. It is that Rankine's manipulation of deictic space throughout the volume forces a reader to continually understand the specifics of her or his own racial and social position, and so the formal texture of *Citizen* presses the question asked during a consideration of the murder of Mark Duggan: "How difficult is it for one body to feel

[56] Rankine, *Citizen*, 71.

the injustice wheeled at another?"⁵⁷ The power and importance of Rankine's *Citizen* is manifold, but it inheres in her adaptation of lyric scaffolding to carry out a performative critique of the racist and unjust ideologies that underwrite subjectivity and personhood in the contemporary world. As she writes, "The world is wrong. You can't put the past behind you. It's buried in you; it's turned your flesh into its own cupboard."⁵⁸ In one of the volume's relatively few lineated passages, Rankine offers a sharp articulation of the alienating experience of being Black in America, of the way in which "a body in the world drowns in it":

> You are you even before you
> grow into understanding you
> are not anyone, worthless,
> not worth you.
>
> Even as your own weight insists
> you are here, fighting off
> the weight of nonexistence.⁵⁹

The harrowing existential dialectic inscribed here is not that of the white subject who has shadowed the volume, but of the Black subject who is insistently made to feel her own nonbeing within a culture structured via racism, despite the literal weight of her body, a "you" that is overexposed within a society that surveils and criminalizes blackness – "because white men can't/police their imagination/black men are dying" – and yet quells Black people's agency.⁶⁰ Rankine's lyric deconstruction of the ideologies of citizenship and subjecthood in *Citizen* is a many-angled and extensive undertaking, and I've only considered a few of its dimensions here. But it demonstrates poetry's capacity to give "form to the crucial contradictions in real existence," as Adorno suggests. *Citizen* faces the world, but it also aims to refashion the threshold between individual being and social relation that is at the heart of poetry's prerogative.

In a related way, the title sequence of Layli Long Soldier's *Whereas* (2017) considers the historical and racialized dimensions of

---

⁵⁷ Ibid., 116. ⁵⁸ Ibid., 63. ⁵⁹ Ibid., 142, 139. ⁶⁰ Ibid., 135.

subjecthood and citizenship within the context of the genocidal history of European colonialism and the devastating consequences of United States policy on Native American tribes and cultures. Written as a response to the 2009 "Congressional Resolution of Apology to Native Americans," "Whereas" criticizes the half-measures of the resolution and offers a countering text. It anatomizes the legalistic and formalized language of the resolution and supplants it with a lyric and personal register that is meant to refute its obfuscating abstractions and massifications with the granularities of lived experience, which Long Soldier specifies in the introduction to the poem:

> I am a citizen of the United States and an enrolled member of the Oglala Sioux Tribe, meaning I am a citizen of the Oglala Lakota Nation – and in this dual citizenship, I must work, I must eat, I must art, I must mother, I must friend, I must listen, I must observe, constantly I must live.[61]

Alternating between prose and long-lined poetry, "Whereas" appropriates the format of the Congressional Resolution – which consists of twenty "whereas" statements, seven resolutions, and two disclaimers – but redirects the energy of "whereas" from that of a legalistic rhetorical motor so that it becomes an anaphoric catalyst for an investigative account of the identity- and activity-based subjectivity that Long Soldier articulates and the larger historical and ideological conditions to which she is subject. While Long Soldier does not aim to speak for Native Americans in general, nor even for her own particular tribe or family, she does aim to speak back to the resolution's mystificatory (and purposive) obliquity and to bring to the surface its treacherous (but unintentional) ironies.

Congress passed the Joint Resolution in December 2009, which was then signed by President Obama and folded into a 2010 Department of Defense Appropriations Act, which provided more than $630 billion for Department of Defense spending to pay for the ongoing wars in Iraq and Afghanistan. The Resolution of Apology was one of 90

---

[61] Layli Long Soldier, *Whereas* (Minneapolis, MN: Graywolf Press, 2017), 57.

amendments to the bill, most of which concerned additional forms of military spending. President Obama signed the bill on December 19 – the last Saturday before Christmas – with no formal ceremony or announcement, and with no members of any Native American tribes present to receive the apology. According to Long Soldier, President Obama "never read the Apology aloud, publicly," although Sam Brownback, the Senator from Kansas who introduced the resolution, later read the apology in front of "five tribal leaders, though there are more than 560 federally recognized tribes in the US."[62] The first official apology on the part of the US government to Native American tribes and citizens, the resolution acknowledges "a long history of official depredations and ill-conceived policies by the Federal Government regarding Indian tribes and offer[s] an apology to all Native Peoples on behalf of the United States."[63] Nonetheless, it is a deeply problematic speech act: a nonapology apology buried within a weapons bill that ensures further "depredations" on a massive scale in other parts of the world, released with no announcement or recognition on the part of the administration, and drained of much of the moral force that it might have so that it could not be harnessed for any legal purposes.

The Joint Resolution's "whereas" statements alternate between legalistic praise poem and belated confession. Statements honoring "Native Peoples[']" long inhabitation of "the present-day United States since time immemorial," their stewardship of the land, their deep spirituality, and their many contributions to the United States are juxtaposed with acknowledgements of the damage and devastation wrought on the civilizations and cultures of Native Peoples by European settlers and the government of the United States. The seven resolutions continue the language of recognition and commendation of Native Peoples before apologizing "on behalf of the people of the United States to all Native Peoples for the many instances of violence, maltreatment, and neglect

---

[62] Long Soldier, *Whereas*, 57.
[63] S.J.Res.14 – "A joint resolution to acknowledge a long history of official depredations and ill-conceived policies by the Federal Government regarding Indian tribes and offer an apology to all Native Peoples on behalf of the United States." *Congress.gov*, December 19, 2009, www.congress.gov/bill/111th-congress/senate-joint-resolution/14/text, accessed on August 26, 2018. All further quotations from the resolution are taken from this web page.

inflicted on Native Peoples by citizens of the United States," expressing "regret for the ramifications of former wrongs," and urging the "President to acknowledge the wrongs of the United States against Indian tribes." The "Resolution of Apology" is strategically drained of agency: the grammatical subject of the "Acknowledgment and Apology" section is "The United States, acting through Congress," but in the two resolutions that include an acknowledgment and an apology, that grammatical subject is relieved of responsibility. The apology is not offered by the subject of the sentence and presumed speech act ("The United States, acting through Congress"), but is rather given "on behalf of the people of the United States." Similarly, the "acknowledgment" of the United States' "wrongs" is not an illocutionary speech act made by "the United States, acting through Congress" that effects what it intends (as in a promise or an order), but is rather a perlocutionary act: the "United States, acting through Congress" "urges the President to acknowledge the wrongs of the United States," but does not itself acknowledge those wrongs. Thus, both the acknowledgment and apology to Native Peoples – that is, the resolution's reason for being – are shunted onto other entities, with the subject of the resolution rhetorically shedding accountability for the litany of wrongs that it enumerates. The "Disclaimer" clinches the resolution's eschewal of responsibility by stating that "nothing in this Joint Resolution" either "authorizes or supports any claim against the United States" or "serves as a settlement of any claim against the United States."

The simple fact that the apology was issued is certainly important, but the circumstances of its occurrence, the rhetorical sleight-of-hand at the heart of the document, as well, of course, as the systemic and centuries-long brutality and discrimination faced by Native Americans that the document so gingerly acknowledges, become both the complex stage upon which Long Soldier lofts her own answering text and the compound object of her critique, one that proceeds indirectly via compositional arrangement and implication rather than by direct rebuttal. Without mentioning the resolution, the first "Whereas Statement" nonetheless censures its deceptive apology by offering its own affective phenomenology of the act of apologizing:

> WHEREAS when offered an apology I watch each movement the shoulders high or folding, tilt of the head both eyes down or straight through me, I listen for cracks in knuckles or in the word choice, what is it that I want? *To feel* and mind you I feel from the senses – I read each muscle, I ask the strength of the gesture to move like a poem.[64]

An apology, in Long Soldier's estimation, is not only a rhetorical or discursive act, and not merely an act of speech. Rather, it must be felt, both by the one who offers it and the one who receives it, as in a later "Whereas Statement" in which the poet recounts a shared meal with her father during which what she takes to be a sneeze is actually her father crying: "I'd never heard him cry, didn't recognize the symptoms. I turned to him when I heard him say *I'm sorry I wasn't there sorry for many things*." Her father's apology for his absence during her childhood is then placed in a broader historical context: "my hand to his shoulder/*it's okay* I said *it's over now* I meant it/because of our faces blankly/because of a lifelong stare down/because of centuries in sorry."[65] The father's genuine apology, both spoken and felt, is juxtaposed with the resolution's paper apology, never actually offered to Native Americans. Such biographically inflected passages alternate with direct considerations of the language of the resolution:

> WHEREAS I query my uneasiness with the statement, "Native Peoples are endowed by their Creator with certain unalienable rights, and among those are life, liberty, and the pursuit of happiness." I shift in my seat a needle in my back. Though "unalienable," they're rights I cannot legally claim if placed within a Whereas Statement. Meaning whatever comes after the word "Whereas" and before the semicolon in a Congressional document falls short of legal grounds, is never cause to sue the Government, the Government's courts say.[66]

---

[64] Long Soldier, *Whereas*, 61 (emphases original).
[65] Ibid., 65 (emphases original).   [66] Ibid., 70.

Long Soldier's "Whereas" statements repeatedly disclose the contradiction at the heart of the resolution – that it is a Congressional document with no legal force – by embedding her own and her family's history and episodes from her development as a poet within its rhetorical frame so as to mark that which the resolution slyly elides: the fact that contemporary Native Americans were neither offered the "Apology" directly nor can understand it to signal the possibility of an improvement in their material circumstances, as the "Disclaimers" make clear.

Long Soldier makes this point in the final set of "Whereas" statements, in which two statements from the resolution are reprinted, though with a series of words removed and replaced by empty brackets: "spiritual," "belief," "Creator," "customs," "traditions," "beliefs," "children," "families," "practices," and "languages." Thus, what appears in the resolution as:

> Whereas Native Peoples are spiritual people with a deep and
> abiding belief in the Creator, and for millennia Native Peoples
> have maintained a powerful spiritual connection to this land,
> as evidenced by their customs and legends;

becomes in Long Soldier's text

> Whereas Native Peoples are [   ] people with a deep and
> abiding [   ] in the [   ], and for millennia Native Peoples
> have maintained a powerful [   ] connection to this land,
> as evidenced by their [   ] and legends.[67]

The final page of the "Whereas" statements reprints the words that were earlier elided, while maintaining the original spacing:

>   [spiritual]
>   [belief]   [Creator]
>   [spiritual]
>   [customs][68]

The logic and force of these typographical manipulations is provided on an intervening page, in which Long Soldier responds to a comment

[67] Ibid., 83. [68] Ibid., 85.

Worlds and Selves 83

posted below a 2013 *New York Times* article about "the federal sequestration of funds from reservation programs," in which the commenter is a fourteen-year-old girl who has recently started a petition on whitehouse.gov asking the government to "*formally apologize and pay reparations to the Native American people.*" The poet imagines a response to the young girl, pointing out that there has already been an apology, and then concretizing the impact of the budget cuts:

> Dear Girl, I went to the Indian Health Services to fix a tooth, a complicated pain. Indian health care is guaranteed by treaty but at the clinic limited funds don't allow treatment beyond a filling. The solution offered: *Pull it.* Under pliers masks and clinical lights, a tooth that could've been saved was placed in my palm to hold after sequestration. Dear Girl, I honor your response and action, I do. Yet the root of reparation is repair. My tooth will not grow back. The root, gone.[69]

The textual alterations that Long Soldier makes to the Congressional document, both in these pages of the "Whereas" statements and in the subsequent "Resolutions" section, model the various forms of cutting and damage the resolution acknowledges but that the US government perpetuates, the primary examples of which are the 2013 budget cuts and the 2016 decision to approve running the Dakota Access Pipeline beneath the Missouri River close to the Standing Rock Indian Reservation, a major water source, archaeological site, and sacred space for the Standing Rock Sioux Tribe as well as several other nearby tribes. The decision sparked massive and longstanding protests and brought national and international attention. The literal "cutting" of the landscape in order to build the pipeline (along with the environmental and health-related damage that the pipeline will cause) is yet another of the "depredations and ill-conceived policies" for which the 2009 Resolution "apologizes" so ineffectually and cynically.

Long Soldier's own "Resolutions" both mutilate the text of the original and attempt to remake its language into gestures of resistance

---

[69] Ibid., 84 (emphases original).

and repair. Her fifth resolution, which is headed with the statement, "*I express commitment to reveal in a text the shape of its pounding,*" shapes the language of the fifth Resolution of the Congressional document – one that expresses regret for "the ramifications of former wrongs" and a commitment to "move toward a bright future" – into the image of a hammer.[70] The sixth resolution braids together statements of principles from two of the Water Protectors at Standing Rock, both of which advocate peaceful protest, nonviolent resistance, and community responsibility. Long Soldier's final resolution again mimics the discourse of the original: "I commend the inventive crafting of a national resolution so mindful of – //boundaries," at which point appears a performative pattern poem that continually reconfigures the document's final resolution, which commends "the State governments that have begun reconciliation efforts with recognized Indian tribes located in their boundaries."[71] The pattern poem repeats ever-varying portions of the clause and includes a large text box down the right-hand side of the page that partitions the sentence and sardonically recapitulates the "boundaries" that are from the perspective of the resolution's subject – "The United States, acting through Congress" – settled facts, but which are from the perspective of the "recognized Indian tribes" located within them evidence of genocide, theft, and systemic crime on the part of the United States. Long Soldier's critique mobilizes all of the textual resources of her own art form in order to lay bare the iniquity behind the 2009 Congressional Resolution and the emptiness of the apology that it offers. Against the resolution's unfeeling abstractions, Long Solder's rerouting of it stresses all that the document evades: the individual, familial, and tribal histories that were erased – "the root, gone" – and the actual taking of responsibility both for the crimes of the past and those that continue into the present.

The final section of "Whereas" rewrites the resolution's disclaimers, stating that "nothing in this book":

(1) authorizes or supports any claim against Layli Long Soldier by the United States; or

---

[70] Ibid., 93. [71] Ibid., 97.

(2) serves as a settlement of any claim against Layli Long Soldier by the United States, here in   the grassesgrassesgrasses.⁷²

These two disclaimers – set in the resistant, reparative space of the volume, "grassesgrassesgrasses" – reverse the forms of agency inherent in the resolution by making Long Soldier the subject of potential litigation that the original disclaimers preempt.⁷³ There are several important things going on in this final rhetorical reoccupation. Most apparently, it is an opportunity for Long Soldier to "sign" her rewriting of the 2009 Resolution: it is an instance of authorial agency. In addition, it lacerates once again the empty pretensions of the resolution by riffing on its null legal force. However, even as these final disclaimers position Long Soldier as the subject of the text – the one who asserts that nothing in it can be used to support a claim or settlement – the addition of the phrase "by the United States" has the effect of redoubling the dangerous and irresponsible authority of the US government. In the original resolution, the disclaimers do not enumerate any potential claimants: the Native Peoples whose claims are preemptively negated in the disclaimer are not mentioned, only the legal subject – "the United States" – against which any such claims might be (fruitlessly) lodged. Long Soldier shrewdly indicates the government's hypocrisy by raising the possibility that claims or settlements may be sought "against" her "by the United States" (perhaps for her deconstruction of the Congressional document) even though such are the precise legal actions that are precluded by the resolution's disclaimers. Even her assumption of an authorial subject produces a potential threat that her volume's last words hope to parry.

---

⁷² Ibid., 101.
⁷³ The final phrase – "grassesgrassesgrasses" – is one of the volume's dominant motifs, gesturing broadly to the literal land and specifically to a notorious comment by the nineteenth-century trader Andrew Myrick, who "is famous for his refusal to provide credit" to starving Dakota people, reportedly saying, "if they are hungry, let them eat grass," as Long Soldier notes in "38" (a stunning poem about the largest legal execution in US history, in which thirty-eight Dakota men were executed in 1862, upon orders from President Lincoln). Myrick was killed during the Sioux Uprising and his mouth "stuffed with grass," an act by the Dakota warriors that Long Soldier categorizes as a poem (ibid., 53).

And this points to the most intriguing implication of Long Soldier's disclaimers: in and through them she binds together the lyric "I," the authorial subject, and the legal person. That is, she goes against the grain of this entire chapter, in which I have tracked the dispersed, mediated, and differential qualities of the subject or "I" as it appears in a poem. Whether in the accounts of Wordsworth, Eliot, or de Man, the tendency is to distance the lyric subject from any actual construal of a person. For Long Soldier in "Whereas," however, it is precisely the rhetorical obfuscation of subjective agency that allows the resolution's grammatical subject – "The United States, acting through Congress" – to shed responsibility and so be incapable of either apology or repair. Her own disclaimers refuse this Janus-faced stance. Rather, they undertake a generative deconstruction: displaying the hollow gestures of intention offered in the Congressional apology allows Long Soldier to reinstall her own person on the far side of the resolution's negations. In so doing she demonstrates the value of poetry to articulate the import of individual life and to address systemic iniquities and injustices via lyric's productive torsions: the resolution's tactical evacuation of the grammatical subject becomes the impetus for Long Soldier's own reconstitution of subjective agency and intention. As Barbara Johnson formulated it in her work on the juxtaposition of "lyric and law," one question that Long Soldier's volume works through is "whether there is a relation between the 'first person' (the grammatical 'I') and the 'constitutional person' (the subject of rights)."[74] The two categories of "person" are certainly not fungible and yet our propensity to suspend our disbelief easily allows the "first person" of a poem to appear as something like a person, even as we understand such an appearance to be something of a ruse. What I've hoped to show in these readings is that contemporary poets have both faced up to this ruse and attempted to make it generative.

In *Poetry and the Fate of the Senses* (2002), one of the most significant accounts of poetry yet written in the twenty-first century, Susan Stewart argues for the centrality of art's, and poetry's especially,

---

[74] Barbara Johnson, "Anthropomorphism in Lyric and Law," *Yale Journal of Law & the Humanities*, 10.2 (1998), 549–574, at 556.

capacity to construct something like a person: "the task of aesthetic production and reception in general is to make visible, tangible, and audible the figures of persons, whether such persons are expressing the particulars of sense impressions or the abstractions of reason or the many ways such particulars and abstractions enter into relations with one another."[75] Stewart understands poetry to do ontological work, to sponsor and represent individual being: "Poetry is both the *repetition* of an ontological moment and the *ongoing process or work* of enunciation by which that moment is recursively known and carried forward."[76] Lyric poetry is, she writes, "the expression and record of the image of the first-person speaker across and through historical and cultural contexts," providing "us with a form on the boundary among sense impressions, somatic memory, individuation of agency, and social context."[77] Seemingly a confutation of New Criticism and deconstructive criticism that subdues or unspools the "figures of persons" that motivate poems by emphasizing their artifactual qualities or their dispersive textures, Stewart's argument aims not to install a new mode of authorial- or biographically-centered criticism, but rather to promote poetry's ability to instantiate figures and images of first-person experience, which is not only a matter of representing what we might call inner and bodily life (the "sense impressions," "somatic memories," and acts of intellectual "individuation of agency" that Stewart mentions), but also of providing a "form on the boundary" between inner life and the social.

It is crucial to keep both valences of Stewart's claim in mind: that poems can construct "figures of persons" and that these are *figures* – we must take on the full denotative and connotative weight of that term. It isn't that lyric poetry is not founded in shadow play, deferral, and absence. It is. But these aspects of lyric's deep structure are also key to its consequence. The "I" of a poem is neither person nor void, but rather a style of textual side-shadowing, a means of producing a space in which the kinds of experiences and activities that

---

[75] Susan Stewart, *Poetry and the Fate of the Senses* (Chicago and London: University of Chicago Press, 2002), 2.
[76] Stewart, *Poetry and the Fate of the Senses*, 15 (emphases original).
[77] Ibid., 41.

typify subjective life – thinking, speaking, feeling, remembering – can be fashioned into form. My aim in this chapter has been to elaborate the complex ways in which poems orbit around matters of subjectivity and the textures of individual experience without simply serving as vehicles for self-identification or authorial scripts that readers rehearse. The "I" or subject of a poem tends in several directions at once, as do the patterns of thought and affect projected within it, and in the following chapter I'll turn more fully to these patterns' textures and to the ways in which poems make spaces in which thinking and feeling happens.

3 Feeling Thought

Thus far, I have suggested that poems, because of the particular kinds of pressure that they place on language, both constitute and elicit acts of attention and play, and that while poems are bound to language's systems of reference and communication, they aren't simply in the game of sensemaking and information-giving, as Ludwig Wittgenstein has suggested.[1] Made of words, as Mallarmé famously counseled Degas, poems make of words something other or further.[2] In Chapter 2 I went on to argue that fundamental to a poem's affordances is its basis within the realm of individual life. This is, once again, not to succumb to an outdated Romanticism, nor to pin a poem's hopes on its ability to express some unique and coherent self, nor to argue for poetry's impregnable solitude or hermeticism. As Adorno has shown, poetry's seeming turn away from the social world is premised upon its immersion in that world and poems that do not register this double condition are self-deluding. The poems that I focused on did not blithely assume the prior unity of a self that might then go about its business of writing a poem; rather, the poem is the liminal, constructive space in which the internally fractured and externally tangled possibilities of subjectivity might be constellated textually, as well as the locus through which ideological and social systems out of the subject's ken might be glimpsed. In this chapter, I turn to a question that follows from the implications of those asked in the previous two: if poems necessarily rely on the stuff of thought – words, sentences – but can't be reduced to species of logical argumentation, information conveyance, or conceptual presentation; and

---

[1] See fragment 160 in Ludwig Wittgenstein, *Zettel*, ed. by G. E. M. Anscombe and G. H. von Wright and trans. by G. E. M. Anscombe (Berkeley, CA: University of California Press, 1970), 28.
[2] As recounted by Paul Valéry, *The Art of Poetry*, trans. Denise Folliot (Princeton, NJ: Princeton University Press, 2014 [1957]), 63.

if poems emerge from the interplay of cognition, imagination, memory, and affect without simply serving as vehicles for a prefabricated or commodified thought or emotion; then how are thinking and feeling intertwined within poems?

The most interesting and productive aspects of this question are not centrally concerned with deciding whose thoughts or feelings are displayed in any given poem. It is helpful to be almost excessively practical about this matter: of course poems have authors (by which I mean some kind of motivating force – poems tend not to self-generate), and often the relationship between the biographical author(s) of a poem and whatever kind of subject is constructed (or elided) in that poem is intricate, confected, and usually at least somewhat occulted. It remains the case that much discussion of poems in classrooms and within scholarship (including this book) silently follows the New Critical elision of the author of a text by using a term like "speaker" or "subject" in order to forestall the tendency toward biographical reading. But it often seems needlessly obfuscatory to pretend away the existence of the actual historical person who we know composed the poem in order to maintain some kind of interpretively sanitized reading environment, especially if the poem is quite clearly biographically inflected. However, it is also crucial to understand the gap that exists – though caused by and spanning a different kind of distance in different cases – between a biographical author and a textual subject, as my readings of volumes by Rankine and Long Soldier try to demonstrate. Just as it is reductive to read a so-called "confessional poet" straightforwardly – as though Plath were simply, baldly confessing – so is it obtuse to carry on as though the poems in *Ariel* (1965) have nothing to do with the circumstances and extremities of the life of Sylvia Plath. An analogous argument can be made about poetry at the other end of the spectrum: it is a form of bad faith to countenance the notion that even those poets who have most strenuously resisted the forms of subjectivity apparent in mainstream lyric, or what Charles Bernstein dismissively calls "official verse culture," produce poetry that is somehow "authorless" or that has escaped the bind that Adorno maps as though from the other side of the knot.³ Indeed, what often holds together poetry that eschews all normative patterns of coherence via whatever manner of conceptual or compositional experiment is the author's name as signal and guarantee. (As I discuss a bit later in the chapter, a related though distinct argument is available for an entire field of postwar New American poetry and the work that comes in its wake: poems by Robert Creeley, Frank O'Hara, Charles Olson, Larry Eigner, and others are in many ways inextricable from their own bodies, biographies, and lifeworlds – indeed the thrust of Olson's argument in "Projective Verse" theorizes the poem as, in part, a textual instrument that can capture and display the poet's own bodily and phenomenological life.)

My account in this chapter of the forms that thought and feeling take in poems is based on a trio of premises. The first premise is that poems have authors and that the relation between a poem's author(s) and the "I" (or speaker, or subject, or figural hollow around which textual energy converges) embedded in the text is productively inscrutable or ambiguous. The second is that a reader's relation with that same "I" is just as productive and just as inscrutable. Whatever amalgam of emotion, feeling, and thought is produced within a poem shuttles, strangely, between. The modernist reframing of Romantic poetics, as I sketched it in Chapter 2, thus remains tremendously generative: poems construct emotions, feelings, impressions, and thoughts, but they do not in any straightforward way belong to or originate in the poet's biographical experience, nor do they simply attach to, or occur at the beck of, the reader. The third premise is that one must respond to a poem as a shaped course of affective and intellectual activity – with all of the meanders and backflows that such a term entails – rather than as a static representation of mental and psychological acts or states that can be simply tagged. Rather than appear as the outcome of a line of intellection and emotion, a poem discloses a crystallized yet open process of thinking and feeling. This chapter aims to show

³ Charles Bernstein, *Content's Dream: Essays, 1975–1984* (Evanston, IL: Northwestern University Press, 2001 [1986]), 246.

how such processes occur and how readers might think their way through them.[4]

One of our most familiar tactics as readers is to approach poems as interior dramas: monologues, whether voiced or unvoiced, produced by agents in particular settings who fashion an affective and intellectual response, often under the pressure of some external or internal force – say, death or desire. The anecdotal, narrative, and imagistic freight that poems carry is entailed to an intertwined course of thought and feeling that often tends toward the symbolic, epiphanic, or parabolic. Reading a poem becomes, then, to return to Wordsworth's language in the "Preface" to *Lyrical Ballads*, a way "to follow the fluxes and refluxes of the mind when agitated by the great and simple affections of our nature."[5] Putting aside the outmoded universality of Wordsworth's account, his capacious sense of a poem as the constructed tracing of a mind's "fluxes and refluxes" is still quite useful within the contemporary context. Such "fluxes and refluxes" represent an amalgam of cognitive activities – perception, memory, projection, reflection, reverie – that comprise a disposition or orientation toward experience, rather than simply the outcome of it. At times, this appears as an elaborate compound of speech act and internal monologue, in which some kind of intellectual problem or affective consideration is worked through, as in Yeats' "Among School Children," Wordsworth's "Lines Composed a Few Miles Above Tintern Abbey," Moore's "Poetry" (the earlier version), or Auden's "In Praise of Limestone," just to name a few anchoring examples. Poems often aim to offer something like the experience of thinking or feeling – thinking about

---

[4] There is a wide range of work on poetry, affect, and the emotions. See especially Charles Altieri, *The Particulars of Rapture: An Aesthetics of the Affects* (Ithaca, NY: Cornell University Press, 2003); Kirstie Blair, *Victorian Poetry and the Culture of the Heart* (Oxford: Oxford University Press, 2006); and Sianne Ngai, *Ugly Feelings* (Cambridge, MA: Harvard University Press, 2005). Also see Helen Vendler, *Poets Thinking: Pope, Whitman, Dickinson, Yeats* (Cambridge, MA: Harvard University Press, 2004).

[5] William Wordsworth, "Preface to *Lyrical Ballads*" [1800/1802], in Stephen Gill, ed., *The Oxford Authors: William Wordsworth* (Oxford: Oxford University Press, 1984), 593–615, 598.

thinking. Stevens' "The Snow Man," for example, aims not to speculate on the contents of a snow man's mind, but to create a figurative space in which it would be possible to think a snow man's thought. Although a form of despair or sadness seems to underlie it, Dickinson's "There's a certain Slant of light" is not the recounting of a set of feelings, but a disclosure of how feeling emerges at the limen of the self and the world, that space of "internal difference – /Where the Meanings, are."[6] More important than the ability to simply present a thought or emotion is a poem's capacity to render via linguistic and poetic form the textures and activities of thinking and feeling.

Understanding a poem in this way requires neither an overweening or determinative account of authorship nor an abdication of the idea of a maker. At the same time, it is possible to preserve a space of readerly agency and activity without resting on the notion of the reader as a co-creator. In *Reckoning with the Imagination: Wittgenstein and the Aesthetics of Literary Experience* (2015), Charles Altieri articulates such an interactive model, one that takes into account both the acts of composition and reception. He suggests that "in art, according to Kant I recognize the presence of a maker everywhere but cannot bring it under a concept because I experience a texture of invention and care for particulars that seems continually free to modify its own processes."[7] Just as the value that Altieri attributes to aesthetic experience necessitates a maker-function, so do his notions of valuation and valuing rely on recognizing "how the text involves our participation in the various ways by which it makes discriminations and on how we might find ourselves endorsing the satisfactions it elicits." He continues, "when we are caught up in aesthetic experience, we have to renounce the direct route, which might provide discursive understanding, in favor of the slow time established by attention to the manner of the presentation. We thereby create a situation in which we can reflect on our orientations

---

[6] Emily Dickinson, *The Complete Poems of Emily Dickinson*, ed. Thomas H. Johnson (Boston and Toronto: Little, Brown and Company, 1955), 118.

[7] Charles Altieri, *Reckoning with the Imagination: Wittgenstein and the Aesthetics of Literary Experience* (Ithaca, NY: Cornell University Press, 2015), 8.

and thematize how the manner establishes significance for the subject matter."⁸ The reader here is a participant in a complex process in which attention and slow reading are privileged over instrumentalizing approaches to the poem at hand, and as the sense of a maker arises in a poem's "texture of invention and care for particulars," a reader's task is to follow the weave of such textures and activate all particulars so that the text's significance might ramify fully. Participation in Altieri's sense, however, expands well beyond acts of noticing, deciphering, and interpretive response. It is also a matter of considering the relation between the poem that discloses itself as a consequence of those readerly actions and our own orientations more broadly. Slowly galvanizing a poem's rhetorical and formal features, we become attuned to its presentation of a distinctly imagined orientation toward the world, and so we come not to identify with the poem but rather to lend it our own cognitive and affective apparatus while we simultaneously think and feel it through.

In "Poetry and Abstract Thought" (1939/1954), Paul Valéry describes such attunement as a "poetic state," one that the poem – as what Stevens calls "the cry of its occasion,/Part of the res itself and not about it" – aims to produce in the reader.⁹ Akin to Eliot's account of the objective status of poetic emotion, Valéry's detaches the poem's emotion from the poet's experience: "A poet's function – do not be startled by this remark – is not to experience the poetic state: that is a private affair. His function is to create it in others."¹⁰ In the same essay, Valéry elaborates on the emotion of poetry:

> The problem can be put in this way: Poetry is an art of Language; certain combinations of words can produce an emotion that others do not produce, and which we shall call *poetic*. What kind of emotion is this?
>
> I recognize it in myself by this: that all possible objects of the ordinary world, external or internal, beings, events, feelings, and

---

[8] Altieri, *Reckoning with the Imagination*, 179–180.
[9] Wallace Stevens, *The Collected Poems* (NY: Vintage Books, 1990 [1954]), 473.
[10] Valéry, *The Art of Poetry*, 60.

actions, while keeping their usual appearance, are suddenly placed in an indefinable but wonderfully fitting relationship with the modes of our general sensibility. That is to say that these well-known things and beings – or rather the ideas that represent them – somehow change in value. They attract one another, they are connected in ways quite different from the ordinary; they become (if you will permit the expression) *musicalized*, resonant, and, as it were, harmonically related. The poetic universe, thus defined, offers extensive analogies with what we can postulate of the dream world.[11]

Valéry understands the emotion of a poem to inhere in the possibility of an enlivening or heightening of particulars: "these well-known things and beings" become charged with significance within the poem's warp and weft. Sensory and imaginative life are quickened in ways that we attribute to aesthetic experience more broadly, and every formal and thematic aspect of a poem is not simply a part of a fixed field of textual features arranged just so, but a node for readerly activity.

Most familiar in the terms of Kantian reflective judgement and within a genealogy of aesthetic philosophy emerging out of Romanticism, we might also consider poetry's solicitation of thought and feeling within contemporary discourses around aesthetics and cognition.[12] In *Feeling Beauty: The Neuroscience of Aesthetic Experience* (2013), G. Gabrielle Starr reframes art's

---

[11] Ibid., 59 (emphases original).
[12] On the relations between philosophy, aesthetic theory, and poetry, see Alain Badiou, *The Age of the Poets and Other Writings on Twentieth-Century Poetry and Prose*, trans. Bruno Bosteels (London and New York: Verso, 2014); Philippe Lacoue-Labarthe, *Poetry as Experience*, trans. Andrea Tarnowski (Stanford, CA: Stanford University Press, 1999); Marjorie Perloff, *Wittgenstein's Ladder: Poetic Language and the Strangeness of the Ordinary* (Chicago and London: University of Chicago Press, 1996); John Gibson, ed., *The Philosophy of Poetry* (Oxford: Oxford University Press, 2015); John Koethe, *Poetry at One Remove* (Ann Arbor, MI: University of Michigan Press, 2000); Maximilian de Gaynesford, *The Rift in the Lute: Attuning Poetry and Philosophy* (Oxford: Oxford University Press, 2017); and Ranjan Ghosh, ed., *Philosophy and Poetry: Continental Perspectives* (New York: Columbia University Press, 2019).

quickened states – those "ghostlier demarcations, keener sounds" that Stevens ponders in "The Idea of Order at Key West"[13] – from the perspective of brain science: "aesthetic experience emerges from *networked* interactions, the workings of intricately connected and coordinated brain systems that, together, form a flexible architecture enabling us to develop new arts and to see the world around us differently."[14] Placing the brain's default mode network at the center of her account, Starr's research – which interweaves aesthetic and philosophical speculation with laboratory experimentation – provides a neurological description of some of the more familiar aspects of aesthetic experience: "We can become so absorbed, so enrapt in the experience of reading, listening, or looking, that the world of perception seems far away; but this happens only because we were so intensely drawn by part of that world of perception to begin with. Even in the noisy confines of an fMRI scanner, art could so grab the attention that auditory processes were suppressed, and inner life began to take over."[15] The sensory apparatus that first encounters and is activated by a work of art then motivates a turn inward, away from the world of the senses and into the "cognitive architecture" where the work of the senses is absorbed and transformed by the attentions of the imagining brain.[16] These attentions are sparked by the art object, but, as Starr notes, this doesn't imply that aesthetic experience is categorically different than everyday experience: "neurally speaking, art moves us by harnessing a key system with extraordinary resources, a system that not only helps make us who we are but also helps us be aware of who we are. Powerful aesthetic experience makes us return to that state of watchful waiting characteristic of core consciousness, but carrying an awareness of the pleasure of looking at an object and contemplating its worth."[17]

[13] Stevens, *The Collected Poems*, 130.
[14] G. Gabrielle Starr, *Feeling Beauty: The Neuroscience of Aesthetic Experience* (Cambridge, MA and London: The MIT Press, 2013), xv (emphasis original).
[15] Starr, *Feeling Beauty*, 63. In addition to *Feeling Beauty*, see Edward A. Vessel, G. Gabrielle Starr, and Nava Rubin, "The Brain on Art: Intense Aesthetic Experience Activates the Default Mode Network," *Frontiers in Human Neuroscience*, 6.66 (2012).
[16] Starr, *Feeling Beauty*, 94.   [17] Ibid., 66–67.

Although it is well beyond the scope of this chapter to delve into the complex field of cognitive aesthetics and the neuroscience of literary experience, it is worth noting that poems, as with literary or imaginative texts more broadly, and as textual "objects" rather than actual art objects, interact with perceptual and cognitive systems in particular ways.[18] The kind of sensory experiences that poems provoke in readers – whether visual, sonic, or, to a lesser extent, haptic or olfactory – are, of course, mediated through the conceptual apparatus of language. If every art, according to Walter Pater, has "its own peculiar and untranslatable sensuous charm," "its own special mode of reaching the imagination," and "its own special responsibilities to its material," then we can understand poems to offer unique instantiations of thought inextricable from sensuous and affective dimensions as mediated by processes of cognition and imagination.[19] Patterns of rhythm, sound, imagery, rhetoric, and figuration not only shape a poem's emergence as a pseudo-speech act and its dramatization of a subjectivity in process, they also spur its processes of thought, even as we understand that poems often resist modes of what John Keats called, in a letter to Benjamin Bailey, "consequitive reasoning" in favor of alternate forms of sequencing and progression.[20] Thinking in images, to adapt a line by Robert Lowell, poems also "think" in sound and rhythm, and by way of juxtaposition, parataxis, disjunction, and contradiction.[21] In the remainder of this chapter, I'll take Altieri's call – reinflected by way of Valéry and Starr – as a methodological cue and so try to elaborate more fully how poems render intellectual and affective experience.

---

[18] On poetry, neuroscience, and cognition, also see Elaine Scarry, *Dreaming by the Book* (New York: Farrar, Straus and Giroux, 1999); Peter Stockwell, *Cognitive Poetics: An Introduction* (London and New York: Routledge, 2002); Nikki Skillman, *The Lyric in the Age of the Brain* (Cambridge, MA: Harvard University Press, 2016); and Semir Zeki, *Inner Vision: An Exploration of Art and the Brain* (Cambridge, MA: The MIT Press, 2010 [1999]).

[19] Walter Pater, *The Renaissance* (New York: The Modern Library, 1919 [1873]), 107.

[20] Robert Gittings, ed., *Letters of John Keats* (Oxford: Oxford University Press, 1970), 37.

[21] See Robert Lowell, *Collected Poems*, ed. Frank Bidart and David Gewanter (New York: Farrar, Straus and Giroux, 2003), 640.

Earlier, I noted that the most straightforward manner in which we galvanize a poem's overlapping textual patterns is by framing it as a kind of drama, that is, by attributing to the poem not only a central figure who usually speaks in the first person, but also a diegetic surround. A poem's diegesis, however, is often much more tenuous than the more certain coordinates and scenery of a novelistic setting or dramatic staging, instead relying heavily on a handful of motifs or images and on the imaginative capacities of the reader to conjure from sparse cues a remarkably full story world – as in Coleridge's "Frost at Midnight," Keats' "To Autumn," or Frost's "Stopping by Woods on a Snowy Evening." It isn't simply that such poems traffic heavily in scenery, but that they network verbal images; deictic scaffoldings of person, place, and time; and an array of perspectival angles in order to create a multidimensional space that is not only "visible" (imaginatively speaking) but also proprioceptively available. Because the diegesis is gestural, uncertain, and malleable – underpinned by pronouns ("I" or "here") of relatively indefinite reference – it becomes a space in which rich readerly participation is both possible and necessary. There is nothing all that specific about the diegetic space of Frost's "Stopping by Woods" – someone's woods, that same someone's house far off, a dark and snow-filled "here" – and for that very reason a reader is licensed to devise a phenomenologically rich setting. The symbolic or thematic freight of the poem reposes upon its minimal scene. Because we can envisage bodies in space – of a horse, of a rider – the features and lineaments of that space might then ramify within the text's tightly rhymed long ballad meter as the various formal and rhetorical components converge upon one another.

A poem in Tracy K. Smith's first volume, *The Body's Question* (2003), provides a powerful instance of this mode of poetic thought and feeling, even though it – like a good deal of English-language poetry of the twentieth century – eschews a traditional or normative metrical pattern.[22] In a familiar anecdotal-epiphanic mode,

---

[22] There are a handful of texts that reckon with the rhythmic structures of nonmetrical verse, or that consider meter and rhythm more broadly within modern and contemporary poetry. See in particular Charles O. Hartman, *Free Verse: An Essay on Prosody* (Princeton, NJ: Princeton University Press, 1980); Annie Finch,

"Mangoes" relates the story of a mother and daughter standing at a bus or rail station, waiting, as we learn, for the husband/father to arrive:

> They wait without luggage.
> They have been waiting
> Since before the station smelled
> Of cigarettes.[23]

A poem of mediated observation – a reader views the pair via the perspective of the implicit poetic narrator – "Mangoes" narrates a nonarrival, maintaining its gaze on the waiting pair as day becomes night. The poem ends with an important shift in perspective and by making explicit the loss that the reader slowly intuits:

> Desire is the woman
> Awake now over a bowl of ashes
> That flutter and drop like abandoned feathers.
> It's the word *widow* spelled slowly in air
> With a cigarette that burns
> On its own going.[24]

No longer standing at the station with her daughter waiting for a man who will never arrive, the woman now sits at a table and the smoke and ash from her cigarette take on the burden of narrating her

---

The Ghost of Meter: Culture and Prosody in American Free Verse (Ann Arbor, MI: University of Michigan Press, 1993); Jon Silkin, *The Life of Metrical and Free Verse in Twentieth-Century Poetry* (New York: St. Martin's Press, 1997); Timothy Steele, *Missing Measures: Modern Poetry and the Revolt Against Meter* (Fayetteville, AR: University of Arkansas Press, 1990); and Andrew Crozier, *"Free Verse" as Formal Restraint: An Alternative to Metrical Conventions in Twentieth-Century Poetic Structure*, ed. Ian Brinton (Bristol, UK: Shearsman Books, 2015). Also see Donald Wesling, *The Scissors of Meter: Grammetrics and Reading* (Ann Arbor, MI: University of Michigan Press, 1996); Derek Attridge, *Poetic Rhythm: An Introduction* (Cambridge: Cambridge University Press, 1995); and Jonathan Culler and Ben Glaser, eds., *Critical Rhythm: The Poetics of a Literary Life Form* (New York: Fordham University Press, 2019).

[23] Tracy K. Smith, *The Body's Question* (Saint Paul, MN: Graywolf Press, 2003), 35.
[24] Smith, *The Body's Question*, 36.

circumstances. The third-person perspective remains, but the angle and proximity both shift subtly: the reader is drawn nearer to the woman, still observing her but now able to see the cigarette's ashes drop into the bowl – the reader is, indeed, disarmingly close to the grieving woman's face. This perspectival act of magnification and convergence is replicated by the transformation of what turns out to be the text's central symbol: not the titular fruit, but the station's ambient cigarette smoke.

In the opening stanza, the smell of cigarettes is largely atmospheric: we don't make a strong connection between the cigarettes and the central characters, apart from reading the smoke as an "objective correlative" of the vaguely oppressive nature of the waiting that the pair must endure. By the end of the poem, however, the cigarette is both the central subject's own device (for smoking, for grieving, for writing out her new status) and the totemic elegiac object. The "cigarette that burns/On its own going" is at once a figuration of the woman's presumed grief and of the husband's death. The ashes dropping into a bowl are, at the diegetic level, those from her cigarette; however, they double as ironic symbols of the absent husband: it is precisely the lack of the husband's body or remains for which the ashes serve as a negative metonym. The temporal hitch in the presentation of the final of images – a bowl of ashes mentioned before the cigarette from which they presumably derive – mirrors the affective course of the poem: the aftermath of the husband's death (though unknown to the two characters) is presented well before any hint of that death is revealed: the poem is, figuratively, a cigarette that's already burned, though we don't know this until the final lines. "Mangoes" offers a two-part vignette – a scene in the station followed by a later scene presumably in an interior, domestic space – in which nothing much happens and which is "epiphanic" only to the degree that it discloses quite slowly its narrative substance. But the diegetic coherence provides a textual logic in which the cigarette's multivalent significance can be fully elaborated: just as it doubles as a writing instrument for the grieving woman so does it function as an image in which the poem's affective logic might be housed. A reader of "Mangoes," drawn closer and closer to the woman and into the room of the poem as the implications of its story become clear, is by the end not only an observer but also a participant, akin to the inwoven figure that closes the text. The cigarette is such a generative image for Smith because it works across the sensorium: a smell and slight haze at the beginning, a visible and tangible remainder toward the end (its actual ash), it is brought nearly up to the reader's own lips in the final lines. It thus becomes not only the symbol at the center of the poem but also a conduit by which to link the text's narrative course and affective substance to the reader's own bodily and cognitive activities – it is composed as an image to think with.

It is possible to lean so heavily on the image of the cigarette in "Mangoes" because Smith's poem converges on itself: details follow from one another and work in conjunction, lines and phrases take their place in a lucid discursive texture, it refers to an imagined or recalled world that is coherent, and its parts operate to form a unity, "the complete consort dancing together," as Eliot is finally able to say in the last part of *Four Quartets*.[25] However, much of the poetry of the past century (as well as a good amount of poetry from further back) has relied on practices of disjunction, juxtaposition, and parataxis, approximating not the consort suggested in "Little Gidding," but what in "East Coker" is described as "a raid on the inarticulate/ With shabby equipment always deteriorating."[26] There are, of course, many modern and contemporary poets whose work is typically "convergent" to some degree, allowing a reader to project something like a diegetic space or a quasi-cohesive subject. Such a list would include major modernists such as Yeats and Stevens; mid-century figures like Brooks, Bishop, Larkin, Plath, and Lowell; and significant poets from the more recent past and present – Heaney, Graham, Derek Walcott, Rita Dove, Robert Hass, and Don Paterson, to name a few prominent figures. For such poets, the basic workings of linguistic reference and denotation, while always under investigation, are maintained. Other poets have privileged a much more fully disjunctive and juxtapositional

---

[25] T. S. Eliot, *Collected Poems, 1909–1962* (New York: Harcourt Brace & Co., 1991 [1963]), 208.
[26] Eliot, *Collected Poems, 1909–1962*, 189.

compositional practice, as modeled by texts such as *The Waste Land* (1922), Pound's *Cantos*, Williams' *Spring and All* (1922), and a good deal of Moore's work. For figures following up on the experiments of Gertrude Stein and other avant-garde practices, the poetic text became not only a space in which to experiment with the relation of parts via forms of collage or montage, but more centrally a site in which some of the basic capacities of language are refused within linguistic forms. The fearsome challenge and wicked thrill of Stein's *Tender Buttons* (1913) is that denotation and reference – and, hence, "meaning" in its typical sense – are so thoroughly undermined. The genealogy of modern poetry is by no means a neat set of lines, and many poets move across the spectrum of conjunctive and disjunctive practices or occupy different places on it at various points of their career, and so my purpose here isn't to argue for the value of one variety of experimental work over another, or even to position the "experimental" as inherently more significant than other styles of poetry. Rather, I'll consider how poems that, as compared to the centripetal tendencies of a text such as "Mangoes," proceed centrifugally can offer modes of thought and feeling even as they do away with or severely problematize means of creating textual coherence – whether diegetic, referential, or narrative. For poems that stress above all else that they are made of words, to return to Mallarmé, by fraying or fissuring the line between words and what they usually lead on to – ideas, images, objects, referents – how is the stuff of thought and feeling made to appear in a text or to occur to a reader?

One of the major forces in postwar poetry has been the idea that the page itself – both the literal page upon which a text is written or typed and the notional page that serves as a lattice or imagined backdrop – can be considered as a compositional field and can serve as something approximating a textual score. Underwritten by modernist experiments in layout and typography such as Mallarmé's *Un coup de dés jamais n'abolira le hasard* [A Toss of the Dice Will Never Abolish Chance] (1897), the two editions of *Blast* (1914–1915), Guillaume Apollinaire's *Calligrammes* (1918), the visual innovations emerging out of Futurism and Dadaism, and Pound's ideogrammatic method, twentieth- and twenty-first century writers have experimented with a variety of visual poetics.[27] Such attention to the visual dynamics of the page as a space of composition has also had a sonic or vocal dimension as well. Most famously articulated by Olson in "Projective Verse" (1950) and extended in different ways by Creeley, Eigner, Denise Levertov, Robert Duncan, Amiri Baraka, and Nathaniel Mackey in the tradition of New American poetry, as well as by figures across the spectrum of English-language literature – from bp Nichol and Allen Fisher to Myung Mi Kim and Catherine Walsh –, what Olson calls "composition by field" aims not only to activate the visual space of the page, but also to transform that space into a means by which to score the physiological and intellectual rhythms of the poet – of breath and perception, of ear and voice. Olson's desire for an unmediated line from the inner workings of the body and mind to their outer realization on the page – "the HEAD, by way of the EAR, to the SYLLABLE /the HEART, by way of the BREATH, to the line" – is, nonetheless, based on his faith in the power of a technology of mediation.[28] The typewriter can, he writes, "indicate exactly the breath, the pauses, the suspensions even of syllables, the juxtapositions even of parts of phrases ... For the first time he can, without the convention of rime and meter, record the listening he has done to his own speech and by that one act indicate how he would want any reader, silently or otherwise, to voice his work."[29] The standardized spacing and formatting possibilities of the typewriter (or of the word processor), in Olson's account, motivate the page as a formal resource and positions it as a conduit between the perceptual and cognitive apparatus of the writer and that of the reader.

Olson's essay and the styles of open field poetics that emerged out of and around it have been the objects of considerable

[27] On visual poetics, see for instance Johanna Drucker, *The Visible Word: Experimental Typography and Modern Art, 1909–1923* (Chicago: University of Chicago Press, 1994); Craig Dworkin, *Reading the Illegible* (Evanston, IL: Northwestern University Press, 2003); and Stephen Scobie, *Earthquakes and Explorations: Language and Painting from Cubism to Concrete Poetry* (Toronto: University of Toronto Press, 1997).
[28] Charles Olson, "Projective Verse" [1950], in *The New American Poetry*, ed. Donald Allen (New York: Grove Press, 1960), 386–397, at 387, 390.
[29] Olson, "Projective Verse," 393.

investigation, elaboration, and critique, but for the particular purposes of this chapter it is enough to point out that so-called composition by field has both a visual and sonic dimension. Working outside of traditional metrical and stanzaic forms, and leveraging the possibilities embedded within practices of free verse, such poetry mobilizes various modes of disjunctive arrangement as lines, phrases, and words are spread across the page in left, right, and center justifications. Such splayed texts ask for a flexible reading practice in order to reckon with spatial patterns and sonic or phrasal rhythms that are stranded from one another but implicitly connected through a series of inscrutable or unfamiliar relays. At times, there might be a consistent diegesis that binds together the text arrayed on a page, but more often formal disjunction brings with it diegetic and discursive disjunction, and so a reader must work to make a path through the text and consider the impact of its distribution as seemingly unmoored pieces of language follow their own logic of construction while simultaneously hanging together on the page. What such works make explicit by way of their inventive arrangements is the chimeric quality of the poem as a linguistic object and act. Approaching a text that operates according to some principle of open field composition requires a double act of readerly construction: we see the page(s) as a concrete array of words and space, and we also begin to divine ways to consider the text as a dispersed act of speaking. To be sure, this doubleness is present in most poetry and isn't at all limited to a certain strain of twentieth-century experimental work. However, because such texts foreground such doubleness by way of their own nonconventional constructions, they demand a particular kind of attention because the usual frames of poetic coherence – stanza shapes, familiar metrical grids, a stable subject and story-space, the typical conventions of even left margins and ragged right margins – have been suppressed or transformed utterly.

For a recent example of this kind of work, I'll turn to a perhaps unexpected poet. Tongo Eisen-Martin is not in any simple way an exemplar of "open field" poetry, if for no other reason than his work appears more than sixty-five years after Olson's formulation of the term. Nonetheless, Eisen-Martin appears to be influenced by certain strands within the New American poetry, especially the work of

Baraka and Ginsberg, and his typical penchant is for a highly distributed, energetically messy page in which the basic unit shifts from sentence to line to phrase to word, and which jumps between prose and lineated sections. Eisen-Martin's work, however, does not merely engage in experiments with the visual dynamics of the page: a San Francisco-born poet who also works as an educator and activist, especially concerning the racialization of crime and extrajudicial (largely police) violence against Black people in the United States, he is also a noted performer of his work. The complex surfaces of his texts – collected in two volumes, *Someone's Dead Already* (2015) and *Heaven Is All Goodbyes* (2017) – must be considered in the context of his own renderings of those poems, which are often performed by memory and during which Eisen-Martin, who typically does not provide the title of a poem before reading it, often strings together disparate individual poems in an unbroken series, ramifying the investigation of the relation between part and whole that occurs at the level of the page. Turning briefly to Eisen-Martin's work allows me to consider the implications of a poem's performance by the poet within the context of this chapter's focus on poetry's capacities for intertwining modes of thought and feeling within verbal forms.

Eisen-Martin's poetry most often concentrates on a set of interconnected topics: racial violence in the United States; the intertwining of race, politics, and rapacious capitalism within contemporary urban space; and the criminalization of blackness as part of the history of American culture. It is disturbing, revolutionary poetry that, like Rankine's and Long Soldier's, interrogates the conditions of individual life in the twenty-first century as such life is enmeshed in systems of oppression, coercion, and unfreedom. The kind of thought and feeling that Eisen-Martin's poetry often provokes is not at all that of Valéry's "poetic state" nor of the kind of heightened, pseudo-spiritual energies that we often associate with lyric poetry. On the page, the poems careen between the left and right margins and among what seem like different voices and snatches from conversations (whether transcribed or imagined). He is a compelling performer, and his ability to recite his work from memory and with a distinctive cadence, affect, and bearing on stage aligns him (in at least certain ways) with varieties of spoken word and slam poetry.[30] However, working against this remarkable stage presence is the disjunctive, often surreal quality of his poems, and his own subtly distanced presentation of them. Eisen-Martin writes about systemic violence and racism, and many of his most memorable lines somehow manage to appear at once as fierce rebuke and offhand punch line. Here are just a few:

> White people will never go home
> – They will make colonialism work[31]
>
> ...
>
> > The start of mass destruction
> > Begins and ends
> > In restaurant bathrooms
> > That some people use
> > And other people clean

---

[30] While artists like Gil Scott Heron, a founding figure within spoken word poetry and an early influence in the history of rap and hip-hop music, and the dub poet Linton Kwesi Johnson are famous in both musical and literary circles, there has not been much general work on spoken word poetry as a hybrid literary-musical genre. There has been a great deal of discussion about the aesthetic merits of slam poetry and the disregard of slam and spoken word poetry by more conservative voices in the academy, and while there is now much more crossover between so-called "page poetry" and "stage poetry," the two cultures remain distinct in many respects. On spoken word and slam poetry, see in particular Susan B. A. Somers-Willett, *The Cultural Politics of Slam Poetry: Race, Identity, and the Performance of Popular Verse in America* (Ann Arbor, MI: University of Michigan Press, 2009); and Javon Johnson, *Killing Poetry: Blackness and the Making of Slam and Spoken Word Communities* (New Brunswick, NJ: Rutgers University Press, 2017). On poetry and performance more generally, see Douglas Oliver, *Poetry and Narrative in Performance* (New York: St. Martin's Press, 1989); Charles Bernstein, ed., *Close Listening: Poetry and the Performed Word* (New York: Oxford University Press, 1998); Laura Hinton and Cynthia Hogue, eds., *We Who Love to Be Astonished: Experimental Women's Writing and Performance Poetics* (Tuscaloosa, AL: University of Alabama Press, 2002); Lesley Wheeler, *Voicing American Poetry: Sound and Performance from the 1920s to the Present* (Ithaca, NY: Cornell University Press, 2008); and Peter Middleton, *Distant Reading: Performance, Readership, and Consumption in Contemporary Poetry* (Tuscaloosa, AL: University of Alabama Press, 2005).

[31] Tongo Eisen-Martin, *Someone's Dead Already* (Oakland, CA: Bootstrap Press, 2015), 60.

...

> My dear, if it is not a city, it is a prison.
> If it has a prison, it is a prison. Not a city.[32]

Taken out of context, such passages resemble instances of lyric critique or ironically gnomic wisdom, and Eisen-Martin sometimes muffles their seriousness in performance by way of a seemingly self-deprecating laugh or sigh, either just before or after the delivery of the line. Within the run of the poem on the page, however, such moments have to contend with the scattered voices that surround them. Here's the full passage of the opening of "Faceless," the first poem in *Heaven Is All Goodbyes*, from which the two previous quotes were drawn:

> A tour guide through your robbery
>
> He also is
>
> Cigarette saying, "look what I did about your silence."
>
> Ransom water and box spring gold
>   – This decade is only for accent grooming, I guess
>
> Ransom water and box spring gold
>   – The corner store must die
>
> War games, I guess
>
> All these tongues rummage junk
>
>   The start of mass destruction
>   Begins and ends
>   In restaurant bathrooms
>   That some people use
>   And other people clean
>
>   "you telling me there's a rag in the sky?"
>   – waiting for you. yes –

---

[32] Tongo Eisen-Martin, *Heaven Is All Goodbyes* (San Francisco, CA: City Lights Books, 2017), 9, 10.

> we've written a scene
> we've set a stage
>
> We should have fit in. Warehouse jobs are for communists. But now more corridor and hallway have walked into our lives. Now the whistling is less playful and the barbed wire is overcrowded too.
>
> > My dear, if it is not a city, it is a prison.
> > If it has a prison, it is a prison. Not a city.
>
> > When a courtyard talks on behalf of military issue,
> > all walks take place outside of the body.
>
> > Dear life to your left
> > Medieval painting to your right
> > None of this makes an impression[33]

Working one's way through this passage, one considers the carceral desolation suggested in the evocations of somber whistling and "overcrowded" barbed wire, and then links that to the reflections on cities and prisons, and then translates that to a military setting, wherein the prison courtyard is exchanged for another space of state-sponsored violence. These transfers are ecstatic and alienating – "all walks take place outside of the body" – and the final stanza above entirely relocates the poem from the space of the prison and military base to the space of the museum. Institutions overwrite one another as the realms of art and culture either participate in the same conditions of oppression as prisons or simply have no effect – "none of this makes an impression." This final line, to be sure, undoes itself, operating crosswise to its literal meaning as Eisen-Martin's poetry piles impression upon impression, with texts continually jumping registers, from statements of political commitment and grim appraisal to casual asides and surreal images. One tries and quickly fails to bring the poem together into a unified context, even as – especially in performance – the speaking subject exerts a centripetal force on the text, though one that constantly threatens to scatter into a gallery of voices talking at once.

---

[33] Eisen-Martin, *Heaven Is All Goodbyes*, 9–10.

Able to link certain details together so as to conjure up the beginnings of a discursive or narrative logic, a reader is quickly stymied when an entirely different context – or no context at all – is brought into play. It isn't that such poetry stifles emotional response or suspends intellectual engagement. Rather, the poem saturates – overcrowds – a reader's reception of it, producing a welter of perceptions, impressions, and thoughts, but deliberately offering no organizing frame in which to place them all.

Eisen-Martin's ability to swing between moments of the most serious kind of critique and protest and passages of odd absurdity makes for a tremendously unnerving reading and listening experience. Uncoordinated bits of conversation are set against oddly angled details: is "Ransom water" a newfangled description, a cryptic command, or an oblique reference to the water system of Ransom, Illinois? Self-reflexive moments that spotlight the poem's status as an aesthetic object that aims to mediate "dear life" vie with what seem like found texts. Passages that are enmeshed in the actualities of political, social, and economic life are at the same time tilted away from direct statements of commitment or protest. Or, what seem like direct statements about the iniquity of contemporary conditions are thrown off-kilter by the non sequiturs or apparently irrelevant details that follow. Drawing on modernist forms of parataxis and collage, and inhibiting typical modes of narrative or discursive conjunction that might otherwise direct a reader's experience of the text, Eisen-Martin's poems flick rapidly among disjunct materials that the page gathers and turns toward the social and political spheres without the sorting mechanism of a single lyric speaker or discursive context. In certain ways, his virtuoso performances can't help but to focus the centrifugal tendencies of his texts within his own speaking body. However, the unruly and unruled energy from which they are built remains as Eisen-Martin's own performances seek not to bring them within an authorial orbit, but rather to maintain the processual, improvisatory thinking that seems part of their conception by transposing it from the scattered space of the page to the syncopated and shifting time of live performance. Such improvisations are redoubled by Eisen-Martin's practice of splicing together poems and parts of poems that appear at a distance from one another in his published volumes or that appear in different volumes. Poems lose their status as autonomous texts and become modular parts within an improvised run in live performance. The logic of disjunction that governs the texts of his poems jumps a level in his performances of those poems.

The forms of disjunction that are apparent in Eisen-Martin's poetry are indicative of techniques that are widespread across contemporary poetry. Phrases, words, and sentences are strewn across a page, and there is no periodic order to their arrangements. Pieces of text are placed into configurations that follow no conventional pattern – they aren't in any usual way stanzas, verse paragraphs, or strophic structures. And while certain passages of his poetry make sense or refer in plausible, if unexpected, ways, many others proceed by splitting the materiality of the signifier from its potential signification, and by eschewing typical patterns of sensemaking. As I have suggested in previous chapters, these modes of defamiliarization or estrangement are crucial to poetry's manifold significance as a form of cultural and political critique as well as the basis of its aesthetic practice. To be sure, because of its thoroughgoing parataxis and its continual enmeshing of unaligned fragments, Eisen-Martin's poetry asks for a good deal from any potential reader, but it also remains conceivable within a structure of intention, and therefore remains available to be thought and felt through, even as the difficulty of bringing its disparate parts together makes the task of readerly response daunting. As writers in the latter part of the twentieth century followed up on modernist avant-garde practices, taking Pound, Stein, or Zukofsky (rather than, or more than, poets like Yeats, Eliot, or Stevens) as their chosen precursors, disjunctive practices and levels of difficulty magnified. Especially with the rise of Language poetry in the 1970s, poets thought more intensely about their writing as a mode of theoretical engagement and critique instead of (or in addition to) a craft or art. In many ways this was a necessary turn away from the ideologies of New Criticism and a resistance to the craft-based poetics of the personal lyric that dominated mainstream publishing and the growing world of university creative writing programs. This isn't the place to recapitulate the history of Language writing (or of university creative writing programs), either from the perspective of its central figures or that of its critics, nor to provide a theoretical account of Language poetry or to parse genealogies of experimental or innovative verse. There is already a massive bibliography – much of it produced by the Language poets themselves – devoted to historicizing and theorizing Language poetry and its influence.[34] Rather, I will focus on one or two implications of Language poetry for how individual readers approach particular poems written either by its practitioners or by later poets who are sometimes brought together under the baggy category of "post-Language poetry." More specifically, I am interested in exploring the ramifications of a significant aspect of Language poetry's technical repertoire – its use of the sentence as the central structuring principle of poetic making – within the broader rubric of this chapter's concerns.

Language poetry is – at once – a theoretical phenomenon, a literary-historical occurrence, a poetic overturning, a conceptual

---

[34] Among many works, see especially Lyn Hejinian, *The Language of Inquiry* (Berkeley, CA: University of California Press, 2000); Barrett Watten, *The Constructivist Moment: From Material Text to Cultural Poetics* (Middletown, CT: Wesleyan University Press, 2003) and *Questions of Poetics: Language Writing and Consequences* (Iowa City, IA: University of Iowa Press, 2016); Bob Perelman, *The Marginalization of Poetry: Language Writing and Literary History* (Princeton, NJ: Princeton University Press, 1996); Charles Bernstein, *A Poetics* (Cambridge, MA: Harvard University Press, 1992) and *Content's Dream: Essays, 1975–1984* (Evanston, IL: Northwestern University Press, 2001 [1986]); Bruce Andrews and Charles Bernstein, eds., *The Language Book* (Carbondale, IL: Southern Illinois University Press, 1984); Ron Silliman, *The New Sentence* (New York: Roof Books, 1987); and *The Grand Piano: An Experiment in Collective Autobiography, San Francisco, 1975–1980* (Detroit, MI: Mode A Press, 2006–2010), ten volumes with contributions by Rae Armantrout, Steve Benson, Alan Bernheimer, Carla Harryman, Lyn Hejinian, Tom Mandel, Ted Pearson, Bob Perelman, Kit Robinson, Ron Silliman, and Barrett Watten. Also see George Hartley, *Textual Politics and the Language Poets* (Bloomington, IN: Indiana University Press, 1989); and Ann Vickery, *Leaving Lines of Gender: A Feminist Genealogy of Language Writing* (Hanover, NH: Wesleyan University Press, 2000).

program, and a social field. Oren Izenberg provides a helpful historical summary:

> Language poetry was conceived as a response to two roughly contemporaneous if incommensurable developments – the American government's involvement in the Vietnam War and the American university's enthusiastic reception of continental literary theory – but its practitioners remain active and visible well after the end of the former and the institutional domestication of the latter. Having survived the historical situation it originally addressed and transcended the most explicit reference to the intellectual framework that underwrites its practice, Language writing promises to outlive as well the institutional ethos (that of the "voice centered" poetry writing workshop) whose dominance initially justified the movement's sense of itself as embattled from the very moment of inception.[35]

Along with certain experimental techniques that were shared among various formations of innovative postwar poetry, one of the central stylistic practices that Language poetry developed is what Ron Silliman named "The New Sentence," in a 1977 essay of that title. Tracing the history of the sentence as a concept and form; marshalling Saussure, Wittgenstein, the Russian Formalists, Quine, Chomsky, Todorov, Barthes, and others; and tracking its prehistory through texts by a handful of writers, particularly Stein, before demonstrating its emergence, uniquely, within "prose of the Bay Area," Silliman eventually arrives at a definition of the "new sentence" as, among other features, a "unit of measure" within a paragraph unit that is related formally (rather than logically or narratively) to the sentences on either side of it, and at a second level to the other sentences that appear in the same paragraph.[36] It is "the first prose technique to identify the signifier (even that of the blank space) as the locus of

---

[35] Oren Izenberg, *Being Numerous: Poetry and the Ground of Social Life* (Princeton, NJ: Princeton University Press, 2011), 139.
[36] Silliman, *The New Sentence*, 63, 91.

literary meaning. As such, it reverses the dynamics which have so long been associated with the tyranny of the signified, and is the first method capable of incorporating all the levels of language, both below the horizon of the sentence *and* above."[37] Although in Silliman's account the "new sentence" is a feature of the prose poem, it extends to and can be adapted within the context of lined poetry. To be sure, different writers might characterize it differently than Silliman and conceive of it along somewhat different lines, but at a broad level the new sentence is the technique that catalyzed Language poetry's formal project.

Concretizing their critique of the ideologies and politics of signification by reenvisioning sentences as purely syntactical forms that do not necessarily coordinate referential content nor serve as the building blocks of larger narratives or discourses, the Language poets revolted against poetry in a number of ways. They capsized the primacy and self-unity of the verbal image, subdued lyric figuration, eschewed the centrality and power of a speaker or "voice," and submerged signification beneath the concretions of words and phrases that refuse to link up into larger structures of sense or meaning. Critics have understood the consequences of their project variously, as – just to give several well-known perspectives – a signal of postmodernism's structural schizophrenia (Jameson), an important intervention that yielded what looks now like a period style (Perloff), or a fundamental unrigging of the poem as the object of attention for poets or critics in favor of poetry as an epitome of generalized linguistic capacity (Izenberg).[38] Aside, however, from literary-historical or critical arguments about Language poetry's place and significance, it is important to understand just how widespread a resource some version of the "new sentence" has become for contemporary writers, whether or not those writers would identify with Language poetry or be described as post-Language writers. And we have barely begun to

---

[37] Ibid., 93 (emphasis original).
[38] See Fredric Jameson, *Postmodernism, or, the Cultural Logic of Late Capitalism* (Durham, NC: Duke University Press, 1991), 25–31; Marjorie Perloff, *Unoriginal Genius: Poetry by Other Means in the New Century* (Chicago and London: University of Chicago Press, 2010), 8–9; and Oren Izenberg, *Being Numerous*, 138–163.

consider its implications for the ways in which we actually *read* contemporary poetry, rather than account for it theoretically or polemically. If we want to understand a poem's significance within the domain of reading – that is, focusing on the ways in which an individual or group of individuals might respond to the particular textures of a poem – then considering the ramifications of "new sentence" techniques is crucial. If Tracy K. Smith's "Mangoes" is an instance of lyric convergence that affords a relatively familiar and accessible mode of readerly participation, and if the more fractured and disjunctive texture of Tongo Eisen-Martin's poetry requires something bordering on readerly construction in order to galvanize the poem's parts, then how might we approach a text that maintains many of the basic forms of linguistic sense – syntax and grammar – but warps their contents or suppresses their logic?

One challenge that arises when facing what seems like the ubiquity of parataxis in much contemporary poetry is to distinguish between parataxis or disjunction as a generative and valuable technique within poetic practice and parataxis as simply an unshakeable sign of contemporary life. As Bob Perelman, a prominent Language poet, wrote in the early 1990s, "parataxis is the dominant mode of postindustrial experience. It is difficult to escape from atomized subject areas, projects, and errands into longer, connected stretches of subjectively meaningful narrative."[39] And how much truer now is Perelman's observation. Sucked into the disjointed, incessant scroll of one's various social media feeds – jerked and jerking from screen to screen – parataxis is simply life's condition. How, then, might a poem based on disjunction or parataxis not simply replicate the frantic mix of distraction and coercion that shapes everyday life? As Barrett Watten, among others, has warned, it is important not to universalize the varieties of disjunction at work in contemporary poetry, nor to understand disjunction merely as an aesthetic technique divorced from its basis within Language writing's project of ideological critique.[40] More broadly, it is important to consider contemporary

---

[39] Bob Perelman, "Parataxis and Narrative: The New Sentence in Theory and Practice," *American Literature*, 65.2 (June 1993), 313–324, at 313.
[40] See Watten, *The Constructivist Moment*, 103–146.

forms of paratactical composition as emerging out of a bevy of discrete modernist practices. As the power of the traditional lyric subject as a poem's centralizing force came into question, and as postwar poetry became more and more likely to incorporate aspects of poststructural theory and posthumanist philosophy into its compositional practices, it became increasingly difficult to conceive of a poem as, at once, an instance of large-scale ideological critique, a presentation of sensuous particulars that connected – somehow – to lived experience, and a mode capable of reflecting back upon the status of those particulars with something more than postmodern irony or superficial glibness. It became more difficult, that is, to fashion poetic texts that one wanted to both consider conceptually and actually read. The most compelling works by Language writers manage this, as do a number of writers in their wake. In such cases, parataxis and constitutive disjunction becomes not only symptomatic or simply resistant, but can take on a positive, generative force.

Lisa Robertson's work is exemplary of the practices that characterize so-called "post-Language" poetry even as it ranges widely across the spectrum of poetic practice. Although she doesn't utilize "new sentence" techniques in any strict sense, Robertson's work draws from Language poetry and avant-garde poetics more broadly, but her books also gain energy by entangling themselves – both archly and critically – in poetry's traditional genres and topoi, as is clear in several of her volume's titles: *XEclogue* (1993), *Debbie: An Epic* (1997), and *The Men: A Lyric Book* (2006). Much of Robertson's poetry is concerned with matters central to the lyric tradition – the limits and textures of selfhood, the interplay between introspection and textuality, the matter of sex, and the force of desire. As Christopher Nealon notes, "she is everywhere an erotic poet, collaging from both modernity and classical tradition new configurations of old figures for pleasure. Her project, in books like *The Weather* and *XEclogue* as well as in *Debbie*, has been to articulate something like a cyborg pastoral."[41] Her writing has also been guided by an attempt to juxtapose a poetry of

---

[41] Christopher Nealon, "Camp Messianism, or, the Hopes of Poetry in Late-Late Capitalism," *American Literature*, 76.3 (September 2004), 579–602, at 591.

sensuous particulars with one of theoretical and philosophical substance. As she writes in "The Seam," the opening poem of *3 Summers* (2016), "[n]ow it's time to return to the sex of my thinking."[42]

Of particular importance for Robertson is devising a mode of lyric writing that can preserve certain practices of lyric expression – "We press out these voices from the inmost parts/to be able to start" – while simultaneously submitting such expressive tendencies to critique so that the ideological conditions that structure them remain in view – "There is no everyday life./That was a bribe from the masters."[43] This often makes for a form of lyric writing whose surface is smooth but whose internal workings are torqued in strange directions, as in this stunning passage from "The Middle":

> Next I realize that all along it's been my body
> that I don't understand.
> I just have to describe what it means
> supernatural, negative and sexual
> and blooming on one side. It's fierce and then
> it's tired. The dog lies on the lawn
> eating apples, me crouched in the
> luxurious secret, whatever
> I have been building, vena cava
> threading to atmosphere, psoas
> ruffling, everything quiet
> rocked only by love, hazard, fate, sleeping –[44]

"The Middle" is a poem covering nineteen pages with no marked internal divisions apart from irregular stanza and page breaks. Some pages contain a single brief free-verse stanza, while others consist of multiple stanzas that spill over to the following page. Overall, there is no particularly obvious pattern of progression – the poem is, in certain ways, all middle. The above stanza is, depending on one's precise mode of reckoning, roughly in the middle of "The Middle," although it doesn't seem to have any special structural significance. There are

---

[42] Lisa Robertson, *3 Summers* (Toronto: Coach House Books, 2016), 10.
[43] Robertson, *3 Summers*, 11, 14.   [44] Ibid., 62.

other passages that contain analogous moments of realization and introspection, and this passage isn't privileged over them. It thus can't be read as the poem's gesture of culmination or conclusion. It would make more sense if it could. Were this stanza to constitute an entire short lyric, or if it assumed a prominent place within a sequence, a reader might be able to contextualize its strange amalgamation of cliché and estrangement. The moments that are most familiar within an economy of expression, such as "I realize that all along it's been my body/that I don't understand," are rebutted by lines that weirdly literalize that initial realization – "vena cava/threading to atmosphere, psoas/ruffling" – which are then countered by a return to lyric atmospherics ("everything quiet") that give way to a final list that doubles down on abstract clichés: "love, hazard, fate, sleeping." The dash that ends the stanza rebuffs the catalogue that precedes it, as though the list might have simply gone on had not sleeping intervened. Instances of imagistic clarity (the dog eating apples) are upset by the uncertainties of syntax that follow. Is "me crouched" the beginning of an independent clause, or part of a surreal list of what the dog is eating? One could read the entire final sentence of the stanza as subordinated to the present-tense verb "lies" – although at the interpretive level this yields little but strange mischief. The one instance in which the grammar of the passage breaks down – "I just have to describe what it means/supernatural, negative and sexual" – is both a second-order reflection on the initial realization and a verbal performance of the nonunderstanding at its heart. It isn't simply that Robertson is ironizing or parodying lyric expressivity, but that she composes a lyric passage that simultaneously provides a mode of sensuous engagement and licenses an overturning of such engagement: what is at issue is not the content of any particular feeling, but the ways in which sensation, feeling, and thought must necessarily straddle distinct domains of conceptualization, as well as the morphing effects of any attempt to represent or figure those physiological, somatic, and psychological crossing patterns.

 Without making this passage representative of Robertson's work, and without making Robertson representative of a certain formation within contemporary poetry, I do want to emphasize that its double motion is indicative: an instance of lyric introspection shot through with self-estrangement. Robertson fashions a formal procedure that tacks between connection and disjointedness, adapting a "new sentence" style both at the level of the poem as a large-scale motion and at the granular movement within verse units. Parts of "The Middle" are placed beside one another but no developmental or narrative logic gains strength. A similar motion characterizes individual stanzas, as in the one above: we work through moments of intensity that are simultaneously placed in relation to one another and repel one another, as in the shift from the register of subjectivity and self-making ("whatever/I have been building") to that of the circulatory system and the musculature. A reader is drawn into a series of intersecting motions as the poem's patterns of thought and affect gather and disperse over a series of lyric durations that systematically refuse to proceed teleologically.

Poetry's significance as a practice of thought and feeling is, in the account that I've been gathering here, inextricably tied to its ability to construct and then provoke in the reader a duration of undetermined attentiveness. The poetics of disjunction that characterize a good deal of recent work are not merely indicative of a capitulation to the commodified atomization of contemporary life nor an eschewal of the poet's function as a maker. To be sure, there are plenty of practices of poetry in which such an eschewal is the primary directive, making the poet-figure into the administrative attendant of a process of textual production that occurs outside of the vicissitudes of aesthetic making, whether by means of a predetermined concept or by a method that fully mechanizes the creation of poetry. It isn't that the designers of such work or those who encounter it don't have thoughts or feelings about it, but that such responses tend to be about the work as a concept or large-scale project rather than induced from a slow working through the work's particulars, by which I mean the specific pressures – figural, semantic, syntactic, rhythmic, sonic, rhetorical – placed upon words and bundles of words within the space of the poem. J. H. Prynne describes the intensely granular nature of what he calls "poetic thought": "The activity of thought resides at the level of language practice and indeed is in the language and is the language; in this sense, language is how thinking gets done and how thinking coheres into thought, shedding its links with an originating sponsor or process of individual consciousness."[45] In Prynne's account, what Wordsworth describes as the "fluxes and refluxes of the mind" are not prelinguistic ephemera that are somehow captured in poems, but rather the specific and constant activity of "language practice" that comprises a text, and that proceeds as a "working encounter with contradiction in the very substance of object-reality and the obduracy of thought."[46] A poem's disjunctive surface is also its method of ongoingness – not as a textual collage, but as a shaped and shaping course that ceaselessly pushes against and reformulates what had come before. Recursive, resistant, radiating backwards and forwards at once, the contemporary poems that ask the most of readers also afford an experience of thinking and affective response that is, crucially, indefinite or uncertain, neither locked within the orbit of authorial power nor a scrim through which the reader can see once again only himself. Identification and instrumentalization are forestalled as localized activity and response take precedence, spurring a reader not toward totalization but differential, dialectic engagement. In a world saturated in empty images, driven by reaction, and premised on unthought, the poems that might matter most offer a space in which the granular intricacies of linguistic materials are shaped so that complex thought and feeling might continue to occur.

---

[45] J. H. Prynne, "Poetic Thought," *Textual Practice*, 24.4 (2010), 595–606, at 596.
[46] Prynne, "Poetic Thought," 597.

4 Recollection

Perhaps one of contemporary poetry's signal strengths is its lack of fixed discursive commitments beyond those galvanized by the shaping forces of the poem at hand. This isn't to say that it is constitutively wayward, ceaselessly navel-gazing, or unmotivated by method or intellectual rigor. Nor is it to say that the multifarious courses of movement that a poem might take are themselves ungoverned by deeper patterns of logic, implication, or association. Rather, it is to say that because poetry often eschews as a determining structure a normative mode of discursive progression such as argument, explanation, or narrative by submitting those modes to other formal logics, it might adapt dimensions of each as an element of its texture or composition without committing fully to its teleologies or entailments. Just as poems take on dimensions of prose autobiographical and narrative genres, so can they take up elements of nonfictional writing or entire areas of discourse and knowledge in an adaptive, critical, or experimental fashion. This also means that they are likely to be taken less seriously than the genres they adapt. There are many poems that tackle a problem of history, that embed themselves in the densities of a particular historical moment, that gather the archival traces of the past, but one wouldn't necessarily go to such a poem for a straightforward account. Instead, we tend to understand poetry that thinks historically to operate meta- or para-historiographically. Such texts approach their chosen historical materials by adopting certain features of historical investigation within poetry's quite different discursive, generic, and formal dynamics. Poetry, under these terms, becomes a matter of rummaging, foraging, gathering, and sorting; an act of arrangement and display; and a mode of research and curation that might suggest a different relation to the past.

In this chapter, I redistribute the accrued connotative weight of a pivotal term in Wordsworth's description of poetry as "emotion recollected in tranquillity" so as to consider a poem's recollective potential from another angle. In certain ways, this chapter's energy reverses or at least redirects that of the previous two: rather than consider poetry's value as linked to its emergence from the space of the subject or its negotiation of the zone between individual and social life, this chapter argues for poetry's ability to recover and reprocess the past as well as the conditions of our present world. Recollection, in this sense, is a practice concerned with approaching external, objective conditions and materials rather than one linked to the representation of introspection and the rendering of subjective states. Recollection becomes something nearer to re-collection, to collecting again: poems can model alternate ways of sifting, constellating, and presenting the stuff of the past. This, in the best instances, does not result in a stylized or pseudo-historiography, but in a mode of counter-historical writing that leverages the affordances of lyric in order to account differently for both past and present by assembling materials according to logics beyond or other than those of nonfiction prose genres – historiography, narrative history, biography, and so on. Such texts often proceed by intertwining personal memory and public history, documentary practices and reflexive meditations on those practices, and theoretical or philosophical speculations with attention to the granular stuff of the textual record.

Throughout much of the twentieth and twenty-first centuries, this tendency has taken on an epic impulse, or at least the impulse to construct very long poems, as writers have sought to follow up on the Poundian project to compose "a poem including history."[1] William Carlos Williams' *Paterson* – published in five books between 1946 and 1958 – and Charles Olson's *The Maximus Poems* – which he worked on for the final twenty years of his life and which appeared in its final form after his death in 1970 – were influenced by Pound but each recollects and reimagines the past (and present) of a particular place:

---

[1] Ezra Pound, "Date Line," in *Literary Essays of Ezra Pound*, ed. T. S. Eliot (New York: New Directions, 1968[1935]), 74–87, at 86.

Williams' Paterson, New Jersey and Olson's Gloucester, Massachusetts. As I discuss in Chapter 3, it has been Olson's underlying theories of poetry, more perhaps than the particulars of *The Maximus Poems*, that have had such a decisive impact on later writers, in particular his ideas about "Projective Verse" or what he calls in that essay "composition by field."[2] "Projective verse" was based on Olson's sense of the poem as a field: "the large area of the whole poem ... where all the syllables and all the lines must be managed in their relations to each other."[3] Olson's notion was not entirely new, and, as I have pointed out, modernist poetry more generally has relied on expanding and transforming the visual conventions that had traditionally typified poetic writing. And poetry that stresses its visual construction long predates modernism. Olson added to and redirected this lineage by joining such modernist experiments in visual arrangement with an archaeological method. The unconventional distributions and bricolage of words, phrases, and sentences across the textual surface becomes a way to symbolize the work of writing and to model the excavatory and archival imagination that inheres in such work. This method of poetic fieldwork – metaphorical though the field may be – continues to run strong, and it is linked to analogous strands of twentieth-century documentary and research-based poetry.[4] From Muriel Rukeyser's *The Book of the Dead* (1938), Charles Reznikoff's *Testimony: The United States, 1885–1915* (1978), and John Montague's *The Rough Field* (1972) to Allen Fisher's massive *Place* (a project begun in the early 1970s but only gathered into a single

---

[2] Charles Olson, "Projective Verse" [1950], in *The New American Poetry*, ed. Donald Allen (New York: Grove Press, 1960), 386–397, at 387.

[3] Olson, "Projective Verse," 391.

[4] For a variety of perspectives, see Brian McHale, *The Obligation Toward the Difficult Whole: Postmodernist Long Poems* (Tuscaloosa, AL: University of Alabama Press, 2004); Lytle Shaw, *Fieldworks: From Place to Site in Postwar Poetics* (Tuscaloosa, AL: University of Alabama Press, 2013), and *Narrowcast: Poetry and Audio Research* (Stanford, CA: Stanford University Press, 2018); and Mandy Bloomfield, *Archaeopoetics: Word, Image, History* (Tuscaloosa, AL: University of Alabama Press, 2016). Also see Michael Davidson, *Ghostlier Demarcations: Modern Poetry and the Material Word* (Berkeley, CA: University of California Press, 1997), and *On the Outskirts of Form: Practicing Cultural Poetics* (Middletown, CT: Wesleyan University Press, 2011); and Paul Naylor, *Poetic Investigations: Singing the Holes in History* (Evanston, IL: Northwestern University Press, 1999).

volume in 2005), C. S. Giscombe's *Giscome Road* (1998), and Susan Howe's career-long project of archival investigation, a significant tendency within contemporary writing has been to gather and re-enliven the historical or personal past, often through the incorporation of earlier texts and materials, and usually via an "open field" poetics that both adapts and departs from Olson's model. Over the course of this chapter, I'll examine several recent texts in order to demonstrate the importance of such modes of compositional recollection within contemporary practice.

Before that, however, it is important to elaborate another aspect of poetry's recollective tendency. For as much as it is still common to construe poems as elaborating some "present" – that uncanny amalgam of compositional, diegetic, and receptive moments (each of which is compound rather than simple) – it is also and more importantly the case that the temporality of any poem is staggered and untimely. As discussed in various ways so far, key to poetry's formal dynamics is its tendency to estrange deixis and so scramble language's usual ability to contextualize and position its agents. Just as the "I" of a poem is significantly more fissile than the "I" spoken in a real-world scenario or within a play or movie, so is the "now" of a poem anything but an indication of present-ness. Any *now* in a poem is striated by its other, *then*, as a reader recollects the poem's temporal and spatial matrix from the position of a different one. This is, in part, an impossible attempt to reconstruct the putative "original" conditions that a poem lays out, but, more significantly, such readerly recollection enmeshes temporal frames: the past of writing impinges upon the future of reception, which is the present of reading. A poem condenses these multiple trajectories as a condition of its discursive uncertainty and as an effect of its form. Poems render untimely textures and readers recollect – that is, collect again – the various temporal logics compounded within them.

This kind of temporal and deictic flux is perhaps most singularly apparent within elegies, for which the unbridgeable gap between the past (before the death of the elegized figure) and the present and future, and so the problem of time and of representing temporality, is the genre's structuring feature. For the most part, poetry's value in the contemporary world is unrelated to what we might think of as its public function. But this is not precisely the case with the elegy. Elegies remain central to the canon of contemporary poetry and also to poetry's larger cultural task. Some of the most famous elegies in the English-language canon have been poems written upon the deaths of poets or other public figures, as in Shelley's "Adonais: An Elegy on the Death of John Keats"; Whitman's "When Lilacs Last in the Dooryard Bloom'd," on the death of Abraham Lincoln; or "North Haven," Bishop's poem for Lowell. This mode of elegiac writing still runs strong, as evidenced – for instance – by the outpouring of elegies for Seamus Heaney after his death in 2013. Others have been elegies written upon the deaths of acquaintances, friends, and lovers, such as Milton's "'Lycidas," written on the occasion of the drowning of his Cambridge colleague Edward King; Tennyson's 133-poem sequence for Arthur Henry Hallam, *In Memoriam, A. H. H.* (1850); or Muldoon's "Incantata," written after the death of his lover, the artist Mary Farl Powers. This strand of elegiac writing continues to be a vital mode for contemporary poets. Several of the most well-regarded poems and book-length projects of the past decade or so are what we might call intimate elegies, written upon the death of a loved one: Mary Jo Bang's *Elegy* (2007), written upon the death of her son; Anne Carson's *Nox* (2010), an elegy for her brother; Denise Riley's "A Part Song," written after her son's death; and Forrest Gander's *Be With* (2018), written after the death of his long-time partner, the poet C. D. Wright. And, of course, certain poets have had a proclivity for self-elegy – Dickinson, Yeats, Plath, Berryman – and countless poets have incorporated elegiac textures or motifs within poems that aren't necessarily elegies proper.[5] Thus, it isn't only that poets continue to write elegies, and that elegies continue to comprise one of the central tasks that poets

---

[5] For several cornerstone accounts of English-language elegy, see Peter Sacks, *The English Elegy: Studies in the Genre from Spenser to Yeats* (Baltimore, MD: Johns Hopkins University Press, 1985); Jahan Ramazani, *Poetry of Mourning: The Modern Elegy from Hardy to Heaney* (Chicago and London: University of Chicago Press, 1994); Max Cavitch, *American Elegy: The Poetry of Mourning from the Puritans to Whitman* (Minneapolis, MN: University of Minnesota Press, 2007); Iain Twiddy, *Pastoral Elegy in Contemporary British and Irish Poetry* (New York and London: Continuum, 2012); and Diana Fuss, *Dying Modern: A Meditation on Elegy* (Durham, NC: Duke University Press, 2013).

undertake, but also that the elegy – its generic lineaments, its formal motors, its affective intensities – has become a general undercurrent, at times, it seems, poetry's default setting, a bearing that can be tracked, albeit loosely, back to Thomas Gray's "Elegy Written in a Country Churchyard."

Conventionally, elegies within the modern period – as distinct from the term's original use in ancient Greek poetics to name a particular metrical and stanzaic form and the subsequent adaptation of that form within Roman love poetry and into the early modern period – mourn loss but also conceive from within that mourning some mode of recompense. They memorialize the dead, constituting what Milton in "Lycidas" calls a "destin'd urn," but they also attempt to construe new life out of death.[6] Typically, this occurs by accentuating the afterlife of the dead, whether by way of a theological turn or a nod toward the dead's posthumous fame. Near the end of Milton's elegy, for example, Lycidas is said to be "not dead" because though he is sunk low "beneath the wat'ry floor" (King drowned in the Irish Sea) he is actually "mounted high/Through the dear might of him that walkt the waves"; that is, Christ's sacrifice has ensured Edward King's eternal life.[7] Analogously, in "In Memory of W. B. Yeats," W. H. Auden projects Yeats' life-after-death by lodging his literary remains into present and future bodies: "The words of a dead man/Are modified in the guts of the living."[8] In both cases, two incompatible temporal logics are pitched against one another, and elegy more generally is governed by two conflicting demands: to enact the process of mourning that ultimately lets the dead be dead, and to harness the power of art to circumvent that process so that the dead are, somehow, still living. Within the poetic tradition these two logics have typically been mediated by nature and grounded in classical forms of pastoral and eclogue: a pastoral elegy spurs its own move toward consolation by placing the seasonal cycle with its promise of spring against the

---

[6] John T. Shawcross, ed., *The Complete Poetry of John Milton* (New York: Anchor Books, 1971), 159.
[7] Shawcross, ed., *The Complete Poetry of John Milton*, 163.
[8] W. H. Auden, *Collected Poems*, ed. Edward Mendelson (New York: The Modern Library, 2007[1976]), 245.

unidirectional arc of an individual life. Interwoven within the poem's form and rhetoric, the cyclicity of one – nature – compensates for the noncyclicity of the other – human mortality. This movement has often been conceived within a Freudian ratio of mourning and melancholia in which melancholia names a failed or refused process of mourning in which the fact of the loved one's death is not accepted but rather introjected pathologically back into the self where it sits like an empty stone. "Lycidas" stages a process of mourning in which, in the end, some kind of consolation is produced such that the poem can conclude by turning contentedly away from the dead and toward tomorrow with its "fresh woods, and pastures new," but such an unvexed maneuver seems less likely now.[9] "The modern elegy," as Jahan Ramazani suggests, "continues the ancient interplay between melancholic and consolatory mourning," even though, overall, it has a "melancholic proclivity."[10]

It isn't simply that modern elegists refuse to mourn properly and instead remain within the ambivalent torsions of melancholia, or that twentieth- and twenty-first-century writers are less likely to have the inbuilt consolations of religious faith to bolster their elegiac maneuvers. Rather, it is more important to notice that, for many poets, elegy is something closer to a structural condition than an occasion for a discrete psychic and aesthetic process. On the one hand, the possibility of staging elegiac recollection via nature is no longer viable because the ideology of pastoral elegy requires a notion of an unadulterated nature that is separate from civilization and so available to serve as the grounds of symbolic recompense. As I will consider in more detail in the conclusion, such an understanding of nature does not suffice, and so one tendency among poets is to elegize the possibility of elegy. On the other hand, many poets are skeptical of art's ability to console unproblematically, and so many contemporary elegies spend a good deal of time undermining the very project that they undertake. If, as I've suggested at various points, the value of poetry in contemporary culture must be premised upon decoupling that value

---

[9] Shawcross, ed., *The Complete Poetry of John Milton*, 164.
[10] Ramazani, *Poetry of Mourning*, 31.

from the presumed power or importance of poets, then this diremption appears with particular sharpness in contemporary elegies. Elegizing the dead is a function that contemporary poets still feel compelled or called upon – or merely licensed – to perform, but also one in which the impossibility of task is constantly on display. Contemporary elegies have been keen to elaborate the contradiction that sits at the heart of the form.

Denise Riley's "A Part Song" is both a stunning instance of the impossible necessity of elegy and an investigation into the ramifications of both elegy's impossibility and its necessity. Comprising twenty short lyrics, "A Part Song" was written in the wake of the unexpected death of Riley's adult son. Rather than accumulate a sequential or cumulative effect, the distribution of the poem into twenty short parts seems designed to forestall or even refute the conventional elegiac progression. It is as though the process of mourning has to begin anew each time. In a number of ways, then, the poem instantiates its title: it is "a part song" in that it is made of short parts that do not necessarily accumulate into larger structures; it is "a part song" because it remains bound to the fact of "apartness" that underlies its occasion; and it is "a part song" because it can only partially and with deep skepticism take up the lyric conventions that are folded into its generic model. The poem begins by placing its own status into question:

> You principle of song, what are you *for* now
> Perking up under any spasmodic light
> To trot out your shadowed warblings?[11]

The underlying logic of elegy is both awkwardly activated and placed under suspicion – a few lyric props are rolled out but made cartoonish as the "principle of song" is anthropomorphized into an unwieldy figure in weird light trotting out once again its dark tune. This kind of sardonic tone is rife within the poem and most often appears in moments of accusatory or grimly parodic self-portraiture: "*What is the first duty of a mother to a child?/At least to keep the wretched thing alive*": "Here's

---

[11] Denise Riley, *Say Something Back* (London: Picador, 2016), 2 (emphasis original).

a denatured thing, whose one eye rummages/Into the mound, her other eye swivelled straight up"; "Oh my dead son you daft bugger/This is one glum mum."[12] As it does in the last of these passages, "A Part Song" occasionally lurches into doggerel, seemingly forcing itself into outmoded metrical and rhetorical patterns as a kind of formal penance, as in the opening lines of a poem set at the son's funeral, the first of five bluntly rhymed, mechanically metered couplets:

> A wardrobe gapes, a mourner tries
> Her several styles of howling-guise[.][13]

Instead of providing an aesthetic means to contend with and so mediate and compensate for the death of the loved one – a turn at the heart of elegy – form here becomes a scourge, its too-neat finish laid bare as a kind of self-reflexive castigation. Across twenty brief episodes, such hyper-stylized moments are, of course, ironically instructive: they remind us again and again that elegy necessarily simplifies or falsifies by gilding the dense contradictions of grief. But they also seek to show that despite a poem's ability to do nothing but provide a scrim atop a vacancy, it must nonetheless perform its inadequate maneuvers for the sake of those who remain after a death, those left, as Riley writes, "in the pale/Blaze of living on alone."[14] Elegy becomes an unfinished wrangling rather than a compensatory motion, a zone in which grief and mourning churn alongside moments of lightness or reprieve that do not necessarily accrue sequential force.

"A Part Song" gives us something like the lived conditions of mourning rather than a smooth process through it. As Riley tells us in the penultimate part, "she do the bereaved in different voices" (tweaking Eliot's initial title for what would become *The Waste Land*, which Eliot took from Dickens' *Our Mutual Friend*), pulling together an array of tones and inflections that nonetheless remain within the ambit of the authorial subject, at least until the poem's final part. At the end of the penultimate poem, Riley – who has once again asked for what can't occur, the return of her dead son – answers her own unanswered

---

[12] Riley, *Say Something Back*, 3, 4, and 6 (emphases original). [13] Ibid., 5.
[14] Ibid., 12.

question by asking for rest: "– Still no? Then let me rest, my dear."[15] The "rest" that is requested here seems to indicate a measure of acceptance: not a wish to die (as in earlier sections of the poem), but a final marking of the elegy's inevitable motion toward unfulfillment. This, however, is forcefully overturned by the final section, a pair of trimeter quatrains in the voice of the dead son who asks first that his sisters and mother *"weep dark tears for me"* and then, in the second stanza, addresses his mother alone:

> *O let me be, my mother*
> *In no unquiet grave*
> *My bone-dust is faint coral*
> *Under the fretful wave*[16]

The poem's previously rigorous immanent critique of its own aesthetic and rhetorical powers gives way to a startling embrace of those powers: the dead figure assumes a speaking role, an instance of what Diana Fuss has described as a "corpse poem."[17] A transformed version of the young man who mourns his lover in "The Unquiet Grave," the English folksong that Riley reworks here, the speaker now takes on the full freight of the elegiac tradition, aligning himself with the drowned figure in Ariel's song in *The Tempest* and later reflexes of that figure in "Lycidas," "The Love Song of J. Alfred Prufrock," and *The Waste Land*, among other texts. Earlier, Riley had referred somewhat mockingly to Mary Elizabeth Frye's popular elegy, "Grieve Not," which is also known by its first line, "do not stand at my grave and weep," and which remains a favorite reading at funerals. Frye's deeply sentimental poem erases the actuality of death by revivifying the dead so as to make the mourners feel better. Quite unexpectedly, Riley adapts Frye's rhetorical strategy whole cloth. This must be, we think, a moment of deep structural irony: Riley ends the poem impossibly, by providing just the kind of aesthetic comfort that she has thus far strenuously resisted. And it is that: in certain ways, the introduction of the revenant can't but scuttle the poem. But it is not only that. Considering what has come before, it is nearly impossible to read this final section as offering anything but the precise opposite of

[15] Ibid., 14. [16] Ibid. (emphasis original). [17] See Fuss, *Dying Modern*, 44–77.

Frye's poem: consolation's negative. This isn't simply a deconstruction of the elegy. Nor is it mere parody, the final instance in the poem's gallery of "different voices," each of whose "shadowed warblings" constitutes a rearguard action to try and justify the poem's progress ("you principle of song, what are you *for* now"), although we certainly are meant to understand the revenant as providing the poem's final and most difficult-to-take "warbling." But, more importantly, Riley's remaking of elegy allows it to hold two incompatible thoughts at once: that the dead necessarily remain so, and that the living – obliged to remember – must continually act as though the first thought doesn't quite hold. The speaker first asks his family to actively mourn him and then asks his mother both to cease her grieving – "*O let me be*" – and to resurrect him: "*O let me be ... In no unquiet grave.*" The imperative here splits along elegy's double, conflictual logic. This isn't evasion or willful blindness, nor is it only an act of ironic displacement in which the final section's speakerly substitution knowingly evacuates the poem's import, such that readers can settle contentedly in that knowingness. Instead, we are called to reckon with the paradoxical demand at the heart of the poem.

In Riley's "A Part Song," elegiac recollection – bringing the dead back to mind – can't but place into relief the impossibility of that task. Mary Jo Bang catches this double motion of intimacy and estrangement in the first poem of *Elegy*:

> I say Come Back and you do
> Not do what I want.
> The train unrolls its track and sends its sound forward.[18]

The entire and unfinished project of elegy sits in miniature within the enjambment's hinge: what at first seems like a successful speech act that retrieves the dead is negated simultaneously. The poem's "you" – which, as for the great majority of Bang's volume, references her dead son – not only does not do what is asked, but also is not even participating in the dialogue into which he is called. To perhaps belabor the obvious: he does not "not do" what she asks him to do not because he chooses not to, but

---

[18] Mary Jo Bang, *Elegy* (Saint Paul, MN: Graywolf Press, 2007), 3.

because he is no longer addressable. This dilemma is, more generally, one faced by any poem that attempts to recollect the past – whether ardently memorializing it, actively reconstruing it, or ambiently instancing it. Implicit in every attempt is the knowledge that what is sought cannot be recovered or considered from a position of epistemological or philosophical certainty, but rather one of partial, biased, and immanent engagement. This troubles poetry's basis in and bid for imaginative autonomy, as well as the idea of a poet as a creative force in the Romantic sense, as in Stevens' great poem, "The Idea of Order at Key West":

> She was the single artificer of the world
> In which she sang. And when she sang, the sea,
> Whatever self it had, became the self
> That was her song, for she was the maker.[19]

The underside of such imaginative freedom is the ceaseless need to co-opt the world beyond in order to aggregate lyric power. Stevens' poem itself is premised upon an endeavor to create the world in words – "She sang beyond the genius of the sea" – but also upon an appropriation and a displacement.[20] The poem's protagonist and diegetic maker – "For she was the maker of the song she sang" – is also the poem's object.[21] The song she sings within the poem is witnessed by the poem's "I," who watches her sing along with his companion Ramon Fernandez, who, as we only realize toward the end of the poem, has been present all along. And the poem's "I" appropriates her song in order to make his own, overwriting it in the process: she is always a third person whose speech and singing are described but not represented. This appropriative mechanism underwrites lyric, and its particular ethical consequences become most pronounced in scenarios in which a poem draws from actual life and the historical record. Geoffrey Hill's early poem, "September Song," elegizes a child who, as a note between the title and the poem tells us, was born on June 19, 1932 – a day after Hill's own birth – and "deported," a euphemism for her placement in a concentration camp by the Nazis, on September 24,

---

[19] Wallace Stevens, *The Collected Poems* (New York: Vintage Books, 1990 [1954]), 129.
[20] Stevens, *The Collected Poems*, 128.   [21] Ibid., 129.

1942. A jagged three-line stanza in parenthesis that appears after the first two stanzas, shearing the poem in two, gets at the core of the problem:

> (I have made
> an elegy for myself it
> is true)[22]

In the midst of trying to reckon with the horrors of that child's life and the historical implications of her death, Hill turns back upon himself and understands that even this attempt to account for a life considerably other to his own (a point that is underlined by the superficial near-coincidence of their birth dates) is fundamentally self-involved. The elegy, he realizes, is "for myself it/is true." It is a text that can't escape the orbit of the authorial subject – it is a self-elegy of a sort – and whose consolatory motions are self-serving. It remains, nonetheless, "true." Beneath the idiomatic, confessional bent of the phrase that is activated initially lies a more straightforward propositional statement. And it is the difficulty of this doubled sense of what is true that both shapes and haunts poetry.

Poetry sits strangely athwart fiction and nonfiction. In a view that goes back to Aristotle and has had many adherents, from Sidney's "The Defence of Poesy" on, the kinds of truth that "poetry" has been said to offer occurs in relation to the ideal and the universal – what might or could or even should be the case – rather than the particular – what was or is the case, which is the realm of the historian. "Poetry," in this sense, implies fictionality of a sort, even though its subjects might be drawn from historical topics. As poetry has reconceived itself over several centuries in relation to the massive expansion of prose fiction, one of the cruces has been its own relation to concepts like "truth" and "fiction." Just as we don't necessarily expect propositional truths from poems, so don't we anticipate poems to deliver biographical truth or historical fact. If we were to learn, say, that Wallace Stevens had never been to Key West, didn't know anyone

---

[22] Geoffrey Hill, *Broken Hierarchies: Poems, 1952–2012*, ed. Kenneth Haynes (Oxford: Oxford University Press, 2013), 44.

named Ramon Fernandez, and never experienced an encounter like the one represented in "The Idea of Order at Key West," we wouldn't care, or at least wouldn't care all that much. We don't demand that the speaker of the poem fully and exclusively align with the biographical truth of Stevens' life, in part because there is no reality of this event outside of the poem itself: even if it had its basis in Steven's own experience, the poem makes no claim to documentary accuracy.

However, when poetry does make a claim on the real, then its own liminal status between fiction and nonfiction comes haltingly to the surface. We've seen one example of this in the case of the elegy: the genre's imaginative endeavors are constantly thwarted or undercut by the facts with which it reckons. As we've seen and as we'll continue to see, this larger conundrum isn't disabling. The impossibility of accessing the past becomes one of the many types of not-knowing upon which poetry and literature are premised. The unspoken "as if" that prefaces a reader's engagement with any fictional or imaginative text – what Coleridge called "that willing suspension of disbelief" – takes on an especially complex dimension in texts that also include historical materials.[23] The notion of compositional and readerly recollection that drives this chapter requires a quite specific calibration of imaginative license and ethical consideration. One of the systemic problems of the lyric "I" – its propensity to appropriate what lies outside of it within its monologic, self-centered drive – is especially pronounced when poets incorporate material of whatever sort that is part of the larger historical record, whether that history exists at the level of the personal, the familial, the local, or the world-historical. Just as the elegist reckons with an impossible desire to both retrieve the dead and to let the dead remain so, so does the poet who approaches the past face a difficult double charge: to find a relation to otherness – whether that of the past or that of some aspect of the poet's present world – and to let that which is exterior to the self remain so. Recollection, as I've been construing the term in this chapter, becomes a way to describe the ways that poetry can

---

[23] Samuel Taylor Coleridge, *Biographia Literaria; or Biographical Sketches of My Literary Life and Opinions* [1817], in H. J. Jackson, ed., *Samuel Taylor Coleridge: The Major Works* (Oxford: Oxford University Press, 2000 [1985]), 155–482, at 314.

provide distinctive perspectives on the past and on the processes by which the past can come back to mind – whether via memory or an archive – while simultaneously providing modes of approaching and relating to that which cannot be fully, or even mostly, known.

Rita Dove's *Thomas and Beulah* (1986), a book-length double sequence based on the lives of Dove's maternal grandparents, is a signal example of one kind of poetic recollection. The note that prefaces the volume provides instructions: "These poems tell two sides of a story and are meant to be read in sequence."[24] After the note, there are two sections of twenty-four and then twenty-one poems, the first from Thomas' perspective and the second from Beulah's. After the two sections, an appendix implicitly provides another set of instructions to readers: a chronology that gives important dates from Thomas' birth in 1900 to Beulah's death in 1969.[25] The chronology includes the major events of each of their lives – their births, their marriage, the births of their children and some of their grandchildren, several key moments that appear in the poems, particular jobs they have, their deaths – which are interspersed with important events that occur in the town of Akron, Ohio, where the poems take place, and several key events in American history. Some of the entries provide sociological detail – "1940: 11,000 Negroes living in Akron (total population: 243,000)" – while others name specific events: "1963: August: The March on Washington."[26] The chronology doesn't aim to be comprehensive – there are only thirty-three entries in total, covering seventy years – and its primary goal, in addition to annotating certain passages in the poems that precede it, is to nudge the reader to extrapolate from the lives of Thomas and Beulah to a broader view of African-American history and culture from the Great Migration to the Civil Rights Movement. Most of the individual poems remain within the realm of personal and domestic life, with larger social and political matters presented implicitly; even the moments in which major historical

---

[24] Rita Dove, *Selected Poems* (New York: Vintage Books, 1993), 137.
[25] As Therese Steffen notes in *Crossing Color: Transcultural Space and Place in Rita Dove's Poetry, Fiction, and Drama*, Dove's maternal grandparents were named Thomas and Georgianna Hurd (Oxford: Oxford University Press, 2001, 96).
[26] Dove, *Selected Poems*, 203, 204.

events are referenced tend to be glancing or sidewise, as in this moment from "Wingfoot Lake (Independence Day, 1964)," which describes a company picnic to which Beulah's daughters have taken her after the death of her husband, during which Beulah remembers watching television the previous summer:

> Last August she stood alone for hours
> in front of the T.V. set
> as a crow's wing moved slowly through
> the white streets of governments.[27]

It is perhaps likely that a reader becomes fully aware that this passage refers to the March on Washington and Martin Luther King's speech only upon glancing at the chronology, which provides a historical scaffolding for the sequence as a whole. Individual poems tend not to provide concrete evidence of their historical setting apart from a few orienting details here and there, which are then confirmed and elaborated in the appended chronology.

Within the macro-history of and surrounding Thomas' and Beulah's lives, to whose central facts Dove adheres, *Thomas and Beulah*'s individual poems move in a loose chronological sequence and present imagined micro-histories: particular instances from their everyday lives that have escaped the historical record, feelings or thoughts that they have at important moments, and confabulated reveries and meditations. In this way, *Thomas and Beulah* takes shape not as a lyric sequence based on the bedrock of chronology, but as a series of short fictions in – for the most part – free verse forms that elaborate precisely that which the chronology can't reveal. Every poem features a third-person narrator focalized through one of the two titular figures, who have become – essentially – novelistic characters. In *Thomas and Beulah*, Dove aspires to construct something like a lineated, episodic historical novella, and she intertwines certain lyric conventions – although not the prominence of a lyric "I" – with a penchant for novelistic detail. For each of her protagonists, she imagines a central conflict that shapes their internal lives and that provides an alternate

[27] Ibid., 198.

frame for the duties, pleasures, and difficulties of their life together. Throughout the rest of his life, Thomas is haunted by the accidental drowning of his friend Lem as they travel the rivers north from Tennessee in their late teenage years. Lem becomes both an elegiac figure and an object of desire through whom Thomas mediates the disappointments of his life, appearing at key moments to help explain Thomas' circumstances, as in "The Stroke," in which Thomas' stroke (or, if we go by the chronology, his heart attack) in 1960 is attributed to Lem, who becomes both cause and cure:

> he knows it was Lem all along:
> Lem's knuckles tapping his chest in passing,
> Lem's heart, for safekeeping,
> he shores up in his arms.[28]

While Thomas' internal conflict is focused on Lem as the lost object, Beulah repeatedly imagines not another person but an alternate version of herself in which she leads a life filled with art, travel, and intellectual engagement, one that has its basis in a moment recounted in a poem entitled "Magic," which depicts Beulah's childhood as an aesthetic, magical space – "Like all art/useless and beautiful, like/sailing in air,//things happened/*to* her" – and ends in a moment when she notices a picture of the Eiffel Tower in the newspaper: "It was a sign//she would make it to Paris one day."[29] This premonition does not, we are led to believe, come true, and Beulah's alternate imagined life – one that resembles, or at least gestures toward, Dove's own life as an artist and writer – remains unrealized outside of the scattered moments of reverie that Beulah finds amidst domestic duties. In both cases, Dove uses the central facts of her grandparents' lives and those of their families, as well as the historical conditions that shape them locally and nationally, to fashion the dialectical inverse of each: a novelistic account of their inner lives that is premised upon – but, crucially, floats free from – an objective, chronological account of their "outer" lives.

A final intriguing detail to mention about *Thomas and Beulah* is Dove's own complex status in relation to the poem. She is, of course, its

[28] Ibid., 169. [29] Ibid., 176 (emphasis original).

author, and because the sequence is based on her own family, we are likely as readers to elide the third-person narrator of the poems with the author. However, she is also a part of the volume's world. As mentioned, the chronology covers the period from 1900 to 1969, while the sequence's diegesis covers the period from 1919 – when Thomas starts his journey from Tennessee to Ohio – to 1969, with the final poem of the volume offering an oblique account of Beulah's death. Dove was born in 1952, and while it may be that she includes a version of her childhood self in a poem called "Roast Possum" that depicts Thomas telling stories with "a granddaughter/propped on each knee," it isn't necessarily the case that Rita Dove herself is one of those two granddaughters, since the chronology gives the birthdates of two other granddaughters – Pauline and Jacqueline, born in 1947 and 1949 – along with a grandson named Malcolm, who was born in 1951.[30] There is no entry for 1952, Dove's year of birth. She has excluded herself from the family story that she tells. It isn't clear how a reader is meant to understand this; surely Dove, who was around ten years old when her grandfather died and around seventeen years old when her grandmother died, was an important part of this story, and it is likely that her grandparents were significant figures in her life, and she in theirs. During her childhood and teenage years, she might not have had a sense of the broader history and chronology upon which *Thomas and Beulah* is built, but she was certainly part of her grandparents' world and would have heard stories about their pasts, and so making no mention of her own birth when she mentions the births of the other grandchildren is curious. One way to understand this elision is to suggest that since the sequence as a whole relies on a third-person omniscient narrator who claims novelistic access to corners of Thomas' and Beulah's lives – their thoughts, unspoken desires and disappointments, stretches of their lifelong internal monologues – it is only Dove the poet rather than Dove the granddaughter who can be incorporated into the world of the text (rather, of course, than the world of the lives from which the text is made, of which Dove was clearly part). That is, the act of recollection that Dove undertakes – which relies on biographical

[30] Ibid., 167.

scaffolding at the global level but novelistic invention at the local level – requires a "suspension of disbelief" that can only be maintained if we understand Dove as the volume's author and narrator but not as a potential character in the text's story world. Considering this, the volume's opening poem, "The Event," which tells of Thomas and Lem traveling north on a riverboat and Lem's drowning, includes an intriguing authorial signature:

> Lem stripped, spoke easy: *Them's chestnuts,*
> *I believe.* Dove
>
> quick as a gasp. Thomas, dry
> on deck, saw the green crown shake
> as the island slipped[.][31]

This is the moment of Lem's presumably accidental drowning as he goes after chestnuts while Thomas watches from the riverboat. "Dove" is a homograph, both a past tense verb and the author's name, and the line shorn of context comprises a sidewise inscription. Reading wrongly, we could say that the first-person statement of belief – which properly attaches to Lem and exists as reported speech – is in fact Rita Dove's, and that it expresses something like an authorial credo, or concession. "*I believe,*" signed "Dove." This indicates a relation to the material to come: what follows is a series of impressions of each of her grandparents that, while not actually true since no one has access to the interior states that the subsequent poems provide, has the feel of what might be true, the touch of the real. Dove signs the poem from the space of fictional belief, from the space of "as is" that allows for disbelief's deferral. She constructs an account of her grandparents' lives by extracting herself as a biographical actor and positioning herself as the medium of fictive recollection. The anecdotal and meditative propensities of poetry, disjointed from lyric's gravitational center in first-person thought and speech, are re-geared so as to take the weight of chronological accuracy and novelistic verisimilitude.

---

[31] Ibid., 141 (emphasis original).

Dove's poetic recollection occurs as a function of the text's multiple generic commitments: *Thomas and Beulah* appears as a sequence of lyric poems, is premised upon a root form of historiography (the chronology), and acts like a novel. In other cases, recollection takes on a more literal weight, as poets set their poems to operate like catalogues or collages. For such poets, the text itself – its visual dimensions, its formal shapes – becomes a space for gathering and scattering. As I've discussed in previous chapters, such practices have been central to modernist and avant-garde writing, whether in the form of Pound's juxtaposition of luminous shards within the *Cantos*, Marianne Moore's layering of disparate found materials within her poems, Walter Benjamin's constellative historiography in *The Arcades Project* (1927–1940, 1982), the chance-based texts of John Cage and Jackson MacLow, or the simple repottings that characterize some varieties of contemporary conceptual poetry. A poem, under these terms, becomes the record of research and often the outcome of a procedure, and in the best cases a reader finds interest both in the process that yielded the poem and the poem itself. (In lesser cases, the interest in the poem is entirely exhausted in the recognition of its concept – one doesn't read such a poem, one "gets" it.)

Caroline Bergvall's "Via" (2005) started, as she writes in a headnote to the text, "by accident," leading to a decision to "collate the opening lines of the *Inferno* translations ['into English'] as archived by the British Library up until May 2000."[32] Ultimately, the project yielded a sound performance and the written text "Via," subtitled "48 Dante Variations," which consists of the original opening tercet of Dante's *Inferno* followed by forty-seven English-language translations arranged in alphabetical order, each tagged with the translator's last name and the date of publication.[33] Here are the first two variations:

[32] Caroline Bergvall, *Fig* (Cambridge: Salt Publishing, 2005), 64.
[33] The implications of the slight discrepancy in the numbering – between the promised "48 Dante Variations" and the forty-seven variations that are actually presented – are important. In her preface, Bergvall notes that, like a good deal of her poetry, "Via" was designed as a performance piece and that Bergvall's own computer-modulated performance of the poem constitutes "the 48th variation" (*Fig*, 64). The published version of the poem in *Fig* does not feature the vocal performance, and so one is left to conclude that the "48th variation" on Dante, in addition to the forty-seven English-language versions, is in fact Dante's original

> 1. Along the journey of our life half way
>   I found myself again in a dark wood
>   wherein the straight road no longer lay
>   (Dale, 1996)
>
> 2. At the midpoint in the journey of our life
>   I found myself astray in a dark wood
>   For the straight path had vanished.
>   (Creagh and Hollander, 1989) [34]

Bergvall describes the two-year process of composing the project as both one of "eery intimacy" and "welcome distance."[35] The mechanical acts of "copying out" the various translations become more arduous than imagined, requiring multiple returns to the library texts in order to check for accuracy. What was conceived of as a procedure – to copy out every English-language version of the opening tercet that exists in the English-language tradition's central library – takes on significantly more weight, although one that only appears as an absence, as the explicit lack of Bergvall's own intervention: "Not to inadvertently change what had been printed. To reproduce each translative gesture. To add my voice to this chorus, to this recitation, only by way of this task."[36] The compositional procedure becomes something closer to a phenomenology: "To come to an understanding of it by standing in it, by becoming it. Very gradually, this transforms a shoe into a foot, extends copyism into writing, and perhaps writing into being ... this was an illuminating, if disturbing, development."[37]

A similar transformation is afforded the reader of the poem, for one of the most unexpected aspects of Bergvall's "Via" is that it is deeply engrossing. Being presented with an alphabetized and numbered catalogue of the same three lines of Dante translated into English forty-

---

Italian tercet, such that the relationship between original and translation undergoes a Derridean deconstruction. As she notes in the headnote to the poem, she did originally copy out a 48th variation of the tercet, but because that variation was copied out in 2003 it "broke the rule of the task, its chronological cut-off point" – the year 2000 is, as she writes, "exactly 700 years after the date fixed by Dante for the start of the Comedy's journey" – and so was removed from the final version (*Fig*, 65, 64).

[34] Bergvall, *Fig*, 67.   [35] Ibid., 65.   [36] Ibid.   [37] Ibid.

seven times doesn't exactly promise readerly adventure, but one finds oneself absorbed in the implications and reverberations of the various choices in phrasing and word order that each translator makes. Bergvall's presentation of the Italian text at the start allows for a recursive reception (one constantly checks back in with the Italian text while reading the English versions), and ordering the translations via the alphabet – from "Along the journey of our life half way" to "When I had journeyed half our life's way" – allows one to see larger-scale patterns develop, such as the fact that "midway" is the most likely word with which English-language translations begin. (Nineteen of the forty-seven variations begin with "midway.")[38] Not only does the text provide a concise compendium in which to study translation practice, it is also able to offer to a reader a version of what the compositional process offered to Bergvall: "To come to an understanding of it by standing in it, by becoming it." The opening tercet of the *Inferno* is a first-person statement of confusion and doubt, and the task of the *Commedia* is to trace the path out of it, from hell to paradise. Bergvall's presentation of that opening tercet performs and then ramifies its consequences. While we understand that "Via" is a textual catalogue of forty-seven different versions of Dante's text rather than a single poetic monologue as is the case in the *Commedia* in which the "I" of the poem is a near-double of the author, we can also take a stranger path and read "Via" as though the "I" approximated a single lyric voice repeating and repeating his predicament.

This, of course, would be seen by many as a form of bad lyric reading – of assuming a monologic speaker whenever we get the chance – and perhaps it is that. But it also honors, from the side of reception, just that task that Bergvall set herself. If we mis-read "Via" as a lyric poem, rather than the outcome of a procedure and conception, then we are left with a pathological form of lyric speaking in which the speaker repeats his stance. But this is precisely the dilemma faced at the start of the *Inferno* and it is precisely – though not pathologically – the task faced by Bergvall in making the poem. Collecting the various translations and copying them out as faithfully as possible is not only an act of "understanding," but also a way to

[38] Ibid., 67, 71.

represent – for both writer and reader – something like the phenomenological or even spiritual conditions of the original poem. I am not saying that Bergvall or a reader "identifies with" or even "relates to" Dante, only that Bergvall's constructive procedures and the readerly effects of those procedural choices end up producing a remarkable structural homology. As we, if we, make a turn from understanding the poem as the result of its procedure to actually moving through the poem line by line, and even though we know we're not reading lyric, the deep-seated conventions surrounding first-person imaginative texts – that is, texts like Dante's *Commedia* – reemerge. Although one knows it isn't the case, one almost can't help but to confect a deictic bridge from one translation's "I" to the next's. Just as one begins to fashion that relation in the course of reading it is thwarted again when the parenthetical interruptions – "(Rossetti, 1865)," "(Heaney, 1993)" – puncture the fantasy of diegetic continuity that had begun to accrue.[39] What remains vital about Bergvall's poem is that it outdistances its procedure: the interest of the text continues well beyond the moment when its procedure is grasped conceptually. Its project of textual collection and arrangement produces a mode of stark and weird readerly attention. We are left, again and again, at the hinge of "midway."

Bergvall's "Via" intertwines two compositional motions: the first a gathering of materials and the second a grouping of those materials according to the convention of the alphabet. There is a very long history of alphabet poetry, from Hebrew Biblical verse, varieties of rune poetry, and the extensive tradition of children's poems to contemporary experiments such as Harryette Mullen's *Sleeping with the Dictionary* (2002), Ron Silliman's massive *The Alphabet* (2008), and, in a different vein, Edward Gorey's *The Gashlycrumb Tinies* (1963). Natalie Harkin's *Dirty Words* (2015), for instance, is a book-length polemical abecedary, providing an A to Z critique – from "Apology" to "Zero Tolerance," complete with cross-references – of the legacies of the history of colonialism and violence against indigenous peoples in Australia. Harkin, a member of the

[39] Ibid., 68.

Narungga people, skewers the racism and doublespeak of contemporary Australian politics, excoriates the government's disastrous environmental policies, and claims both textual and ideological space to celebrate indigenous practices and memorialize those who she refers to as her "elders-ancestors-guides."[40] The alphabet structure provides Harkin a powerful means of mobility: organizing what she calls her "sing-chant-rage" around a thematic index allows her the latitude to move between the past and present and to construct an ongoing and synthetic argument.[41] Harkin stitches in as epigraphs and intertexts historical documents and quotations by present-day politicians and powerbrokers that demonstrate the longstanding and ongoing racism of Australian settler culture, as well as responses from Aboriginal individuals and groups protesting that treatment. Harkin's poetry tends toward direct response, with poems of praise to particular Aboriginal figures and ancestors alternating with addresses to specific politicians that critique their statements and policies and lament more broadly the iniquities of past and present. The alphabet structure allows the totality of Harkin's critique to ramify beyond its individual parts and the quite specific contexts of many of her poems, and to aggregate into something like a specimen index of Australian anti-Aboriginal, colonialist discourse combined with a competing index of anti-colonial response.

In Harkin's *Dirty Words*, as in Bergvall's "Via," the alphabetic scaffolding provides a new frame in which to make sense of the materials that are gathered – in Bergvall's case the forty-seven found texts, and in Harkin's the combination of discrete poetic texts of her own design and the many intertexts that ground her critique. The alphabet provides centripetal force. Other poetic projects undertake a mode of centripetal recollection – bringing disparate materials together, whether composed passages or found text – but do not submit them to a structural logic. In this kind of work, phrases, words, and stanzas may sit adjacent to one another on the page, but they do not necessarily cohere or even articulate with one another. Of course,

---

[40] Natalie Harkin, *Dirty Words* (Melbourne: Cordite Books, 2015), 45.
[41] Harkin, *Dirty Words*, 28.

parataxis and juxtaposition have been central poetic tactics for a long while and have been nearly default features of much poetry from the past century. And we've seen numerous examples of juxtapositional poetry in previous chapters. Within the recollective mode that is the focus of this chapter, however, parataxis takes on a much more ardent spatial dimension. If such a poem takes on the metaphorical dimensions of a "field," in Olson's sense, then the page is construed as a textual surface with an imagined depth. Words and phrases exist in a set of relations governed not by grammar or stanza, but by placement and proximity. And these arrangements – these practices of gathering and scattering – can take on broader conceptual force as the page is asked to function like a textual canvas with its visual and material aspects brought into the domain of meaning. Describing her 2002 volume *Commons*, Myung Mi Kim gives a sense of these complex textures of the page:

> *COMMONS* elides multiple sites: reading and text making, discourses and disciplines, documents and documenting. Fluctuating. Proceeding by fragment, by increment. Through proposition, parataxis, contingency – appropriating nerve, line, song[42]

This passage occurs in "Pollen Fossil Record," the last of the volume's four named sections, which is both a series of notes on the texts that come before it and a continuation of the collaging practices of those texts. Moving between an archival imagination and an Olsonian drive to conceive of the page as a means of catching the specific phenomenological and historical conditions of one's existence, Kim's poetry is based on a practice of constellation and fragmented display. Boundaries between textual units are ambiguous and provisional, and large-scale structuring mechanisms are avoided in favor of a mode of immanent composition in which, as she writes elsewhere in "Pollen Fossil Record," "the book emerges through cycles of erosion and accretion."[43] For Kim, this practice concerns "the meaning of

---

[42] Myung Mi Kim, *Commons* (Berkeley and Los Angeles, CA: University of California Press, 2002), 107.
[43] Kim, *Commons*, 107.

becoming a historical subject" and makes for poetry that resides "in disrupted, dilated, circulatory spaces, and [] is the means by which one notates this provisional location that evokes and demonstrates agency – the ear by which the prosody by which to calibrate the liberative potential of writing, storehouse of the human[.]"[44] The page becomes the lattice within which the "historical subject" comes into being as an accumulation of disjointed fragments and in relation to broader forces that shape and wreck the possibilities of such subjectivity: war, environmental degradation, economic injustice, colonialism and its aftereffects. The techniques of fragmentation and constellation that underlie her work is a means of what she calls in *Penury* (2009) "trolling sense," which we might understand as the description of a poetics keen to search the very ground of language and language-making in order to catch the fluctuational dynamics of subjective agency and critique the ideological and material forces that subtend that agency.[45]

There is perhaps no more powerful contemporary instance of the kind of recollective poetics that I have been considering in this chapter, one that harnesses both gathering and scattering as aesthetic and critical practices, than M. NourbeSe Philip's *Zong!* (2008), a book-length project of historical reckoning. *Zong!* takes as its subject one of the most well-known incidents in the history of the transatlantic slave trade. In the penultimate section of *Zong!*, "Notanda," an extensive essay that both provides the historical context for the volume and recounts the process of its composition, Philip lays out the facts of the matter: "In 1781 a fully provisioned ship, the *Zong*, captained by one Luke Collingwood, leaves the West Coast of Africa with a cargo of 470 slaves and sets sail for Jamaica. As is the custom, the cargo is fully insured."[46] Because of Collingwood's "navigational errors," a journey that should have taken "six to nine weeks" took "four months," during which 60 slaves died from dehydration, another 40 jumped overboard, and 150 were thrown overboard under the orders of

[44] Ibid., 108, 111.
[45] Myung Mi Kim, *Penury* (Richmond, CA: Omnidawn, 2009), 83.
[46] M. NourbeSe Philip, *Zong!* (Middletown, CT: Wesleyan University Press, 2011 [2008]), 189.

Collingwood, who reasoned that, as Philip writes, "the massacre of the African slaves would prove to be more financially advantageous to the owners of the ship," who will receive compensation from their insurers for the loss of "cargo," than if the slaves died of "natural causes."[47] After the ship returned to England and the ship's owners – the Messrs Gregson – submitted a claim for their lost cargo, their insurers – the Messrs Gilbert – refused to pay and the resulting court case found the insurers liable, who then appealed to a higher court, which decided that a new trial should be held, although there is no evidence that another trial ever took place or that an insurance payment was ever made. Philip uses a 1783 report of the court's decision in the appeal, known as Gregson v. Gilbert, the only-known document relating to the mass murder on the Zong, as the base text of her entire volume, as a "word store," in order to, as she writes, "lock myself into this particular and peculiar discursive landscape in the belief that the story of these African men, women, and children thrown overboard in an attempt to collect insurance monies, the story that can only be told by not telling, is locked in this text."[48] *Zong!*, then, aims both to approach this event via the historical record and to register at every moment that the event can't be known via that record: as Philip writes, in what stands as the volume's mantra, "there is no telling this story; it must be told."[49]

The Zong case was crucial for the eventual abolition of slavery in England, and it has been a popular topic for a number of contemporary writers. Philip's *Zong!* is unique for remaining entirely within the bounds of the archival record and relying on cutting up and rearranging it, what she describes as "the fragmentation and mutilation of the text."[50] Philip adamantly refuses to reimagine events such that they might be narrated, as that would do "a second violence, this time to the memory of an already violent experience."[51] The poems that constitute the volume – a "non-telling of the story that must be told" – must remain within the zone of "disorder, illogic, and irrationality," because both the events on which they fasten and the textual record of

---

[47] Philip, *Zong!*, 189. [48] Ibid., 191. [49] Ibid., 189. [50] Ibid., 198.
[51] Ibid., 197.

those events claim "order, logic, and rationality" to explain away their brutality and barbarism.[52] This accords with Philip's broader practice and her sense of the task of postcolonial Anglophone poetry. In her earlier volume, *She Tries Her Tongue, Her Silence Softly Breaks* (1989), she writes that the African Caribbean writer must "use language in such a way that the historical realities are not erased or obliterated, so that English is revealed as the tainted tongue it truly is. Only in so doing will English be redeemed."[53] In the case of *Zong!*, this theoretical commitment yields a book of broken language, a compendium of fragments that derive from and explode the 1783 court transcript, ultimately comprising what Philip calls a "hauntological" text.[54] It faces the dilemma upon which elegy pivots, but ramifies that dilemma by trying to approach a particular instance of historical mass murder in which the victims are not only lost to history, but whose status as property in the eyes of the English legal and economic culture that captured them in Africa and shipped them across the Atlantic denied them the forms of personhood upon which any sort of remembrance or retrieval might be premised.

Zong! is a long, complex volume in ten parts (if one includes the glossary and fictional manifest, Philip's "Notanda," and the text of the Gregson v. Gilbert transcript, which is the very last item in the volume), and I can't hope to provide anything like a full account of the book in this chapter's final turn. But I can at least indicate a few of its central features so as to suggest its scope and import. The first section, "Os," Latin for "bone," consists of twenty-six numbered poems followed by six unnumbered poems, each of which uses the page-space as a lattice upon which to fix and arrange certain words from the trial transcript in order to anatomize the various iniquitous logics that it presumes. "*Zong! #1*" is a concrete poem in which a handful of letters – primarily those in the word *water* – are strewn in varying combinations across and down the page as though mimicking both the motion of waves and the acts of murder around which the historical case and

[52] Ibid.
[53] M. NourbeSe Philip, *She Tries Her Tongue, Her Silence Softly Breaks* (Charlottestown, PEI, Canada: Ragweed Press, 1989), 19.
[54] Philip, *Zong!*, 201.

the poem revolves. The rest of the poems in the first section maintain the integrity of the individual words and phrases that Philip culls from the 1783 trial transcript, and we can read this initial poem as both preparing the volume's mid-ocean space and foreshadowing the more thoroughgoing typographical breakdowns that will feature in subsequent sections. The textual shapes change from page to page, sometimes appearing as a single series of words and short phrases, sometimes toggling between differently justified text columns, sometimes cycling through more elaborate permutations, and sometimes unspooling in more haphazard patterns. Except in very limited instances – combinations of two or three, or very occasionally four, words – grammar and syntax are abandoned, and certain words reappear from poem to poem as Philip returns again and again to the trial text. At times, one can glimpse discursive cohesion, as in this passage from "*Zong! #8*":

> the good of overboard
> justified a throwing
>
>   of property
>   fellow
>
> creatures[55]

But for the most part, Philip chooses a particular cache of words from the trial text and iterates them in a variety of sequences and configurations so as to isolate and dismantle their logic and force. A horizontal line appears at the bottom of each page in the opening section, beneath which appear a list of names – "Aba Chimanga Naeema Oba Eshe" or "Wafor Yao Siyolo Bolade Kibibi Kamau," just to give two examples.[56] In the second part of "Os," subtitled "Dicta," the horizontal line remains, but no names are below it, and no additional names appear in footers until the very end of the penultimate section, "Ferrum." Philip creates names for those Africans who were thrown overboard at the orders of Collingwood: even had the Zong's manifest or other associated documentation survived, the names of the individual Africans who were on the ship is lost to history: they would not

[55] Ibid., 16. [56] Ibid., 4 and 5.

have been listed by their names, but rather by their general type in terms of gender, age, and other physical characteristics. Such an act of imaginative reach starkly performs the elegiac crux outlined earlier in the chapter. Within the regime into which the Africans were forcibly taken and then forcibly killed, they had no names. Thus, Philip undertakes the risky act of providing names for them: this is perhaps a knowing instance of authorial hubris, but it is also an attempt to render poetically an absence. Philip can't and must provide epitaphs as part of her attempt to fashion an account of what happened on the Zong atop the chasm of the historical record.

This double impulse – which sits at the heart of poetic recollection as I've been outlining it here – drives *Zong!*. The first section draws entirely from the storehouse of the Gregson v. Gilbert report. Subsequent sections – which comprise more than two-thirds of the volume – break apart the text, scattering the letters and words of the report into its constituent parts and their combinations. This exponentially increases the available lexis (the entire alphabet appears in the transcript), and it allows Philip to turn from marking absences to conjuring presences. As the volume proceeds, the pages get thicker and thicker with text – three- and four-word assemblages of mainly mono- and disyllabic words strewn in wave-like fractals down the page – and a series of voices and scenes gathers. Rather than a found-poetry project bound to what lies beyond its ken, the choice to break up the text of the 1783 transcript – to turn a word-hoard back into an alphabet – allows *Zong!* to become a generative text. Preternaturally or even magically so; as Philip suggests in the invaluable "Notanda," the authorial function in *Zong!* straddles two positions: "censor" and "magician."[57] Philip recounts the moment at which the poem found "its own form, its own voice": "every word or word cluster is seeking a space directly above within which to fit itself and in so doing falls into relation with others either above, below, or laterally. This is the governing principle and adds a strong visual quality to the work."[58] This turn also takes on the brutal spatial logic of the slave ship, and the sense of downward motion built into the pages' architectures mimics

[57] Ibid., 199. [58] Ibid., 203.

the manner in which the enslaved Africans were killed. For Philip, this compositional structure also allows for the resurrection in which the "cacophony of voices – wails, cries, moans, and shouts that had earlier been banned from the text" return.[59]

On the following page of this book, there appears a full page taken from early in "Sal," part two of Zong!, which gives a good sense of the texture that emerges from Philip's practice (Figure 4.1). The final line of the previous page of Zong! consists of two bits of text set at a distance from one another: "she f" and "alls falling." Coalescing Philip's assemblages allows for this passage:

> she falls falling found a rose found africa under water proved
> justice dangerous the law a crime she died

After a description of one woman being thrown overboard, and the contextualization of that death within the unjust justice and unlawful law that allowed and encouraged it, the text provides a visual and even aural analogue for the woman as she drowns in the water. About halfway down the page the text reorchestrates several of its key words from multiple perspectives, and the "cacophony of voices" that converge in the text are both diegetic and extradiegetic: some bits of text attach to the collective dead – "us us *os* /save us *os*" – while others come from outside of the text's imagined space, as in the phrases that appear at the bottom of the page and that seem to address the dead. Toggling between "slave" and "*salve*," this passage faces squarely the difficult task that Philip attempts. The more straightforward meaning of "*salve*" here is the Latin term for "hello" or "be well." And it is this term that Philip gives in the multilingual "Glossary: Words and Phrases Overheard on Board the *Zong*," for which she gives the meaning as "hello, good-bye."[60] Coming after the first-person plural words that attach to the drowned Africans, the word "slave" repositions them, which they would not have used to describe themselves, and so we conclude that this word attaches either to one of the white slavers on the ship or to an abstract narratological function. In which case, it is difficult to place the word

[59] Ibid., 203.   [60] Ibid., 183.

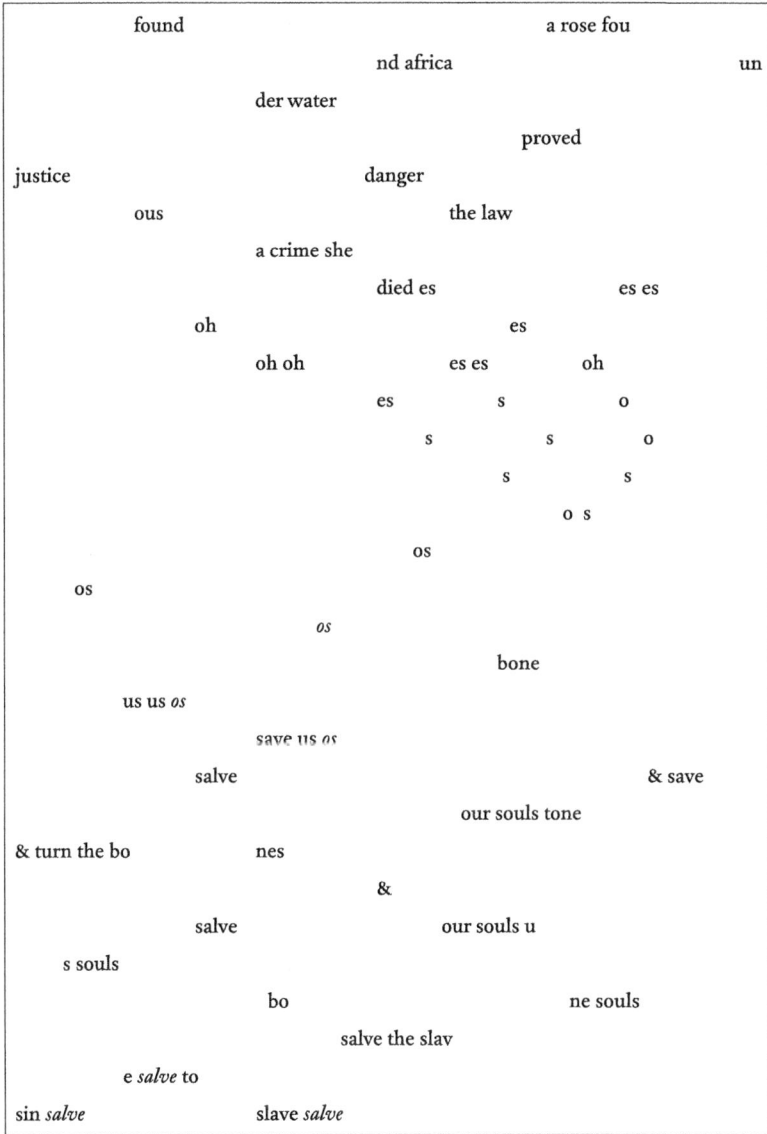

Figure 4.1 M. NourbeSe Philip, *Zong!* (Middletown, CT: Wesleyan University Press, 2011 [2008]), page 63

"*salve.*" Such a speech act in Latin is not functional: within the circumstances of the passage, no one would or could use this to address anyone else, and so it likely wouldn't have been heard on board. And reading *salve* as an English word is problematic, if not completely disbarred: whatever else it may be, *Zong!* is not a "salve." It does not comfort or heal, but asks the reader to undertake significant challenges – simply deciphering each page takes effort and time – while acknowledging at every moment that such "healing" or recompense is not possible.

As the pages thicken and their fractures intensify, the text's repetitions gather more and more momentum, and even as Philip disallows narrative, we are given snatches of diegesis: scenes of capture and enslavement, moments of violence and terror – barely glimpsed – from aboard the Zong, instances of chant or song or prayer, small proto-narrative germs that are refused coherence or continuance. Several voices reappear from section to section, such as one belonging to a white Englishman, perhaps part of the crew, whose letters back to his beloved "Ruth" appear in tattered strands and express both the force of his love and the depth of his shame. Although Philip declares in the "Notanda" that she has allowed herself "to surrender to the text" and so is "'absolved' of 'authorial intention'," there are certainly moments of self-reflexivity in which the authorial function is made apparent.[61] There are occasional inclusions of pseudo-stage directions (*"act s   ix sce   ne o /   ne"*), moments of extradiegetical pronouncement ("let the play begin we   each act the part"), and even the occasional allusion, as when a bit of one of Ariel's songs from *The Tempest* suddenly appears: "s how the so   ng go   es where the/bee suc   ks there   do the s[.]"[62] These moments of self-conscious literariness cut against Philip's declaration of non-intention and in so doing complicate her project: what slowly emerges, in fleeting textual moments, is a recognition that even as narration is barred, dramatic staging becomes central: the voices that are conjured and assembled do not tell full stories, nor do they interact outside of their juxtaposition within Philip's textual assemblages, but

[61] Ibid., 204.   [62] Ibid., 147, 127, 135.

they do require orchestration. From an initial impulse of nonintervention, in which the 1783 report would provide all of the content, we've moved toward a quite different model of authorial construction, one that might eschew the prerogative of creative intention, but certainly takes up the function of authorial arrangement, although even this aspect of the text's discursive and generic system is reinflected by another feature of Philip's design.

The cover and title page of *Zong!* feature most prominently the title and the author's name, as we would expect. Below that, however, we are given a second quasi-authorial inscription: "as told to the author by Setaey Adamu Boateng." Just as Philip imagines names for the nameless dead who are thrown overboard the Zong, so does she imagine a figure who relays their stories to Philip. Setaey Adamu Boateng is also described in Philip's biography on the volume's back cover as "the voice of the ancestors revealing the submerged stories of all who were on board the *Zong*." Here, we have another variation on or departure from the typical author function that we expect in poems. And at this point we can say that among the requirements of the type of recollective poetics that I've been tracking here is the refashioning of that function. As the poet of *Thomas and Beulah* can assume a position as novelistic narrator of her grandparents' lives only by extracting herself as a biographical person within those lives, and as Bergvall reconstrues the act of composition by basing it in a mode of rigorous, attentive copying and ordering, so does Philip institute an additional authorial scrim between herself and the text. As Philip remakes her project, from one that reposes entirely on the found text to one that fully dismantles that found text in order to spur new composition (a structural arc suggested by the progress of each section's epigraphs), the paradox in which the poem situates itself becomes more starkly outlined. The impasse faced by elegy and other modes of poetic recollection is redoubled here by the fact of the archival void: it isn't only that one must mourn deaths, but that one must mourn the deaths of those who can't be named. Because of the circumstances of their capture and their mid-ocean deaths, their lives will leave no trace.

The historian or scholar may aim to make such archival silence speak, to understand the lack of actual historical material as itself a negative form of historical material, and this is the tack Philip takes at first when she remains within the ambit of the 1783 report's "word store." In the volume's opening sections, as she notes, the authorial function acts in part as "censor," managing the silences of the historical record. The volume turns when Philip moves from "censor" to "magician," from one bound to the past's silences to one who proceeds by way of poetry's alternate logic of "as if," which in this case requires the construction of an overtly fictional edifice who reveals "the submerged stories" that Philip's text mediates and displays. In this light, the volume's final major section, "Ebora," the Yoruban term for "underwater spirits," is both the most flagrant and most fitting conclusion to *Zong!*[63] This final section consists of seven pages in which pages from previous sections are overprinted in light grey, such that many of the words and phrases are unreadable within a "dense landscape of text."[64] Philip explains this final section as one governed by chance and caused by a mishap with Philip's printer, which superimposed multiple pages on top of one another while printing them. This same printer malfunction occurred when Philip tried to print each section of the book, although it only affected the first few pages of each section before printing the rest correctly. Philip takes these self-haunted pages – the outcome of an unaccountable technological glitch – and installs them as the volume's conclusion. The "underwater spirits" of those thrown overboard, who are channeled via another kind of spirit, Setaey Adamu Boateng, are now conjured by a malfunctioning laser printer. Another faulty transcript is produced. We can understand this as a radical abdication of authorial responsibility or as a literalization of the poetics of conjuring that has generated much of *Zong!*

And, in the end, we must understand it as both. For a volume in which "order, logic, and rationality" are tools of barbarism and civilizational violence, and one in which the tidying motions of narrative are forbidden, such a move toward illegibility may just well be

[63] Ibid., 184. [64] Ibid., 206.

required, both to emphasize the impossibility of the authorial act that has taken place and to display the compositional facades that enabled it. As we look at the only occasionally legible final section, we decouple the text we see from the titular figures, the spirits of the dead, who are putatively represented by and within the scumbled pages. And we are given to understand that Philip's mode of gathering and scattering, and poetic recollection more broadly, offers a way of engaging with the past that is unique among genres: rather than a discourse of explanation, narrative, or synthesis, the acts of recollection that poems undertake offer both glimpses of the stuff of the past while simultaneously asserting via their formal and generic machinations the paradox that underwrites those glimpses. It isn't only that that which has been lost to time is irretrievable, but that it is irretrievable and that we must nevertheless seek to retrieve it. The texts I've gathered in this chapter demonstrate multiple ways that poetry can serve as a means of historical investigation, even as they suggest again and again that such an investigation cannot proceed simply as a search for knowledge about the past, and even as they recognize that any such knowing is shot through with its opposites – not-knowing and imagining. The value of such investigations is not in spite of their reliance on these counterepistemological tasks but indeed rooted in them.

Conclusion

Throughout this book I've argued that the poems that matter do so because they are able to catch and mark something of the vital complexity of individual life as that life is shaped in language. Able to maneuver around certain discursive obligations that are expected from other kinds of writing (both fiction and nonfiction), and tending to handle words as aesthetic materials with their own densities, textures, and rhythms (rather than exclusively as communicative tokens), poems often move laterally, by association and implication as well as by more familiar discursive paths. This makes them especially capable of presenting the fluxes, swerves, and fissures that characterize interiority, and of constructing varieties of subjective response to internal and external conditions – that limen where subject and environment meet and constitute one another. Implicit within this argument is that poetry is less good at other tasks, whether those that might be better undertaken by novels or other genres for which large-scale narrative and world-building are central or – it probably goes without saying – those whose primary purpose is informational or expository.

At the same time, suggesting that poetry's import hinges on its relation to subjective life does not, as I hope I've shown by now, mean that it is simply an aesthetic remnant of a ruined notion of the enlightenment subject. Poetry is bound up in the same ideologies that shape modernity's systemic turmoil and damage, and because language is by definition shareable, there isn't a space apart from the social and the political in which poems or poets can take refuge from society and politics. But those same constraints – that is, the fact that poetry is made of language and so cannot cordon itself off from the ideologies carried in language – make it possible for poems to rework those constraints immanently, and so to suggest modes of individual and social relation that cut against the governing ideologies of the present.

To be sure, there are plenty of poems that repose too easily in a species of lyric subjectivity too near the self-satisfactions and aggrandizements that dominate our instrumentalized, transactional cultural landscape. However, this does not mean that poetry should (or even could) give up on the project of articulating the intricacies, affordances, and obligations that structure the intersection of individual and social life. This intersection is enacted – offset and in miniature – when a reader encounters a poem. Poems can provide a form of textual encounter that is categorically different than those offered in other literary and nonliterary genres by modeling a relation that is based neither on identification nor spectatorship, but on a processual and productive uncertainty. Neither offering itself up to be fully co-opted or incorporated by the reader (the lyric *I* and *you* are never quite the readerly *you* and *I*), nor presenting a textual diegesis that can be observed from a distance, a poem asks for recognition and participation rather than appropriation or objectification. Even as I've shied away from suggesting that the encounter between person and poem is analogous to the encounter between person and person or that great poems are necessarily models of ethical relations, I have tried to make it clear that the kinds of linguistic density and obliquity that often typify the poems that I value most are not merely signs of artistic gamesmanship or willful hermeticism (though they are sometimes that), but rather features and effects of the aim to render the full, vertiginous complexity of our various and differential experiences. Such poems rarely grant clear answers or even ask fully formed questions, but they do compose paths in and of language that disclose what it's like to be in the world.

This argument comes under heavy pressure in a time of global political and ecological crisis: what is poetry's place, if it has one, within conceptions of the future, if we have one? Poetry has long served as a means to reckon with large-scale cultural change and civilizational crisis – whether we think of the epic tradition from Homer forward, Milton writing in the English Civil War, Dickinson and Whitman writing during the American Civil War, or Celan writing after the Holocaust – even if that function has been somewhat less pronounced over the course of the last century, as the scale of fully industrialized global wars have made it nearly unthinkable within the terms of lyric. An analogous, though amplified, crisis of representation faces poets who aim to consider the sheer scope of climate change: the more-than-human timescale of the geological changes that humans have wrought within the Anthropocene, that debatable but valuable term that marks the period in history when human activity – primarily the extraction and burning of fossil fuels – has altered the planet's systems.[1] Although the fate of poetry seems trivial in the face of global warming and other forms of environmental destruction, and although it has never been more stupifyingly clear that "poetry makes nothing happen" and will be of no immediate help in the global political fight to curb civilization's dependence on fossil fuels and our propensity to damage – both blindly and willfully – the planet in nearly every possible way, poets have begun the intractable task of imagining responses to what seem like impossible questions: If poems have, embedded within them, some notional and projected future, then how does a poet write toward a future that may well be entirely wrecked? If the crises that we face, particularly the catastrophic crisis of climate change, can't be conceived of or imagined at the level of the individual, how might poetry – an imaginative endeavor on an immutably human scale – be useful? Why should anyone spend time on poetry when we face the increasingly likely prospect of cataclysmic changes to the world and much of the life within it?

To ask about the value of poetry at the end of the world – an overdramatization perhaps, but nonetheless – is to ask about the value of any cultural or artistic endeavor in such a time: The imaginative actions of art have no direct effect on emissions or deforestation or on the systemic injustice of the effects of global warming, but

---

[1] Paul Crutzen and Eugene Stoermer introduced the term "Anthropocene" in wide circulation in a brief note in the newsletter for The International Geosphere-Biosphere Programme as a way to name a post-Holocene epoch in which human activity plays a key part in the planet's ecological and geological developments, the start of which they date to the late eighteenth century (see Paul J. Crutzen and Eugene F. Stoermer, "The 'Anthropocene'," *Global Change Newsletter*, 41 [May 2000], 17–18). Even as its geological scope is still under debate, it has become a nearly ubiquitous term beyond scientific domains.

they do help shape a culture's notion of itself – its past and future – and so imaginatively grappling with what lies ahead is a minor though vital adjunct to actually changing the path we're on. By way of conclusion, I will address two aspects of this matter, each of which poses specific difficulties for poets. The first problem, which I've already noted, concerns the profound disjunction between the timescales and temporal vectors of poems and the timescale of climate change within the scope of planetary history. The second is the problem for poets of what has been called, most famously by Bill McKibben in a book of that title, "the end of nature," which indicates not only the realities of the magnitude of human intervention in, and interruption and destruction of, the natural world, but also the loss of an idea that has long structured our sense of nature and its relation to human culture: that nature is immutable, primeval and pristine, endlessly regenerative, and both entirely apart from human civilization and an accessible refuge from society. This ideology of nature is one of poetry's deep premises, not only for nature poets or ecopoets and not only since the Romantic period. The double loss of this idea – that it is both no longer viable and was always something of a mystification – is, for poets, a subject and a dilemma.

In *The Great Derangement: Climate Change and the Unthinkable* (2016), Amitav Ghosh articulates the challenges for writers facing the implications of climate change:

> Are the currents of global warming too wild to be navigated in the accustomed barques of narration? But the truth, as is now widely acknowledged, is that we have entered a time when the wild has become the norm: if certain literary forms are unable to negotiate these torrents, then they will have failed – and their failures will have to be counted as an aspect of the broader imaginative and cultural failure that lies at the heart of the climate crisis.[2]

---

[2] Amitav Ghosh, *The Great Derangement: Climate Change and the Unthinkable* (Chicago and London: The University of Chicago Press, 2016), 8.

He goes on to consider this from the perspective of the changed future:

> In a substantially altered world, when sea-level rise has swallowed the Sundarbans and made cities like Kolkata, New York, and Bangkok uninhabitable, when readers and museum-goers turn to the art and literature of our time, will they not look, first and most urgently, for traces and portents of the altered world of their inheritance? And when they fail to find them, what should they – what can they – do other than to conclude that ours was a time when most forms of art and literature were drawn into the modes of concealment that prevented people from recognizing the realities of their plight? Quite possibly, then, this era, which so congratulates itself on its self-awareness, will come to be known as the time of the Great Derangement.[3]

Ghosh's "Great Derangement" is a function of our capacity for self-deception, the ubiquity of our self-interest, our absorption by the rhythms of consumer capitalism and the culture industry, and our inability or unwillingness to look for too long at what is painful or difficult – "human kind/Cannot bear very much reality," Eliot writes in *Four Quartets*.[4] But the navigational difficulties and ideological derangements that Ghosh diagnoses here are also based in the incommensurability between the timescales of literature (and any other cultural production) and the timescales of planetary history. Although the effects and incidents of climate change are and will continue to be observable, and although it is clear that those effects will be deeply felt within the lifetimes of many of the people now living on the planet, the full disaster of global warming occurs over a duration beyond that of human history. As David Wallace-Wells notes: "warming at the level necessary to fully melt ice sheets and glaciers and elevate sea level by several hundred feet promises to initiate rolling, radically transformative changes on a timescale measured not in decades or centuries or even millennia, but in the millions

---

[3] Ghosh, *The Great Derangement*, 11.
[4] T. S. Eliot, *Collected Poems, 1909–1962* (New York: Harcourt Brace & Co., 1991 [1963]), 176.

of years. Alongside that timeline, the entire lifespan of human civilization is rendered, effectively, an afterthought; and the much longer span of climate change becomes eternity."[5] Reckoning imaginatively with such a scenario within aesthetic forms that are premised upon human timescales (from single lives to generations to civilizations) is a matter of a profoundly negative capability. It is difficult not to be stupefied by any one of the eventual large-scale effects of global warming or of the long-term environmental implications of our most seemingly trivial, and often thoughtless, behaviors and choices. Not only are we awed by the sight of the glacier palming the mountain range, we are also overwhelmed to conceive the timescale of the glacier's formation, itself an afterthought compared with the range's own. The glacier's slow melt – quickened by human activity – can be measured and observed, but the ramifications of its total loss are remote from any single person's life. What would be needed to fully grasp and convey those durations is a mode of speculative poetry that operates entirely outside of the terms by which poems have long been made, outside – that is – of the scale and scope of human experience: an inhuman poetry to represent the consequences of our human acts.

One work that does manage to be deeply human and inhuman at once, and one that catches the Anthropocentric sublime while having – at least explicitly – nothing to do with climate change or global warming is *Sea and Spar Between* (2010) by Stephanie Strickland and Nick Montfort. An electronic text, *Sea and Spar Between* is, as the authors point out in a prefatory statement, "a poetry generator which defines a space of language populated by a number of stanzas comparable to the number of fish in the sea, around 225 trillion."[6] There are essentially three works that travel under the title *Sea and Spar Between*. The first two are manageable: the "poetry generator" itself, a 502 line JavaScript code written by Strickland and Montfort that lays out the rules for generating and

---

[5] David Wallace-Wells, *The Uninhabitable Earth: Life After Warming* (New York: Tim Duggan Books, 2019), 203.
[6] Stephanie Strickland and Nick Montfort, "Author(s) Statement," *Sea and Spar Between* [2010], in *Electronic Literature Collection, Volume 3*, ed. Stephanie Boluk, Leonardo Flores, Jacob Garbe, and Anastasia Salter (Cambridge, MA: Electronic Literature Organization, 2016), http://collection.eliterature.org/3/work.html?work=sea-and-spar-between, accessed July 5, 2019.

presenting 225 trillion stanzas; and a 930 line text titled "cut to fit the toolspun course," which we might think of as an annotated edition of the code, containing the 502 lines of code plus the authors' comments arrayed around it.[7] The third work is entirely unmanageable: the 225 trillion quatrain output of the poetry generator, the totality of which cannot be read by any single reader, not only because reading those 900 trillion lines would take around 214 million years at thirty seconds per stanza (also dwarfing exponentially the duration of human civilization), but also because the nature of the program's interface makes it nearly impossible to "read" the stanzas in any kind of orderly fashion. Upon navigating to the page "containing" *Sea and Spar Between*, one is placed randomly within what Strickland and Montfort describe as "an immense lattice of stanzas," a grid of stair-step quatrains in blue text against a lighter blue background – stanzaic fish in a sea of pixels.[8] The rules for navigating from quatrain to quatrain and adjusting the display are quite simple (typing in x/y coordinates, arrowing up and down, using the mouse or specific keys to zoom in and out, and so on), but the program is extremely sensitive to a user's touch, so that every click and flutter of a finger hurries one on to another sector of the "immense lattice," which though not infinite and not random, is made to feel so. One can either simply stare at the quatrains that appear on the screen and suppress the urge to involve oneself tactilely in the reading process (the difficulty of which reminds us of the importance of touch for reading, whether in print or on screen), or try and activate the usual coordination between hand and eye only to be presented with a jittering, scrolling screen that shuttles too quickly across the lattice. Only an exceedingly small portion of the whole text is available in a single screen-view (on the eleven-inch screen I am currently writing on, I can comfortably read fifteen stanzas per screen – sixty lines – but can zoom out so that seventy-seven stanzas, too small to decipher, can be made to appear at once), and any attempt to manipulate the text takes one to a different set of coordinates. It isn't only that one couldn't possibly

---

[7] The "work archive" for *Sea and Spar Between*, including both the original code and the glossed version, as well as the work itself are available at http://collection.eliterature.org/3/work.html?work=sea-and-spar-between, accessed July 5, 2019. "cut to fit the toolspun course" is available at http://digitalhumanities.org/dhq/vol/7/1/000149/resources/source/000149.html, accessed July 5, 2019.

[8] "cut to fit the toolspun course," line 121.

read all 225 trillion stanzas, but even if one could, the nature of the user interface ceaselessly hinders any course of continuous reading or of orienting oneself in relation to a text that is at once thrilling and monstrous. One is always at sea.

Sea and Spar Between is, in this sense, an inhuman text, one that is designed to confound human attempts to read it, and critics and "readers" tend to focus on this aspect of the poem's overwhelming, oceanic sublimity.[9] A digitally born poem that is not conceivable as a print-based artifact and that requires a thorough reconstruction of what it means to "read" or "encounter" a text, *Sea and Spar Between* pushes against a number of fundamental conventions of poetry.[10] At the same time, *Sea and Spar Between* is an example of a quite familiar genre: the found poem. Like Bergvall's "Via," *Sea and Spar Between* consists of preexisting texts: in this case, selections from Herman Melville's *Moby Dick* and the poems of Emily Dickinson. The title itself is taken from a Dickinson poem (#879), and "based on [their] long acquaintance with the distinguishing textual rhythms and rhetorical gestures of Melville and Dickinson," Strickland and Montfort selected characteristic words and phrases from the source texts and generated a set of rules by which those words might be arranged and combined.[11] *Sea and Spar Between* is formally homogeneous – every one of its 225 trillion stanzas appears as

---

[9] See in particular Stuart Moulthrop and Justin Schumaker, "Along the Folds: Sea and Spar and Portals Between," *CounterText: A Journal for the Study of the Post-Literary*, 2.2 (2016), 130–139.

[10] Such overturnings are central to electronic literature's *modus operandi*. For a brief but invaluable primer on digital poetry, see Stephanie Strickland, "Born Digital" (2009), *Poetry Foundation*, www.poetryfoundation.org/articles/69224/born-digital, accessed July 5, 2019. Also see C. T. Funkhauser, *Prehistoric Digital Poetry: An Archaeology of Forms, 1959–1995* (Tuscaloosa, AL: University of Alabama Press, 2007) and *New Directions in Digital Poetry* (New York and London: Continuum, 2012); ed. Adalaide Morris and Thomas Swiss, *New Media Poetics: Contexts, Technotexts, and Theories* (Cambridge, MA: The MIT Press, 2006); Loss Pequeño Glazier, *Digital Poetics: The Making of E-Poetries* (Tuscaloosa, AL: University of Alabama Press, 2002); N. Katherine Hayles, *Electronic Literature: New Horizons for the Literary* (Notre Dame, IN: University of Notre Dame Press, 2008); David Jhave Johnson, *Aesthetic Animism: Digital Poetry's Ontological Implications* (Cambridge, MA: The MIT Press, 2016); and Craig Dworkin, "Poetry in the Age of Consumer-Generated Content," *Critical Inquiry*, 44 (Summer 2018), 674–705.

[11] Stephanie Strickland and Nick Montfort, "Author Statement," http://directory.eliterature.org/individual-work/4897, accessed July 5, 2019.

a quatrain made of two stair-step couplets – and the small lexis that constitutes the data set makes its rhetorical texture relatively homogeneous as well, and quite repetitive. Strickland and Montfort's process of generating the data set was designed to catch particular stylistic traits of each writer that could then be mashed continually together, and so it often seems as though we are reading the longest Emily Dickinson poem ever written by Herman Melville. Here are two stanzas generated from *Sea and Spar Between*:

> loose-fish
>   but graspless is the sun
> one air one air one art one rest
>   artless move and go –
>
> fix upon the beespun course
>   nailed to the plank
> circle on
>   another! today![12]

There is genuine rhythmic and sonic interest in many of the stanzas, which are filled with often arresting and incantatory variations on a small core of lexical and phrasal elements, and because stanzas that are close together often feature similar words slightly rearranged (the following stanza after the above passage begins, "circle on/but graspless is the sky"), one can trace their implications as they appear and morph kaleidoscopically. In this sense, the text conforms to some of our basic expectations of poetry: that it be sonically dense and rhythmically active, that it regard words as compositional materials to be shaped. The interpretive problem is that one can only do this kind of reading in isolated pockets – no momentum can be built because the interface insists that one keep losing one's place within the ever-generating lattice of stanzas.

Of course, this is key to the gist of the poem: the "Editorial Statement" accompanying the work on the *Electronic Literature Collection* website suggests that "*Sea and Spar Between* allegorizes

---

[12] These stanzas appeared at the following coordinates: 276,12 and 276,13. See https://nickm.com/montfort_strickland/sea_and_spar_between/, accessed July 5, 2019.

the relationship of the reader to a digital sublime."[13] It does so by stacking two forms of sublimity. The "digital sublime" is allegorized via the natural sublime, that sense of astonishment and terror in the face of nature that is at the heart of accounts of the sublime by Longinus, Burke, and Kant. Two oceans – one water, one data – are intermingled, and a reader (or viewer, or helpless navigator) is set adrift within it. The compositional method by which these two sublimities are twined together is at once procedural, algorithmic, and freely composed. Out of a process that is quite familiar from other kinds of procedural texts – the selection of a corpus, the invention of a set of rules by which that corpus will be manipulated and presented – and via a series of authorial activities that are adamantly human – their interpretation of and selection from Dickinson's and Melville's work – Strickland and Montfort create a poem that confounds our modes of approaching it. The attempt to apprehend the process by which *Sea and Spar Between* came about is relatively straightforward, even for those who do not necessarily understand all of the technical details of the JavaScript code. But the attempt to "read" *Sea and Spar Between* is anything but: it rebuts reading and instead produces a suite of affective and intellectual responses surrounding that rebuttal, which are likely to vary among readers and modulate within any given reader's experience. I am dumbfounded by the unthinkable size of the poem and its 900 trillion lines. As when thinking about other kinds of immensities, I am alternately terrified at the scope before me and relieved to be able to look away and fasten onto some more reasonable set of proportions. Even as I attempt to find meaning and pleasure in one of its stanzas, I am unable to carry forward a close reading of the text because it keeps slipping away every time my fingers – intentionally or not – move the cursor. I can only satisfy a desire to engage with and attend to the text several isolated stanzas at a time, provided that my hands remain immobilized on the keyboard. The minor melancholy that arises at this point – the text is elusive on every level – is mixed with both relief and boredom as the inevitable

---

[13] *Sea and Spar Between*, http://collection.eliterature.org/3/work.html?work=sea-and-spar-between, accessed July 5, 2019.

actions of fingers and thumbs clicking and scrolling produce that sort of digital mindlessness that we know all too well.

We might even say that *Sea and Spar Between* asks us merely to do what we're already good at: to be, again drawing from *Four Quartets*, "distracted from distraction by distraction."[14] One perfectly reasonable response to encountering this text is to operate it mindlessly for a little while, and then turn to something else. Just another feed for us to scroll through. But something else is at work here: what Strickland and Montfort ask us to do is not merely to stare and go slack, but to actively register the massive scalar differences that constitute the project: the unthinkable mass of its trillions of stanzas, the very cognizable process by which the authors created it, and the particular interest that any individual stanza holds, even if we are flummoxed when we attempt to read consecutively for long. A lyrically minded apotheosis of lyric, *Sea and Spar Between* continually produces the immense gap upon which it is founded: between the human-sized acts of composition that constitute it – Melville's, Dickinson's, Strickland's, Montfort's – and the inhuman outcome of those acts. In this, it not only allegorizes a "digital sublime" but also suggests obliquely the problem at the heart of the Anthropocene: our inability to conceive of, and therefore to care about and so change, the ramifications of our individual and collective actions.

It takes a text as overwhelming as *Sea and Spar Between* to concretize these asymmetries of scale, and most poems – disinclined to contain trillions of lines – must find other ways to evoke the disjunction of scale through which we must imagine what Ed Roberson calls, in the title poem of *To See the Earth Before the End of the World* (2010), the "subtle collapse of time between large//and our small human extinction."[15] Roberson begins the poem – which opens the volume – by sardonically framing the impending effects of climate change as an opportunity for tourism: "People are grabbing at the chance to see/the earth before the end of the world."[16]

---

[14] Eliot, *Collected Poems, 1909–1962*, 178.
[15] Ed Roberson, *To See the Earth Before the End of the World* (Middletown, CT: Wesleyan University Press, 2017[2010]), 3.
[16] Roberson, *To See the Earth Before the End of the World*, 3.

Contemplating the multiple timescales at which creation and destruction occur before focusing on the temporality of glacial melt, the poem ends by thinking all the way back to primitive hunter-gatherers to suggest that the earliest forms of human violence presage the changes wrought within the industrial age:

> we just now see
>   our own lives taken by
> taking them out.   Hunting the bear,
> we hunt the glacier with the changes come
>   of that choice.[17]

For Roberson here, the Anthropocene doesn't simply name the period in which large-scale human activity began to reshape the ecosystem, whether one dates it to the invention of the steam engine in the mid-eighteenth century or some other moment early in the industrial age, or focuses on the period after 1945, when a layer of radioactive material becomes evident in the geological record, which marks what is sometimes called "The Great Acceleration," as the burning of fossil fuels has rapidly expanded since the middle of the twentieth century. Instead, Roberson suggests that the entire bent of human civilization entails the damage that we have brought about. In a companion poem later in the same volume, entitled "We Look at the World to See the Earth," he telescopes human and natural history along different lines:

> We look upon the world
> to see ourselves in the brief moment that we are of the earth
>   *a small fern in a crevice of the cliff face*[18]

Any one's single life is aligned with the collective and the civilizational ("the world"), each of which is a "brief moment" as compared to the planet's history ("of the earth"), and the stark image of the fern in the rock face provides a metaphorical analogue that relies on an identical scalar disjunction. This passage also suggests the second topic I'll take up in this final chapter: the ongoing relation between poetry and "nature" when the logic of that relation no longer holds. If most modes of poetic practice are unable to represent the scope of

[17] Ibid.   [18] Ibid., 22 (emphasis original).

climate change because they are fitted to the exceedingly brief lifespans of individuals and cultures, then poetry may also be ill-equipped to reckon with those changes because they wreck several of poetry's deepest foundations, foremost of which is its reliance on bankrupt ideologies about the "natural" world – all, that is, that is not human – and the human relation to that world. The importance of nature for poetry is so deep as to be nearly unnoticeable, not only poetry's reliance on the ideologies of the pastoral, but also poetry's leveraging of its own significance by way of the sublimity of the natural world. To put the matter in the form of two questions: What is the status of a "nature" poem well after the death of "nature," both the idea of nature as an unchanging refuge from the world and as a consequence of ongoing ecological devastation? When, as McKibben writes, "there is no future in loving nature," how might poetry respond to the loss of what for so long subtended it?[19]

One strategy has been to maintain the basic scene and scaffolding of a fairly recognizable genre of post-Romantic meditative nature poetry – a coherent lyric speaker in a particular landscape – and to refit them so that they might dispense with the outmoded or ideologically bankrupt aspects of that form while representing more fully the complexities of the relation between nature and human activity, registering more forcefully the damage that we've caused, and stirring readers to act differently. A number of the most significant environmental poets – such as Robinson Jeffers, Gary Snyder, W. S. Merwin, Wendell Berry, and John Burnside – have worked along such lines. If nature can no longer be positioned as a space of redemption and refuge from the depredations of modernity, or as the unproblematic source and backdrop for a speaker's epiphanies, then it remains possible for poets to adjust the tone or tenor of such stances while keeping their basic shapes. The lyric speaker is still stationed in or near a "natural" environment but focuses on its various forms of ruin or destruction, often conjoining praise and lament while articulating what has been lost and expressing a mixture of self-reflexive critique and hopeless hope. A number of poems in Jorie Graham's *Sea Change* (2008) are

---

[19] Bill McKibben, *The End of Nature* (New York: Random House, 2006 [1989]), 180.

good examples of this kind of approach, as is Alice Oswald's "Dunt: A Poem for a Dried-Up River," in which Oswald reaches back to poetry's roots in incantation and ritual as a way to figure the loss of the river. Other writers employ the kind of documentary, research-based poetics that I describe in the previous chapter to investigate and call attention to particular instances or types of ecological damage, such as Evelyn Reilly's *Styrofoam* (2009), Mark Nowak's *Coal Mountain Elementary* (2009), and Jennifer Scappettone's hybrid work about toxic waste sites near her childhood home on Long Island, *The Republic of Exit 43: Outtakes & Scores from an Archaeology and Pop-Up Opera of the Corporate Dump* (2016). Positioning themselves as far as they can from earlier forms of ecopoetry and familiar lyric stances, and drawing considerable energy from the lineage of environmentalist texts inaugurated by Rachel Carson's *Silent Spring* (1962), such works act as dossiers of environmental damage even as they are assembled and presented according to often subterranean logics, combining modernist forms of collage and parataxis with a data- and information-heavy style more typical of the digital age.

What unites varieties of ecopoetry – and the above paragraph should be regarded as nothing more than the barest of sketches – is a shared project, as Forrest Gander suggests: "it's been suggested that ecopoetries, by offering revised, less dogmatically binary perspectives of interaction between human and nonhuman realms, suggest ways of *being* in the world that might lead to less exploitative and destructive histories."[20] Gander is surely correct, and his claim is broad enough to encompass a huge swath of poetry – indeed, it might cover nearly the entire canon of modern and contemporary environmentally minded poetry as well as critical approaches to it.[21] It is difficult, however, to

---

[20] Forrest Gander and John Kinsella, *Redstart* (Iowa City, IA: University of Iowa Press, 2012), 15 (emphasis original).
[21] Key critical texts within the field of ecopoetics include John Elder, *Imagining the Earth: Poetry and the Vision of Nature* (Urbana, IL: University of Illinois Press, 1985); Leonard M. Scigaj, *Sustainable Poetry: Four American Ecopoets* (Lexington, KY: University Press of Kentucky, 1999); Jonathan Bate, *The Song of the Earth* (Cambridge, MA: Harvard University Press, 2000); Jed Rasula, *This Compost: Ecological Imperatives in American Poetry* (Athens, GA: University of Georgia Press, 2002); John Felstiner, *Can Poetry Save the Earth? A Field Guide to Nature Poems* (New Haven, CT: Yale University Press, 2009); Terry Gifford,

get from the inarguable ethical substance of Gander's suggestion – that what is needed are "less dogmatically binary perspectives of interaction between human and nonhuman realms" – to specific forms of poetic practice. The "perspectives" that poems offer are not isolatable from their specific textual patterns, and so once again – and as always – we are brought back to the question of form. If poetry has any place in the project of registering the stakes of the ecological catastrophe that is upon us, then it must offer something that isn't better found somewhere else. The particular and wrenching difficulty in this regard is that the basis of poetry's value and import as an art – that it is a sensitive and nuanced means by which to reveal and portray the granularities of individual experience within social and historical conditions – is also its potential weakness. It relies on multifarious patterns of linguistic complexity and interest in order to construct spaces in which specific instances of subjectivity can be shaped and so offered as significant. The types of poetry for which I've advocated don't necessarily lend themselves to the kinds of collective, political effort that is needed at the largest of scales. They might even be seen to take part in the hegemony of economic and political ideologies that privilege the individual and its interests and so are part of the root problem. The challenge, as Ghosh points out, is a significant one: "at exactly the time when it has become clear that global warming is in every sense a collective predicament, humanity finds itself in the thrall of a dominant culture in which the idea of the collective has been exiled from politics, economics, and literature alike."[22]

Green Voices: Understanding Contemporary Nature Poetry, 2nd ed. (Nottingham: Critical, Cultural and Communications Press, 2011); Tom Bristow, *The Anthropocene Lyric: An Affective Geography of Poetry, Person, Place* (Basingstoke: Palgrave Macmillan, 2015); Sam Solnick, *Poetry and the Anthropocene: Ecology, Biology and Technology in Contemporary British and Irish Poetry* (London and New York: Routledge, 2017); Lynn Keller, *Recomposing Ecopoetics: North American Poetry of the Self-Conscious Anthropocene* (Charlottesville, VA: University of Virginia Press, 2017); Angela Hume and Gillian Osborne, eds., *Ecopoetics: Essays in the Field* (Iowa City, IA: University of Iowa Press, 2018); Margaret Ronda, *Remainders: American Poetry at Nature's End* (Stanford, CA: Stanford University Press, 2018); and John Farrier, *Anthropocene Poetics: Deep Time, Sacrifice Zones, and Extinction* (Minneapolis, MN: University of Minnesota Press, 2019).

[22] Ghosh, *The Great Derangement*, 80.

In a time of ecological catastrophe, and considering the snares I've mentioned, what do we need poems to do? If other modes of writing do a better job of explaining environmental issues, constructing narratives about climate change, and stirring their readers to act, what role do poems play? And if one familiar poetic archetype – the coherent lyric speaker meditating amidst or about nature – is ideologically wrenched, then what kinds of poetic practice remain viable? Interestingly, Timothy Clark suggests that poetry might be better positioned than other literary forms to represent "the true complexity of environmental issues":

> One advantage of poetry is that its removal from the conventional constraints of prose narrative renders it more open to representing multiplicity, and even contradiction and indeterminacy, and to do so without its readers necessarily feeling the lack of some clear storyline. The dominance in poetry of versatile and often plural kinds of metaphor and other kinds of figurative language further removes it from the constraints of narrative linearity felt in most kinds of prose.[23]

For Clarke here, poetic complexity is a strength, although there are clearly limits to how far poets might go. Later, he asks, "how often do readers of poetry wish to be subjected to a linguistic space that enacts lack of control, limited ability to comprehend, personal guilt and complicity, and a sense of the helpless? Are other aesthetic techniques that enable a sense of harmony and moderate cognitive control simply illusory?"[24] Poems that evoke a sense of "harmony" are still likely "illusory," but poems that are difficult or complex – "a linguistic space that enacts a lack of control" – are now placed under suspicion as well. Subsequent to this passage he seems to turn his argument more fully around: "The most forceful ecopoetry would surely be one that managed to retain great accessibility and clarity while at the same time being formally and technically inventive."[25] Initially, poetry's

---

[23] Timothy Clark, *The Value of Ecocriticism* (Cambridge: Cambridge University Press, 2019), 59.
[24] Clark, *The Value of Ecocriticism*, 76.   [25] Ibid., 77.

formal mobility and density is a strength, and then it comes under question, and then Clark tries to split the difference by promoting a species of poetry that is both accessible and inventive. Poems that centralize the natural world in a familiar lyrical vein, even while taking cognizance of human-caused environmental damage, are perhaps too likely to be "illusory," offering readers simply the sort of pleasure that they expect from poems – a bad pleasure, in this case, because merely a kind of aestheticized mystification. However, experimental, "inventive" works, such as the books by Scappettone or Reilly, prove too rebarbative: it becomes too difficult to articulate the densely layered inscrutabilities of the text and the substantial demands that it places on the reader with the project's more clearcut political and ecological stance.

Rather than focus on the tensions striating Clark's argument, I want to see his hesitations about how poetry might best approach the matters of ecological destruction and climate change as indicative of precisely the lurch in which poets find themselves, one that isn't limited to the matter of difficulty and accessibility, and one that has appeared in other guises throughout this volume. The very features of poetry that source its value, and the formal means by which it elaborates those features, are also those that it must reimagine within the larger project of addressing the future – and perhaps it is this practice of placing constant pressure on its own devices and materials that marks the part that poems might play. Poems may delineate that fissile and uncertain space in which the unthinkable scope of global warming and planetary history is registered – as it must be – by an individual subject, whose response is likely to be, as Margaret Ronda suggests, one of "unresolvable affects and bewildering sensations."[26] In this way, and to return to Clark's original assessment, it is not just poetry's tendency toward multiplicity or complexity that makes it a useful genre in which to consider the overwhelming scales of climate change, but – more significantly – poetry's ability to render contradiction. If it is likely to remain difficult to avoid, on the one side, a kind of stumbling Beckettian hope, and, on the other, a fatalistic patter or recessive

---

[26] Ronda, *Remainders: American Poetry at Nature's End*, 6.

despair, then it might also be that poems can find ways to limn the experiential stutter in which such incompatible feelings and responses arise. Poems might pattern the inevitably discrepant affects that accompany the consideration of a civilizational crisis that feels both immediately critical and out of range.

Juliana Spahr's "Dynamic Positioning," published in *That Winter the Wolf Came* (2015), is a powerful text in this regard, and I'll close by turning to it briefly. Spahr has written a handful of celebrated poems about ecological damage and environmental destruction, and like those earlier poems – especially "Unnamed Dragonfly Species" and "Gentle Now, Don't Add to Heartache" – "Dynamic Positioning" is characterized by a limpid rhetorical texture and a preponderance of concrete detail. In those earlier poems, Spahr incorporates scores of plant and animal names as she details species endangerment, extinction, and habitat destruction, offering the poems both as catalogues of loss and as dynamic allegorical structures in which the figures in the poems begin to come to knowledge of their own lifelong participation in environmental degradation. "Gentle Now, Don't Add to Heartache," in particular, might be read as a lyric parable about our coming to understand how we "lost nature." Adapting several of her stylistic signatures – repetition and variation, cataloguing, accretion – to quite different effect, "Dynamic Positioning" gives an account of the Deepwater Horizon disaster in 2010. The Deepwater Horizon was a semisubmersible offshore oil drilling unit that was drilling on behalf of British Petroleum about forty miles off the Louisiana coast. The rig exploded and started a fire that killed eleven people on board, injured seventeen others, and caused a huge oil spill in the Gulf of Mexico. It is one of the largest environmental disasters, so far, in United States history.

At first glance, "Dynamic Positioning" does not accord with the suggestion that I made earlier that poetry's task might be to figure the contradictions and ambivalences that often characterize responses to climate change. Nor does Spahr in "Dynamic Positioning" seem to be too interested in the matter of global warming's inconceivable scope. Rather, the poem is – on the surface – relatively straightforward. In recounting the course of the Deepwater Horizon disaster, Spahr relies on just those discursive tools that poems so often eschew or submerge: narrative, exposition, and explanation. The poem begins by explaining its title and the deepwater drilling process:

> It is dynamic positioning that
> Allows a semi-submersible the
>
> Ability to hover there over
> The well. It is a thirty-six inch tube,
>
> A casing, that extends down to allow
> The drill and bit to be rotated there;
>
> The drill then spudding in; the seafloor, dark,
> And giving way.[27]

The poem's adherence to couplets made of ten-syllable lines constitutes its own form of "dynamic positioning," as the syntax bends and breaks to accommodate the syllable count. Spahr moves very slowly as she tells "the story of This Well," naming the components of the drilling process, and layering detail upon detail about the rig and well and the circumstances leading up to the explosion in a flat style:

> It is a blowout preventer, a series of valves
> That seal off the excessive pressure should
>
> The wellhead kick then blowout. There are all
> These variables. Various valves. Pressures.
>
> Buoyancies. Mixes of cement. Currents. Claims.
> Humans. Bow spring. Top plug. Shoe track. Floatshoe.
>
> I could go on and on here calling the
> New muses of innovation, common
>
> Vocabulary, that covers over the
> Elaborate simplicity of this,

---

[27] Juliana Spahr, *That Winter the Wolf Came* (Oakland, CA: Commune Editions, 2015), 43.

> This well, Macondo well, was drilled by
> Deepwater Horizon and it went through
>
> Five thousand feet, through the abyssal zones,
> The epipelagic with its sunlight
>
> The mesopelagic with its twilight
> The bathypelagic with its midnight ...
>
> This well then went on reaching for the oil
> Another thirteen thousand feet. When it hits
>
> The pay zone, down through it, down deeper, deep.
> This well, Macondo well, was exploratory.
>
> This story then begins with other wells,
> But I will tell the story of This Well[.][28]

As the poem goes on to relate the various testing and corner-cutting and troubleshooting that led up to the explosion, Spahr slows the pace and ratchets the tension as we approach the time when the explosion occurs. The line breaks become more severe as the explosion is described:

>   The drill press
> Ure, the volumes of gases, fluids, drill-
>
> Ing mud, seawater, then is steadily in-
> Creasing. And it begins again. Or be-
>
> Gins some more. First as mud. A mud that roar-
> Ing, rained.[29]

Each explosion and its aftermath are recorded as the "Deepwater Horizon [is] gutted stem/To stern."[30] After sixty-nine couplets detailing the disaster, the poem ends with seven couplets that undertake an act of Yeatsian elegiac naming: the eleven men who died are named, but the speaker swerves away from providing detail about their lives before moving on to name those who escaped. Here are the final five stanzas:

---

[28] Spahr, *That Winter the Wolf Came*, 44, 45.   [29] Ibid., 48.   [30] Ibid.

> I will not tell
> You their lives, their loves, their young children, their
>
> Relationship to oil. Our oil. The well
> Exploded. They then died. Some swam away.
>
> Some floated away in boats. Donald Vidrine,
> Curt Kuchta, Jimmy Wayne Harrell. I did
>
> Not die. I watched it then burn on a
> Flat screen. Anthony Brian Hayward, Steven
>
> L. Newman, David Lesar watched. And
> Susan Birnbaum too, watching.[31]

The three men named in the third couplet above all had supervisory positions on the rig. Anthony Brian Hayward was the CEO of British Petroleum at the time of the disaster, Steven L. Newman was the CEO of Transocean Limited, the drilling company that owned the rig, and David Lesar served as the CEO of the Halliburton, the oilfield services company that provided the cement meant to seal the well. All three companies faced investigations and litigation in the wake of the disaster. Susan Birnbaum served as the Director of the United States Minerals Management Service and was therefore putatively in charge of monitoring the drilling companies to ensure compliance with safety regulations. As the ten-syllable pattern breaks down, the poem closes with an elegiac litany followed by a list of those who share in the blame, one of whom is the poet herself, who takes part in the same fossil-fuel based global economy as do those CEOs and rig workers and who watches the explosion on the "[f]lat screen" of her computer or television.

The power of this poem's final turn is twofold. First, the poet includes herself among the guilty, and by extension the reader as well. For we, like Spahr, "did/Not die." And second, the specificity of these final two instances of the "I" ("I did/Not die. I watched it then burn") adds a different dimension to the poem's presentation of subjectivity

---

[31] Ibid., 49.

and so beckons a reader to think more carefully about how the speaking subject has been constituted. The first three instances in which an "I" appears, each of which are included in the extracts above, partake of the storyteller's or narrator's "I" more so than the lyric "I." Each is largely functional and generalized, ruddering the poem from one section to another. The first one activates a cliché – "I could go on and on" – and the second provides an *in medias res* speech-act that tells us what we already know: "I will tell the story of this well." The third is an inversion of the second, stating what the "I" will not do: "I will not tell/You their lives." And the fourth and fifth present a biographically situated "I": Juliana Spahr, alive, sitting in front of her screen watching the disaster. What interests me here is the way in which these various "I"s recalibrate the "you" that they address. The first three are blank "I"s: because they carry with them little substance or reference and because they are largely operational, they are unlikely to detain a reader. The final two "I"s are quite different, and if a reader could glide easily over the first three, the final two tug a reader into a different relation to the "I" and to the poem. Similarly, the "you" produced as an effect of the first three "I"s is relatively nondescript: it can be passively occupied by a reader without much trouble and without much thought. The "you" produced by the final two "I"s is endlessly differentiating: a reader is thrown back on the specificity of herself as a consequence of Spahr's own shift in relation to the poem's "I." This pronominal modulation becomes another form of "dynamic positioning" and a reader moves from being outside of the text to being called into it. In retrospect, the third instance of the "I" is the pivotal one: "I will not tell/You their lives." Not only by including "You" and so drawing a reader explicitly into the poem, but also by doing so while simultaneously suggesting via negation the specific fullness of the lives that were lost in the explosion. The poem both refuses and is unable to provide information about the particular lives of the eleven dead men, instead bringing together all of the figures in the text – those named, "I," "you" – into alienated relation: "Our oil." The "[f]lat screen" on which the speaker – Spahr – watches the Deepwater Horizon disaster is replicated formally, and the reader is required to account for herself or himself just as fully as those persons who are more directly responsible, and just as fully as the poet herself.

One might argue that by placing each figure in a position of guilty, helpless "watching," Spahr simply offers us a familiar structure of anthropogenic feeling. As Clark asked, "how often do readers of poetry wish to be subjected to a linguistic space that enacts lack of control, limited ability to comprehend, personal guilt and complicity, and a sense of the helpless?" But something more important is at work here. Spahr's careful composition of the poem's form and explanatory narrative is everywhere evident, but just as important – if more subtle – is her composition of a textual relation that undergoes a transformation from the beginning to the end. The "I" and the "you" implied at the start are not those that appear at the end. The poem performs – and asks a reader to perform – a process by which a far-off disaster is not simply an opportunity for spectatorship, but a space in which we must see ourselves in the "[f]lat screen," not simply as guilty individuals but as subjects who must take cognizance of our relation with others via the unthinkable systems in which we exist. The import of Spahr's poem is that it concretizes via its formal dynamics the complex interfolds that structure inner life and social relation. Poems can present the intricacies of subjective being and historical experience by activating the full capacity of that being's most basic medium – language. They also – via their formal and imaginative textures – can help to glimpse new modes of being and experience. Called into a poem's unfolding and asked to track its branching paths, a reader might even extend the implications of this form of attention beyond the poem itself, subtly adjusting one's own sense of things.

The climate and ecological crisis in which the globe and all its inhabitants are ensnared is – in part – structured by our inability to imagine and carry out forms of individual well-being that aren't at the same time deeply damaging to others – both actual others in the present and potential others in the future. That is, the lifestyles of those who contribute most to global warming – the wealthy inhabitants of wealthy nations primarily in the global north – are inextricable from the poverty of people in other parts of the globe. In the same way, our species-life on the planet – especially since the beginning of the industrial age and most especially since its severe quickening since the mid-twentieth century – is premised upon a carbon economy and the ceaseless extraction of fossil fuels and other resources that will endanger future life of all kinds. The direst omens suggest that we have already wrecked the future – that the earth will become too hot to support human civilization as it has developed over the past 10,000 years, and also perhaps life as we know it. Facing such existential threats, it is certainly reasonable to conclude that poetry – that art more broadly – doesn't matter at all. It becomes ever more difficult, and ever more necessary, to think otherwise. The poems that do so won't save us, but it is essential that we continue to have the capacity to imagine and read in such ways as great poems ask if we are also to muster the will to curb our capacity for ruin.

Index

Address, 10, 11, 32, 47
Adorno, Theodor, 40, 60, 62–65, 66, 77, 89, 90–91
   "On Lyric Poetry and Society," 62
Agamben, Giorgio, 25, 27
   "The End of the Poem," 24
Alienation
   historical alienation, 60–63
   in lyric poetry, 53, 56–57, 59–63, 65
   racism and, 77
Alphabet poetry, 142–143
Altieri, Charles, 93–94, 97
   Reckoning with the Imagination: Wittgenstein and the Aesthetics of Literary Experience, 93
Anderson, James Craig, 73
Anthropocene, 158, 167
Apollinaire, Guillaume
   Calligrammes, 102–103
Aristotle, 132
Armantrout, Rae, 67–68
   "Anchor," 68
   "Yoohoo," 67
Ashbery, John, 52–53, 56, 70
   "As One Put Drunk into the Packet-Boat," 53
   "Definition of Blue," 52
   "Hop o' My Thumb," 68–69
   Self-Portrait in a Convex Mirror, 53
Attention, poetry and
   feeling and, 118
   necessity of, 19–20
   play and, 22–23
   power of poetry, 20–21
   recognition and participation, demand for, 157
   thought and, 118
Auden, W.H., 12, 13
   "In Memory of W.B. Yeats," 125
   "In Praise of Limestone," 92
Australian indigenous peoples, 142–143
Authorship
   fictional authorship, use of, 153
   self, relation with author, 91
   subject versus, 90–91
Avant-garde poetry, 44–48, 102, 110, 115, 139

Bailey, Benjamin, 97
Baldwin, James, 72–73
Ball, Hugo, 33
Bang, Mary Jo
   Elegy, 124, 130–131
Baraka, Amiri, 103, 104–105
Barthes, Roland, 112
Baudelaire, Charles, 19, 60–63
Benjamin, Walter, 19–20, 60–63, 66
   The Arcades Project, 139
   "On Some Motifs in Baudelaire," 60
Bergvall, Caroline, 153
   "Via (48 Dante Variations)," 139–142, 143, 163
Bernstein, Charles, 90–91
Berrigan, Ted
   Sonnets, 45–46
Berry, Wendell, 168
Berryman, John, 124
   Dream Songs, 45–46, 51
Bhabha, Homi, 72–73
Bierce, Ambrose
   The Devil's Dictionary, 43–44
Birnbaum, Susan, 176
Bishop, Elizabeth, 43, 101
   "At the Fishhouses," 42
   "North Haven," 124
Blanchot, Maurice, 72–73
Blast, 102–103

Bök, Christian
 Eunoia, 45
Borges, Jorge Luis
 The Book of Imaginary Beings, 43–44
Bridges, Robert, 23–24
British Petroleum, 173, 176
Brooks, Cleanth, 5–6
Brooks, Gwendolyn, 26, 101
 "We Real Cool," 25
Brown, Michael, 73
Brownback, Sam, 79
Browning, Elizabeth Barrett, 55
 Aurora Leigh, 50
Browning, Robert
 The Ring and the Book, 51
Burke, Edmund, 165
Burnside, John, 168

Cage, John, 44–45, 139
Carroll, Lewis
 "Jabberwocky," 33, 34
Carson, Anne
 Autobiography of Red, 50
 Nox, 124
Carson, Rachel
 Silent Spring, 169
Celan, Paul, 157–158
Chomsky, Noam, 112
Civil Rights Movement, 134
Clark, Timothy, 171–173, 178
Clarke, Austin, 50
Climate change
 collective versus individual and, 170
 overview, 178
 role of poetry in addressing, 157–158, 159–161, 169–178
 temporal structure of poetry and, 158–159
Cobbing, Bob, 33
Cognition, poetry and, 95–97
Coleridge, Samuel Taylor, 133
 "Frost at Midnight," 98
 "Kubla Khan," 53–54
Collage, 8, 109, 139
Collingwood, Luke, 145–146, 148–149
Collins, Billy, 15
"Composition by field" (Olson), 102–105, 122
Conceptual poetry, 44–48, 139
Congressional Resolution of Apology to Native Americans (2009), 78–87
Contrapuntal structure, 23–24, 27

Counterhistorical writing, poetry as, 121
Crawford, John, 73
Creeley, Robert, 91, 103
Critical race theory, poetry and, 71–72
Crutzen, Paul, 158

Dadaism, 33, 102–103
Dakota Access Pipeline, 83–84
Dante, 139–140
 Commedia, 141–142
 Inferno, 139–142
Davis, Jordan Russell, 73
Deepwater Horizon disaster (2010), 173–176, 177–178
Degas, Edgar, 89
Deixis, 10–11, 65–67, 72, 76–77, 98, 123–124
De Man, Paul, 9, 58–59, 60, 66, 86
 "Semiology and Rhetoric," 59
Department of Defense Appropriations Act (2010), 78–79
Dialectical nature of poetry, 23–26
Dickens, Charles
 Our Mutual Friend, 128
Dickinson, Emily, 124, 157–158, 163, 164, 165, 166
 "There's a certain Slant of Light," 93
Diegesis, 65–67, 75, 98–102, 104, 131
Digital poetry, 161–166
Disjunction, 101–102, 103–104, 106, 110, 114–115, 119
Douglass, Frederick, 72–73
Dove, Rita, 101
 "The Event," 138
 "Magic," 136
 "Roast Possum," 137
 Thomas and Beulah, 134–139, 153
 "Wingfoot Lake (Independence Day, 1964)," 134–135
Dramatic poetry, 49–51
Duffy, Carol Ann, 55
Duggan, Mark, 73, 76–77
Duncan, Robert, 103
Dworkin, Craig, 15, 40–41

Ecopoetry, 169–178
Eigner, Larry, 91, 103
Eisenhower, Dwight D., 32–33
Eisen-Martin, Tongo, 104–110, 114
 "Faceless," 107–108

Eisen-Martin, Tongo (Cont.)
  Heaven Is All Goodbyes, 105, 106–108
  Someone's Dead Already, 105, 106
Electronic literature, 161–166
Electronic Literature Collection, 164–165
Elegies, 39–40, 123–132, 133, 147, 153
Eliot, T.S., 9, 15, 29, 35, 50, 55, 57–58, 60, 61, 66, 86, 94, 110
  "East Coker," 101
  Four Quartets, 21, 101, 160, 166
  "Little Gidding," 30, 101
  "The Love Song of J. Alfred Prufrock," 10, 22, 47, 129
  "The Music of Poetry," 34–35
  "Tradition and the Individual Talent," 9, 59
  The Waste Land, 51, 101–102, 128, 129
Elizabeth I, 11
Ellison, Ralph, 72–73
Emotion
  experience versus, 94–95
  in lyric poetry, 55–57
  self and, 55–57
England, slavery in, 146
English Civil War, 157–158
Enjambment, 24, 25, 42, 71, 130
Environmental crisis
  collective versus individual and, 170
  overview, 178
  role of poetry in addressing, 157–158, 159–161, 169–178
  temporal structure of poetry and, 158–159
Epic poetry
  decline of, 49–51
  recollection and, 121
Evaristo, Bernardine
  The Emperor's Babe, 50
Experimental poetry, 33–34, 47, 102, 112, 172

Fanon, Frantz, 72–73
Feeling, poetry and
  generally, 89–90
  aesthetics and, 95–97
  attention and, 118
  cognition and, 95–97
  emotion versus experience, 94–95
  figuration and, 118
  interactive model, 93–94
  internal monologue, poetry as, 92–93
  in lyric poetry, 55–57
  "open field" poetry and, 102–110
  performance and, 105
  perspective and, 98–100
  response to poetry and, 91–92
  rhythm and, 118
  self and, 55–57
  verbal imagery and, 98, 100–101
Feminist politics, poetry and, 71–72
Figuration
  feeling and thought and, 118
  lyric poetry and, 58–59
  objective correlative and, 9
  overview, 5
  play and, 41
  rhyme and, 39
First person, use of, 86–87, 98. *See also* Self, poetry and
Fisher, Allen, 103
  Place, 122–123
Fisher, Roy, 69–71
  A Furnace, 69–71
Form of poetry
  elegies, 39–40, 123–132
  hybrid models, 7–8
  materiality, 5–6
  mixed models, 7–8
  overview, 4
  sonnets, 7, 38–40, 45–46
  temporal structure (*See* Temporal structure of poetry)
Freud, Sigmund
  Beyond the Pleasure Principle, 61
Frost, Robert, 34–35
  "Stopping by Woods on a Snowy Evening," 98
Frye, Mary Elizabeth
  "Grieve Not," 129–130
Frye, Northrop, 23
Fuss, Diana, 129
Futurism, 102–103

Gander, Forrest, 169–170
  Be With, 124
Garner, Eric, 73
Genre
  climate change and, 168, 172
  elegy as, 133
  environmental crisis and, 168, 172
  lyric poetry as, 50
  overview, 5

poetry compared to other genres, 13, 51, 120, 121, 157
sentence/line dichotomy and, 27–28
sound and, 40
temporality and, 123–124
Ghosh, Amitav, 159–160, 170
Ginsberg, Allen, 104–105
"Howl," 24–25
Giscombe, C.S.
Giscome Road, 122–123
Global warming. *See* Climate change
Goldsmith, Kenneth
Day, 45
Gorey, Edward
The Gashlycrumb Tinies, 142
Graham, John J., 101
Shetland Dictionary, 43
Graham, Jorie
"San Sepolcro," 66–67
Sea Change, 168–169
Grammar, poetry and, 24–27
Gray, Thomas
"Elegy Written in a Country Churchyard," 124–125
Great Migration, 134
Gregson v. Gilbert case (1783), 146, 147–148, 149, 152–153

Hadfield, Jen
"Gish," 43–44
Nigh-No-Place, 43–44
Hallam, Arthur Henry, 124
Halliburton, 176
Harkin, Natalie
"Apology," 142
Dirty Words, 142–143
"Zero Tolerance," 142
Harshav, Benjamin, 36–37, 41
Hass, Robert, 101
Hayes, Terrance
American Sonnets for My Past and Future Assassin, 45–46
Hayward, Brian, 176
Heaney, Seamus, 15, 43, 101, 124, 142
"Requiem for the Croppies," 38–40, 41
Wintering Out, 43–44
Hejinian, Lyn
"The Rejection of Closure," 4
The Unfollowing, 45–46

Herbert, George
"Easter Wings," 41
Heron, Gil Scott, 106
Hill, Geoffrey
"September Song," 131–132
History, poetry and
counterhistorical writing, poetry as, 121
historical alienation, 60–63
historiography, 120
transhistorical value of poetry, 1–2, 3
Holocaust, 131–132, 157–158
Homer, 157–158
Hopkins, Gerald Manley, 23–24
Horkheimer, Max, 62
Howe, Susan, 122–123
Hughes, Ted, 15
Huizinga, Johan
Homo Ludens, 23
Hurricane Katrina, 73

Innovative poetry. *See* Experimental poetry
Internal monologue, poetry as, 92–93
Irish Rebellion (1798), 38
Izambard, Georges, 52–53
Izenberg, Oren, 112, 113

Jackson, Virginia, 49–50
Jakobson, Roman, 32–34, 35, 37, 40
Jameson, Fredric, 113
Jeffers, Robinson, 168
Jena Six, 73
"John Henryism," 73
Johnson, Barbara, 86
Johnson, Linton Kwesi, 106

Kant, Immanuel, 93, 95, 165
Keats, John, 97
"Ode to a Nightingale," 53–54
"To Autumn," 6, 98
Kim, Myung Mi, 103, 144–145
Commons, 144
Penury, 145
"Pollen Fossil Record," 144–145
King, Edward, 124, 125
King, Martin Luther, 134–135

Language poetry, 110–115
Larkin, Philip, 15, 101
Lesar, David, 176
Levertov, Denise, 103

Index

Lincoln, Abraham, 124
Longinus, Dionysius, 165
Long Soldier, Layli, 90, 105
   "38," 85
   Whereas, 77–87
Lowell, Robert, 97, 101, 124
Loy, Mina, 71–72
"Lyricization" (Jackson), 49–50
Lyric poetry
   generally, 49
   address, 10, 11, 32, 47
   alienation in, 53, 56–57, 59–63, 65
   depersonalization in, 57–59
   emotion in, 55–57
   feeling in, 55–57
   figuration and, 58–59
   as genre, 50
   "I," 47, 52, 54, 55, 65, 69–71, 133 (*See also* Self, poetry and)
   modernity and, 63–65
   nature poetry and, 167–169
   self in, 52–53
   subject, 52, 54–55, 63–65, 71, 86, 115
   thought in, 55–57

Mackey, Nathaniel, 103
MacLow, Jackson, 44–45, 139
Mallarmé, Stéphane, 89, 102
   Un coup de dés jamais n'abolira le hasard, 102–103
March on Washington (1963), 134–135
Marlowe, Christopher
   "The Passionate Shepherd to His Love," 47
Martin, Trayvon, 73
Marx, Karl, 61
Materazzi, Marco, 72–73
McKibben, Bill, 159, 168
Melville, Herman, 163, 164, 165, 166
   Moby Dick, 163
Meredith, George
   Modern Love, 45–46
Merwin, W.S., 168
Meter
   in elegies, 129
   play and, 41, 42
   rhyme and, 25–26
Mill, John Stuart, 8, 9, 48, 55–58, 61
Milton, John, 157–158
   "Lycidas," 124, 125, 126

Modernism
   collage in, 109, 139, 169
   disjunction in, 110
   expression in, 8–9
   Language poetry and, 114–115
   "open field" poetry and, 102–103, 122–123
   parataxis in, 109, 169
   Romanticism versus, 91
   sound poetry, 33
   subject in, 8–9
Montage, 8
Montague, John
   The Rough Field, 122–123
Montfort, Nick
   Sea and Spar Between, 161–166
Moore, Marianne, 15, 43, 101–102, 139
   "The Pangolin," 41–42
   "Poetry," 13, 92
Morris, Tracie, 33
Muldoon, Paul
   "Incantata," 124
   "When the Pie Was Opened," 25–26
Mullen, Harryette, 44–45
   "Any Lit," 46–48
   Recyclopedia, 44
   Sleeping with the Dictionary, 44–45, 46, 142
Myrick, Andrew, 85

Nabokov, Vladimir
   Pale Fire, 50
Narrative poetry, 49–51, 100–101, 102, 109, 120, 150–153
Native Americans, 78–87
Nealon, Christopher, 115
New Criticism, 58, 68–69, 87, 90, 110–111
Newman, Steven L., 176
Nichol, bp, 103
Nowak, Mark
   Coal Mountain Elementary, 169

Obama, Barack, 78–79
O'Hara, Frank, 19, 91
Oliver, Mary, 15
Olson, Charles, 103–104, 121–123, 144
   The Maximus Poems, 121–122
   "Projective Verse," 91, 103, 122
   "Open field" poetry, 102–110, 122–123

O'Sullivan, Maggie, 26–27, 33
  "Riverrunning (Realisations)," 26
  "Starlings," 26–27
Oswald, Alice
  "Dunt: A Poem for a Dried-Up River," 168–169
Oulipo, 44–45
Oxford English Dictionary, 43

Pararhyme, 39
Parataxis, 101–102, 109, 110, 114–115, 143–145
Pater, Walter, 97
Paterson, Don, 101
Perelman, Bob, 114
Performance
  feeling and thought and, 105
  "open field" poetry and, 105, 107, 109–110
  pronouns and, 10–11
  sentence/line dichotomy and, 27–28
  time and, 6–7
Perloff, Marjorie, 113
Perspective in poetry, 84, 98–100, 134, 150, 169–170
Philip, M. NourbeSe
  She Tries Her Tongue, Her Silence Softly Breaks, 147
  Zong!, 145–155
Plath, Sylvia, 101, 124
  Ariel, 90
  "Daddy," 53–54
Plato, 20–21
  "Cratylus," 36
"Poetic function" (Jakobson), 32–34, 35, 37
"Poetic mode" (Tsur), 31–32, 34, 35, 37
"Poetic thought" (Prynne), 118–119
Pope, Alexander, 39, 41
  "An Essay on Criticism," 35–36, 38
Postmodernism, 113
Pound, Ezra, 110, 121–122
  "Hugh Selwyn Mauberley," 19
  Cantos, 42–43, 51, 101–102, 139
Powers, Mary Farl, 124
Procedural poetry, 44–48
Pronouns in poetry, 10–11, 59–60, 65–67, 74–76, 98
Proust, Marcel, 61

Prynne, J.H., 16, 118–119
Pushkin, Alexander
  Eugene Onegin, 50

Quenau, Raymond, 44–45
Quine, Willard Van Orman, 112

Racism, poetry and
  African-Americans and, 72–78, 134–135
  alienation and, 77
  anecdotes of racism, 73
  Australian indigenous peoples and, 142–143
  deixis, use of, 76–77
  Native Americans and, 78–87
  "open field" poetry and, 104–110
  second person, use of, 74–76
  slave trade and, 145–155
Ramazani, Jahan, 15, 28, 126
Rankine, Claudia, 90, 105
  Citizen, 72–77
  Don't Let Me Be Lonely, 72
Raworth, Tom, 19
Recollection, poetry and
  African-Americans and, 134–135
  alphabet poetry and, 142–143
  collage and, 139
  counterhistorical writing, poetry as, 121
  defined, 121
  elegies and, 123–132
  epic poetry and, 121
  fictional authorship, use of, 153
  fiction versus nonfiction, 132–139
  juxtaposition and, 143–145, 152–153
  parataxis and, 143–145
  research-based poetry and, 122–123, 139
  self and, 133
  slave trade and, 145–155
  third person, use of, 138
Reilly, Evelyn, 172
  Styrofoam, 169
Research-based poetry, 122–123, 139, 169
Reznikoff, Charles
  Testimony: The United States, 1885–1915, 122–123
Rhyme
  figuration and, 39
  meter and, 25–26
  overview, 5

Rhyme (Cont.)
    as play, 22–23
    sound and, 30–31, 38–39
    triplets, 38–39
Rhythm
    contrapuntal structure and, 23–24
    in digital poetry, 164
    feeling and thought and, 118
    objective correlative and, 9
    "open field" poetry and, 104
    overview, 5
    play and, 42
    thought and, 97
Rich, Adrienne, 71–72
Richards, I.A., 37
Riley, Denise, 66
    "A Part Song," 124, 127–130
    The Words of Selves: Identification, Solidarity, Irony, 59–60
Rimbaud, Arthur, 52–53
Roberson, Ed, 166–167
    To See the Earth Before the End of the World, 166–167
    "We Look at the World to See the Earth," 167
Robertson, Lisa, 115–118
    Debbie: An Epic, 115
    The Men: A Lyric Book, 115
    "The Middle," 116–118
    "The Seam," 116
    3 Summers, 116
    The Weather, 115
    XEclogue, 115
Romanticism
    aesthetics and, 95
    Modernism versus, 91
    poets versus poetry and, 3
    self and, 53–54, 89, 91
    subject in, 8–9
Ronda, Margaret, 172
Rossetti, Dante Gabriel, 142
Rukeyser, Muriel
    The Book of the Dead, 122–123
Russian Formalists, 40, 112

de Saussure, Ferdinand, 112
Scappettone, Jennifer, 172
    The Republic of Exit 43: Outtakes & Scores from an Archaeology and Pop-Up Opera of the Corporate Dump, 169
Schwitters, Kurt
    "Ursonate," 33
Second person, use of, 74–76
Self, poetry and
    alienation and, 53, 56–57, 59–63, 65
    author, relation with, 91
    capitalism and, 60–63
    in contemporary poetry, 54–55
    depersonalization and, 57–59
    elegies and, 131
    emotion and, 55–57
    feeling and, 55–57
    historical alienation and, 60–63
    in lyric poetry, 52–53
    modernity and, 60–63
    problematic nature of, 47–48, 53–54
    reader, relation with, 91
    recollection and, 133
    Romanticism and, 53–54, 89, 91
    space and, 67–71
    thought and, 55–57
    time and, 67–71
Seth, Vikram
    Golden Gate, 50
Shakespeare, William, 72–73
    The Tempest, 129, 152
Shelley, Percy Bysshe
    "Adonais: An Elegy on the Death of John Keats," 124
    Cenci, 50
    "A Defense of Poetry," 20–21
Shklovsky, Viktor
    "Art as Technique," 37
Sidney, Philip, 8–9
    "The Defence of Poesy," 7, 132
Silliman, Ron
    The Alphabet, 142
    "The New Sentence," 112–113
Slam poetry, 105–106
Smith, Tracy K.
    The Body's Question, 98
    "Mangoes," 98–102, 114
Sonnets, 7, 38–40, 45–46
Sound, poetry and
    "defamiliarization" and, 37
    dialectical process in, 36–37
    experimental works and, 33–34
    genre and, 40
    human audition and, 32
    mode and, 40

"poetic function" (Jakobson) and, 32–34, 35, 37
"poetic mode" (Tsur) and, 31–32, 34, 35, 37
rhyme and, 30–31, 38–39
sense and, 35–37, 40–44
sonic play, 30–31
Sound poetry, 33
Space, poetry and, 67–71
Spahr, Juliana
  "Dynamic Positioning," 173–178
  "Gentle Now, Don't Add to Heartache," 173
  That Winter the Wolf Came, 173
  "Unnamed Dragonfly Species," 173
Speech act, poetry as, 28–30
Spoken word poetry, 105–106
Standing Rock Indian Reservation, 83–84
Standing Rock Sioux, 83–84
Starr, G. Gabrielle, 97
  Feeling Beauty: The Neuroscience of Aesthetic Experience, 95–96
Stein, Gertrude, 71–72, 110
  Tender Buttons, 102
Stevens, Wallace, 17–18, 54, 94, 101, 110
  "Bantams in Pine Woods," 34
  "The Idea of Order at Key West," 95–96, 131, 132–133
  "The Snow Man," 11, 92–93
Stewart, Susan, 87–88
  Poetry and the Fate of the Senses, 87
Stoermer, Eugene, 158
Strickland, Stephanie
  Sea and Spar Between, 161–166
Subject. *See also* Self, poetry and
  authorship versus subject, 90–91
  lyric subject, 52, 54–55, 63–65, 71, 86, 115
  in Modernism, 8–9
  poetry as emanation of subject, 8–9
  in Romanticism, 8–9
Swinburne, Algernon Charles
  Atalanta in Calydon, 50
Syntax, poetry and, 24–27

Temporal structure of poetry. *See also* Recollection, poetry and
  climate change and, 158–159

  environmental crisis and, 158–159
  indeterminate nature of, 6–7
  overview, 67–71
  staggered and untimely nature of, 123
Tennyson, Alfred Lord
  Idylls of the King, 50
  In Memoriam, A.H.H., 124
Third person, use of, 138
Thomas, Dylan
  "Fern Hill," 53–54
Thought, poetry and
  generally, 89–90
  aesthetics and, 95–97
  attention and, 118
  cognition and, 95–97
  emotion versus experience, 94–95
  figuration and, 118
  interactive model, 93–94
  internal monologue, poetry as, 92–93
  in lyric poetry, 55–57
  "open field" poetry and, 102–110
  performance and, 105
  perspective and, 98–100
  "poetic thought" (Prynne), 118–119
  rhythm and, 97, 118
  self and, 55–57
  verbal imagery and, 98, 100–101
Tichborne, Chidiock, 11
Time. *See* Temporal structure of poetry
Todorov, Tzvetan, 112
Transocean Limited, 176
Tsur, Reuven, 31–32, 34, 35, 37

United States Minerals Management Service, 176

Valéry, Paul, 97, 105
  "Poetry and Abstract Thought," 94–95
Verbal imagery, 98, 100–101
Voice in poetry, 6–7, 9–10, 129

Walcott, Derek, 101
  Omeros, 50
Wallace-Wells, David, 160–161
Walsh, Catherine, 103
Watten, Barrett, 114

Whitman, Walt, 157–158
  "Song of Myself," 24–25, 51
  "When Lilacs Last in the Dooryard Bloom'd," 124
Williams, Serena, 72–73
Williams, William Carlos, 5–6, 15, 21
  "Asphodel, That Greeny Flower," 21
  Paterson, 121–122
  Spring and All, 101–102
Wittgenstein, Ludwig, 40, 89, 112
Wordsworth, William, 47–48, 56–57, 58, 60, 61, 66, 86, 92, 119, 121
  "Lines Composed a Few Miles Above Tintern Abbey," 92
  Lyrical Ballads, 29, 56, 92
  "Preface" to *Lyrical Ballads*, 56–58, 59, 92
  The Prelude, 51
Wright, C.D., 124

Yeats, W.B., 25, 27, 43, 50, 101, 110, 124, 125
  "Among School Children," 11, 92
  "A General Introduction for My Work," 23–24
  "The Song of Wandering Aengus," 42

Zidane, Zinedine, 72–73
Zong (ship), 145–146
Zukofsky, Louis, 110

Printed in Great Britain
by Amazon